THE CRISIS OF REPRESENTATION
IN EUROPE

THE CRISIS OF REPRESENTATION IN EUROPE

Edited by
JACK HAYWARD

FRANK CASS • LONDON

First published 1995 in Great Britain by
FRANK CASS & CO. LTD
Newbury House, 900 Eastern Avenue
London IG2 7HH

and in the United States of America by
FRANK CASS
c/o ISBS
5804 N.E. Hassalo Street,
Portland, Oregon 97213-3644

British Library Cataloguing in Publication Data

Crisis of Representation in Europe. –
(Special Issue of "West European
Politics", ISSN 0140-2382)
  I. Hayward, J. E. S. II. Series
  324.94

  ISBN 0-7146-4656-3 (cloth)
  ISBN 0-7146-4184-7 (paper)

Library of Congress Cataloging-in-Publication Data

A catalog record for this book is available from the
Library of Congress

This group of studies first appeared in a Special Issue on 'The Crisis of Representation in Europe' of *West European Politics*, Vol. 18, No. 3 (July 1995), published by Frank Cass & Co. Ltd.

Typeset by Frank Cass & Co. Ltd.
Printed in Great Britain by
Antony Rowe Ltd

Contents

Preface

JACK HAYWARD

Representation long predated universal suffrage. The advent of mass democracy in a world in which elites were accustomed to take decisions (including political decisions) meant that the legitimacy of those in positions of authority was open to challenge from below. The notion of popular sovereignty implied that the people should not merely support those in power but exercise power themselves. This claim was circumvented in the nineteenth and early twentieth centuries by the view that direct democracy being impracticable in large states, it was both necessary and desirable that power should be entrusted to the few by the many. However, the latter could withdraw their consent periodically at elections, when competing candidates solicited their votes.

Where the intermediating organisations between the government and the governed, notably political parties and organised interests, operated effectively in synchronising the wishes of the public and the actions of those in office, the political system managed with the indirect influence of the people on the politicians. However, the latter – never enjoying a particularly high public regard – have in recent years suffered a measure of discredit (often deserved) that has induced a disaffection with the process by which legitimate authority has been transmitted upwards from the people. The current crisis has been a long time in the making, but it has come to a head as a result of the apparent incapacity of European political systems, in many of the individual states and collectively in the European Union, either to satisfy the basic expectations of their citizens or to leave them in peace.

The contributions that follow are the revised versions of papers presented to a workshop held in Oxford in October 1994, thanks to financial support from the British Academy, *West European Politics* and the University of Oxford European Studies Fund. They start from a fundamental interrogation about whether representative institutions within the European Union can exist without a European people, and argue that this requires the separation of citizenship from any ethnic-based sense of nationhood. European governance as a composite international, supranational and infranational set of disaggregated processes is then investigated. The two articles on political parties consider the way in which they have become simultaneously closer to government and lost touch with their electorates, as well as the problems that national parties have had in developing a European party system. Recourse to referendums as a way of providing public support for major decisions relating to the European Union is then examined to demonstrate that the results reflect the popularity of the government asking the question rather than public attitudes on the issue itself.

The enduring importance of national parliaments is emphasised in providing representative legitimacy as a basis of the developing European Union institutions, despite the fact that they have receded in their capacity to exercise control over their own national governments. The need for consensus between states, rather than majority rule, reinforces the view that it is not the lack of the development of a European party system or a more powerful European Parliament to which the representative failings of the present arrangements should be attributed.

The problems posed by pursuing European integration in a context of economic recession are discussed in terms of alternative explanations: an economic determinism that will lead to a resurgence of the integrative impetus, with the resumption of expansion and a decline in unemployment, or a structuralist interpretation in which the loss of political impetus derives mainly from the end of the Cold War and the globalisation of economic competition that remove the incentives to regional European integration. The technocratic emphasis, which largely excluded public involvement in the working of European institutions from their inception, has meant that as intergovernmental bargaining has reached the limits of the practicable in an enlarged Union, the protagonists of closer integration have not been able to mobilise public support for a policy of incremental federalism pursued by stealth. This has led some to seek European integration through subnational mobilisation at the regional level, which is closer to the public in its preoccupation with day-to-day policy decisions.

The current lack of public enthusiasm for European integration was reflected in the dishearteningly low turnout for the 1994 European elections, which continued to concentrate on national issues despite desultory efforts to promote transnational party campaigns. Populist protest found expression in the votes for parties and movements that adopted an anti-Establishment stance. The unwillingness of national political leaders to create effective democratic European institutions, particularly evident in the United Kingdom, France and Denmark, has led part of their publics to retreat into a backward-looking and defensive (if not defeatist) preoccupation with their own interests.

The process of European integration has, hitherto, not proceeded in a linear fashion. It has advanced with pauses and retreats. The tension between what the modernising and extrovert political, economic and administrative elites see as desirable objectives, and the reticences, suspicions and repulsions felt by their more traditionalist and introvert mass publics, is now new. The current challenge to Europe's leaders is to persuade their peoples that what most of their representatives regard as indispensable should be implemented in the coming years. It is a matter of concern that so many of them have for the present chosen to lie low, a reflection of the contemporary crisis of representation.

The Editor and authors would like to thank the discussants at the workshop – David Butler, Vernon Bogdanor, David Hine, Iain Mclean, Martin Westlake and Vincent Wright – for their comments on the first drafts of the contributions that follow.

European Democracy and Its Critique

J.H.H. WEILER

with

ULRICH R. HALTERN and FRANZ C. MAYER

After presenting a 'standard version' of the European Union's democratic deficit thesis, the European democratisation debate is broadened in four directions. First, the issue of demos and the political boundaries of the Union is considered, presenting competing notions of European peoplehood. Then European governance is presented as taking one of three forms: international, supranational and/or infranational. A differentiated democratic discourse is proposed to reflect the multiple-form governance of the Union. The notion of democracy itself is then subjected to the same differentiated approach with a brief examination of various models of democracy and of the insight they can offer to European governance. Finally, the issue of Union competences – as a form of disaggregating power – is introduced as an important element in the democratisation debate.

The output of European governance is like that of a state, even a super state: an endless stream of laws in increasingly varied areas of public and private life. They are binding on governments and individuals as part of the law of the land. Indeed, they are a higher law of the land – supreme over conflicting state laws. The structure and process of European governance, by contrast, is not at all, in many of its features, like that of a state. In particular it lacks many of the features we associate with democratic government.

This essay, contributing to the post-Maastricht discussion about democracy in, and democratisation of, the European Union is non-linear: no central thesis is developed and sustained. Instead, we shall first present a 'Standard Version' of the critique of democracy in the Union. The Standard Version is non-attributable. It is an aggregate of public opinion data, politicians' statements, media commentary, and considerable learned analysis. It is an uneasy attempt to capture the core of the present discussion on European democracy. We share much of the critique in the Standard Version and take responsibility for its shortcomings. Our purpose is not to set up a caricature that we shall later debunk. The remaining four uneasy pieces are meant instead to explore unstated or unexplored premises of the Standard Version and to widen the range of issues which we believe should be part of the discussion, a work-in-progress agenda for further reflection.

Who is the Demos? Much democratic theory presupposes a polity (usually a State) and almost all theories presuppose a demos. Democracy, in a loose sense, is about the many permutations of exercise of power by and for that demos. Indeed, the existence of a demos is not merely a semantic condition for democracy. In the case of Europe we cannot presuppose demos. After all, an article of faith of European integration has been the aim of an ever closer union among the *peoples* of Europe. Demoi, then, rather than demos. Can there be democratisation at the European level without there being a transcendent notion of a European people? Is there a European demos around which, by which, for which, a democracy can be established? How should or could it be defined? How could or should it fit into political theory? These are some of the questions we shall address.

What is the Polity? Although in a formal sense we can speak of the Union as a single polity, from the perspective of governance and power – its exercise, control and accountability – the notion of a European polity is no less uneasy than the notion of European peoplehood. We will present a description of European governance which has (at least) three principal facets: international, supranational and infranational. Our argument is simple. In this sense there are three polities, or three regimes, or three modes of governance. This trichotomy creates fundamentally different permutations of power distribution in the overall European polity. The problems of democracy manifest themselves in different ways which need to be explored.

Which Democracy? An interesting feature of the democratisation discussion in Europe, especially the blueprints for change, concerns the very understanding of democracy. Very rarely, if at all, is there more than cursory acknowledgement of the uneasy co-existence of competing visions and models of democracy which, in turn, should inform both diagnosis, prognosis and possible remedy of democratic shortcomings. Typically and endearingly there is an implicit projection onto Europe of a national self-understanding of democratic governance. The task is rendered more complex by the need to juggle models of democracy with the Union's permutations of governance. We shall offer some pointers in that direction.

Democracy over What? This issue is notorious. What should be the limits of the Union's jurisdiction? Is there anything one can add to the issue of 'subsidiarity', competences and jurisdiction? We shall explore jurisdictional lines as part of governance process and institutional structure rather than addressing the substantive problem of allocating material competences.

In broadening the discussion in the ways we propose, the result we have in mind is a Revised Version, not a revisionist version of the democracy debate.

THE CRITIQUE OF DEMOCRACY IN EUROPE: 'THE STANDARD VERSION'

The democratic problems of European integration are well explored. The phenomenon is frequently labelled as the 'Democratic Deficit' of the Community, but whatever nomenclature is employed, the principal features are well known.

European Integration has seen many, and increasingly important, government functions transferred to 'Brussels', brought within the exclusive or concurrent responsibility of the Community and Union. This is problematic in a variety of ways. Though the formal political boundaries of the state have remained intact, in the areas of transfer of responsibility to the Union the functional political boundaries of the polity have been effectively redrawn. If critical public policy choices about, say, international trade, environmental protection, consumer protection or immigration come exclusively or predominantly within Community responsibility, for those matters the locus of decision-making is no longer the state but the Union. Even if the Union were to replicate in its system of governance the very same institutional set-up found in its constituent states, there would be a diminution in the specific gravity, in the political weight, in the level of control of each individual within the redrawn political boundaries. That is, *arguendo*, an inevitable result of enlarging the membership of the functional polity (when a company issues new voting shares, the value of each share is reduced) and from adding a tier of government thereby distancing it further from its ultimate subjects in whose name and for whom democratic government is supposed to operate. We can call this Inverted Regionalism. All the real and supposed virtues of regionalism are here inverted.

Inverted Regionalism does not simply diminish democracy in the sense of individual disempowerment, it also fuels the separate and distinct phenomenon of de-legitimation. Democracy and legitimacy are not co-terminus. One knows from the past of polities with arguably democratic structure and process which enjoyed shaky political legitimacy and were replaced, democratically, with dictatorships. One knows from the past and present of polities with an egregiously undemocratic governmental structure and process which, nonetheless, enjoyed or enjoy high levels of legitimacy.

Inverted Regionalism, to the extent that it diminishes democracy or is thought to have that effect, will undermine the legitimacy of the Union.

The perceived perniciousness of Inverted Regionalism and its delegitimation effect will be/are enhanced by three factors:

– The reach of the Community or Union into areas which are, or are thought to be, classical symbolic 'state' functions in relation to which 'foreigners' should not be telling 'us' how to run our lives. These areas, socially constructed and culturally bound, are not fixed. They range from the ridiculous (the British pint) to the sublime (the right-to-life of the Irish abortion saga).

– The reach of the Community or Union into areas which are, or are thought to be, matters left to individuals or local communities and in relation to which 'government' should not be telling 'us' (the people) how to run our lives.

– The perception, whether or not rooted in reality, that there is no effective limit and/or check on the ability of the Community or Union to reach into areas previously thought to be the preserve of the state or of the individual.

Inverted Regionalism is only one aspect of the alleged democratic malaise of European Integration. A feature of the democratic process within the member states, with many variations, is that government is, at least formally, subject to parliamentary accountability. In particular, when policy requires legislation, parliamentary approval is needed. National parliaments, apart from exercising these 'power functions', also fulfil a 'public forum' function described variously as information, communication, legitimation, etc. The argument is that Community and Union governance, and Community institutions, harm these principal democratic processes within the member states and within the Union itself.

Community and Union governance pervert the balance between executive and legislative organs of government of the state. Member state ministers are reconstituted in the Community as the principal legislative organ with, as noted above, an ever widening jurisdiction over increasing areas of public policy. The volume, complexity and timing of the Community decisional process makes national parliamentary control, especially in large member states, more an illusion than a reality. In a majority decision environment, the power of national parliaments to affect outcomes in the Council of Ministers is further reduced. The European Parliament does not offer an effective substitution. Even after Maastricht, the powers of the European Parliament in the legislative process leave formal and formidable gaps in parliamentary control. So Union governance results in a net empowerment of the executive branch of the states.

The European Parliament is debilitated not only by its formal absence of certain powers but also by its remoteness. The technical ability of MEPs to link and represent actual constituents to the Community process is seriously compromised in the larger member states by simple reasons of size. Its abstract representation function of 'the people' – its public forum function – is also compromised, by a combination of its ineffective powers (the real decisions do not happen there), by its mode of operation (time and place), by its language 'problem', by the difficulty (and lack of interest) of media coverage. Paradoxically, over the years, one has seen a gradual increase in the formal powers of the European Parliament, and a decrease in the turn-out to European elections. And when the people do turn out, these elections are dominated by a national political agenda, a mid-term signal to the national party in power. This is the opposite of American politics, where State elections are frequently a mid-term signal to the federal government. The non-emergence of true trans-European political parties is another expression of the phenomenon. Critically, there is no real sense in which the European political process allows the electorate 'to throw the scoundrels out', to take what is often the only ultimate power left to the people, which is to replace one set of 'governors' by another. In its present state, no one who votes in the European elections has a strong sense at all of affecting critical policy choices at the European level, and certainly not of confirming or rejecting European governance.

Community governance might also have a distorting effect if one takes a neo-corporatist view of the European polity. Under this view, the executive and legislature do not monopolise policy-making but are important actors in a broader arena involving public and private parties. The importance of parliament under this model is to give voice and power to diffuse and fragmented interests whose principal political clout derives from a combination of their electoral power and the re-election drive of politicians. Other actors, such as big industry or organised labour, whose 'membership' is far less diffuse and fragmented, exercise influence through different channels and by different means such as political contributions, control of party organisation, and direct lobbying of the administration. When policy areas are transferred to Europe, there will be a weakening of diffuse and fragmented national interests, deriving from the greater difficulty they will experience in organising themselves at the transnational level compared to, say, a more compact body of large manufacturers (e.g., the tobacco industry). In addition, the structural weakness of the European Parliament has a corresponding effect on these interests even if organised. Electoral power simply carries less weight in Euro-politics.

Since the outcome of the Community legislative process becomes the supreme law of the land, national judicial control of primary legislation – in those systems which have such control (e.g., Italy, Germany, Ireland) – is compromised, too. The European Court of Justice, like the European

Parliament, does not offer an effective substitution, since, inevitably, it is informed by different judicial sensibilities, in particular in relation to interpreting the limits of Community competences. Since the governments of the member states are not only the most decisive legislative organ of the Community, but also fulfil the most important executive function (they, much more than the Commission, are responsible for the implementation and execution of Community law and policy) they escape, also, national parliamentary (typically weak) and national judicial (typically stronger) control of large chunks of their administrative functions. Domestic preferences are, arguably, perverted in a substantive sense, as well. A member state may elect a centre government and yet might be subject to centre left policies if a majority of, say, centre left governments dominate the Council. Conversely, there might even be a majority of, say, centre right governments in the Council, but they might find themselves thwarted by a minority of centre right governments or even by a single such government where Community decisional rules provide for unanimity. Both in Council and in the European Parliament, the principle of proportional representation is compromised whereby enhanced voice is accorded citizens of small states, notably Luxembourg, and, arguably, inadequate voice accorded citizens of the larger states, notably Germany.

Last a feature which is said to pervade all Community governance, and negatively affect the democratic process, is its overall lack of transparency. This is not just a result of the added layer of governance and its increased remoteness. The process itself is notoriously prolix, extremely divergent when one moves from one policy area to another and, in part, kept secret. 'Comitology' is an apt neologism – a phenomenon that requires its very own science, which no single person has mastered.

This concludes the Standard Version. Our argument is that it represents some kind of 'received knowledge', though we have tried to be careful in my claims about its veracity. It is true if it corresponds to some objective reality; it is real, albeit in a different way, if it is believed to be true. Probably no one subscribes to all of its tenets. We will not criticise it directly, but instead turn to certain features which have been absent from the debate or have been underplayed in the Standard Version.

DEMOCRACY WITHOUT A DEMOS?

For decades lawyers have been speaking loosely about the 'constitutionalisation' of the Treaties establishing the European Community and Union. In part this has meant the emergence of European law as constitutionally 'higher law', with immediate effect within the 'legal space' of the Community. The political science of European integration, which had lagged in noticing the phenomenon and understanding its importance, has in recent times been addressing it. But, so far, most searching and illuminating analysis has been on constitutionalisation as an element in understanding governance, with most attention given to the newly discovered actors (e.g., the European Court and national courts), to the myriad factors which explain the emergence and acceptance of the new constitutional architecture, to the constraints, real or imaginary, which constitutionalism places on political and economic actors and to the dynamics of interaction between the various actors and between legal integration and other forms of integration. In very large measure, all these phenomena have been discussed in positivist terms, as understood both in political science and law.

There is an underlying issue which has received less attention. By what authority, if any – in the vocabulary of normative political theory – can the claim of European law to be both constitutionally superior and with immediate effect in the polity be sustained? Why should the subjects of European law in the Union, individuals, courts, governments feel bound to observe the law of the Union as higher law, in the same way that their counterparts in, say, the USA, are bound, to and by, American federal law? It is a dramatic question, since constitutionalisation has taken place and to give a negative answer would be subversive. This is partly why the critique of European democracy is controversial. One can, it seems, proclaim a profound democracy deficit and yet insist at the same time on the importance of accepting the supremacy of Union law. .

One of the most trenchant critiques of authority to emerge recently has come from a certain strand of German constitutional theory and can be entitled the No-Demos thesis. Interestingly, it found powerful expression in the so-called Maastricht decision of the German Federal Constitutional Court. The decision, formally unanimous, contains conflicting strands. We shall present the robust version culled from decision and constitutional writing. It is also a strand in the theory of the European Nation-State.

The No Demos Thesis

The following is a composite version of the No Demos thesis culled from the decision of the German Court itself, and some of the principal exponents of this thesis.

The people of a polity, the *Volk*, its demos, is a concept which has a subjective – socio-psychological – component which is rooted in objective, organic conditions. Both the subjective and objective can be observed empirically in a way which would enable us, on the basis of observation and analysis, to determine that, for example, there is no European *Volk*.

The subjective manifestations of peoplehood, of the demos, are to be found in a sense of social cohesion, shared destiny and collective self-identity which, in turn, result in and deserve loyalty. These subjective manifestations have thus both a descriptive and also a normative element.

The subjective manifestations are a result of, but are also conditioned on, some, though not necessarily all, of the following objective elements: common language, common history, common cultural habits and sensibilities and – this is dealt with more discretely since the 12 years of National-Socialism – common ethnic origin, common religion. All these factors do not alone capture the essence of *Volk* – one will always find allusions to some spiritual, even mystical, element as well. Whereas different writers may throw a different mix of elements into the pot, an insistence on a relatively high degree of homogeneity, measured by these ethno-cultural criteria, is typically an important, indeed critical, element of the discourse. Here rests, of course, the most delicate aspect of the theory since the insistence on homogeneity is what conditions in its statal operationalisation the rules for inclusion and exclusion. When, say, Jews were excluded from full membership in many European nation-states as equal citizens, it was often on the theory that being a Christian was essential to the homogeneity of the people.

The 'organic' nature of the *Volk* is a delicate matter. We call 'organic' those parts of the discourse which make, to a greater or lesser degree, one or more of the following claims. The *Volk* predates historically and precedes politically the modern state. Germany could emerge as a modern Nation-State because there was already a German *Volk*. The 'nation' is simply a modern appellation, in the context of modernist political theory and international law, of the pre-existing *Volk* and the state is its political expression. It is on this view that the compelling case for German (re)unification rested. One could split the German state but not the German nation. Hence, maybe unification of the State but certainly only *re*unification of the people. Anthropologically, this understanding of being German, which means being part of the German *Volk*, is 'organic'. It has, first, an almost natural connotation. You are born German the way you are born male or female – though you can, with only somewhat greater ease, change your national identity (even then you will remain an 'ex-German') and to the extent that ethnicity continues to play a role – muted to be sure – in this discourse of the *Volk*, ethnicity is even more immutable than gender. There is no operation which can change one's ethnicity. The implication of this is that one's nationality as a form of identity is almost primordial according to this view, taking precedence over other forms of consciousness and membership. I may have solidarity with fellow Christians elsewhere, fellow workers elsewhere, fellow women elsewhere. This would make me a Christian German, a Socialist German, a feminist German or, at most, a

German Christian, a German Socialist, a German feminist. I cannot escape my *Volkish*, national identity.

No one today argues that the 'organic' is absolute. One can, after all, 'naturalise', acquire membership in a new nation, but does not the word 'naturalisation' speak volumes? And one can, more as an hypothesis than a reality, imagine that should the objective conditions sufficiently change, and a measure of homogeneity in language, culture, shared historical experience develop, a subjective consciousness could follow and a new *Volk*/nation emerge. But, realistically, these mutations are possible over 'geological' time, epochal not generational.

Volk fits into modern political theory easily enough. The German Constitution may have constituted the post-war German state, but it did not constitute the German people except, perhaps, in some narrow legal sense. The *Volk*, the Nation, understood in this national, ethno-cultural sense is the basis for the modern State. It is the basis in an older, self-determination sense of political independence in statehood. Only nations 'may have' states. The state belongs to the nation, its *Volk*, and the Nation (the *Volk*) 'belongs' to the state. Critically, *Volk*/Nation are also the basis for the modern democratic state. The nation and its members, the *Volk*, constitute the polity for the purposes of accepting the discipline of democratic, majoritarian governance. Both descriptively and prescriptively (how it is and how it ought to be) a minority will/should accept the legitimacy of a majority decision, because both majority and minority are part of the same *Volk*, belong to the nation. That is an integral part of what rule-by-the-people, democracy, means on this reading. Thus, nationality constitutes the state (hence nation-state) which in turn constitutes its political boundary, an idea which runs from Schmitt to Kirchhof.[1] The significance of the political boundary is not only to the older notion of political independence and territorial integrity, but also to the very democratic nature of the polity. A parliament is, on this view, an institution of democracy not only because it provides a mechanism for representation and majority voting, but because it represents the *Volk*, the nation, the demos from which derive the authority and legitimacy of its decisions. To drive this point home, imagine an *anschluss* between Germany and Denmark. Try and tell the Danes that they should not worry since they will have full representation in the Bundestag. Their screams of grief will be shrill not simply because they will be condemned, as Danes, to permanent minorityship (that may be true for the German Greens too), but because the way nationality, *in this way of thinking*, enmeshes with democracy in that even majority rule is only legitimate within a demos, when Danes rule Danes. Demos, thus, is a condition of democracy. By contrast, when democrats like Alfred Verdross argued for a Greater Germany, this was clearly not motivated by some proto-fascist design, but by a belief that the German-speaking 'peoples' were in fact one people in terms of this very understanding of peoplehood.[2]

Turning to Europe, it is argued as a matter of empirical observation, based on these ethno-cultural criteria, that there is no European demos – not a people not a nation. Neither the subjective element (the sense of shared collective identity and loyalty) nor the objective conditions which could produce these (the kind of homogeneity of the ethno-national conditions on which peoplehood depend) exist. Long-term peaceful relations with thickening economic and social intercourse should not be confused with the bonds of peoplehood and nationality forged by language, history and ethnicity. At this point we detect two versions to the No Demos thesis. The 'soft' version of the Court itself is the *not yet* version. Although there is no demos now, the possibility for the future is not precluded *a priori*. If and when a European demos emerges, then, and only then, will the basic political premises of the decision have to be reviewed. This is unlikely in the foreseeable future. The 'hard' version does not only dismiss that possibility as objectively unrealistic but also as undesirable. It is argued (correctly in my view) that integration is not about creating a European nation or people, but about the ever closer Union among the peoples of Europe. However, what the 'soft' and 'hard' version share is the same understanding of peoplehood, its characteristics and manifestations.

Soft version or hard, the consequences of the No Demos thesis for the European construct are interesting. The rigorous implication of this view would be that absent a demos, there cannot, by definition, be a democracy or democratisation at the European level. This is not a semantic proposition. On this reading, European democracy (meaning a minimum binding majoritarian decision-making at the European level) without a demos is no different from the previously mentioned German-Danish *anschluss* except on a larger scale. Giving the Danes a vote in the Bundestag is, as argued, ice cold comfort. Giving them a vote in the European Parliament or Council is, conceptually, no different. This would be true for each and every nation-state. European integration, on this view, may have involved a certain transfer of state functions to the Union, but this has not been accompanied by a redrawing of political boundaries which can occur only if, and can be ascertained only when, a European *Volk* can be said to exist. Since this, it is claimed, has not occurred, the Union and its institutions can have neither the authority nor the legitimacy of a Demos-cratic state. Empowering the European Parliament is no solution and could – to the extent that it weakens the Council (the voice of the member states) – actually exacerbate the legitimacy problem of the Community. On this view, a parliament without a demos is conceptually impossible, practically despotic. If the European Parliament is not the representative of *a* people, if the territorial boundaries of the EU do not correspond to its political boundaries, than the writ of such a parliament has only slightly more legitimacy than the writ of an emperor.

What, however, if the interests of the nation-state would be served by functional cooperation with other nation-states? The No Demos thesis has an implicit and traditional solution: cooperation through international treaties, freely entered into by High Contracting Parties, preferably of a contractual nature (meaning no open-ended commitments) capable of denunciation, covering well-circumscribed subjects. Historically, such treaties were concluded by heads of state embodying the sovereignty of the nation-state. Under the more modern version, such treaties are concluded by a government answerable to a national parliament often requiring parliamentary approval and subject to the material conditions of the national democratic constitution. Democracy is safeguarded in that way.

Democracy and membership

There is much that is puzzling in the reasoning of the German Court. If the concern of the German Court was to safeguard the democratic character of the European construct in its future developments, and if its explicit and implicit thesis was that in the absence of a European demos, democracy can be guaranteed only through member state mechanisms, it is hard to see how, employing the same sensibilities, it could have given a democratic seal of approval to the already existing European Community and Union. Whatever the original intentions of the High Contracting parties, the Treaties establishing the European Community and Union have no international parallel, and national procedures to ensure democratic control over international treaties of the state are clearly ill suited and woefully inadequate to address the problems posited by the European Union.

One could suggest, explicitly or implicitly, that the current situation of the Union has been democratically legitimated by national processes – for example the successive approvals of the Community by the German parliament – but this is problematic and somewhat embarrassing. First, successive approvals of Treaty amendments (such as the Single European Act and the various acts of accession of new member states) imply a very formal view of democratic legitimation. Is it not just a little bit like the Weimar elections which democratically approved a non-democratic regime? Is it not the task of a constitutional court to be a counter-balance to such self-defeating democratisation? Member state mediation does have a powerful impact on the social and formal legitimacy of the European construct, but it has done little to address the problems of deficient democratic structures and processes. If the current democratic malaise of the Union can be said to have been cured by the simple fact that national parliaments have endorsed the package deal in one way or another, the Court would have engaged at worst in another form of fiction about the reality of the Union and the democratising power of national structures and institutions, at best in adopting a formal and impoverished sense of what it takes to ensure democracy in the polity.

The Court could have highlighted, embarrassing as this may have been, the democratic failings of the Community, uncured by Maastricht, in which all European and member State institutions (including courts) connived. Since, despite these failings, the Union was formally legitimated, the Court could, for example, have approved the Treaty, but insisted that the existing gap between formal legitimation and material democratic deficiency must be regarded as temporary and could not be accepted in the medium and long term. In this way the Federal Constitutional Court would have thrown its formidable power behind the pressure for democratisation. For all its talk about democracy, the Court, by adopting the view it has on *Volk*, State and Citizenship, has boxed itself into a further untenable situation. Stated briefly: if the judges who subscribed to the decision truly believe that a polity enjoying democratic authority and legitimate rule-making power must be based on the conflation of *Volk*, State and Citizenship, that the only way to conceive of the demos of such a polity is in thickly homogeneous ethno-cultural terms, then, whether one admits it or not, the future of European integration poses a huge threat. The problem is not that there is not now a European demos; the problem is that there might one day be one. The emergence of a European demos in a European polity enjoying legitimate democratic authority would signify – on this understanding of polity and demos – the replacement of the various member state *demoi*, including the German *Volk*. This would be too high a price to pay for European integration. Since on their reading there is only a simple choice – either a European State (one European *Volk*) or a Union of States (with the preservation of all European *Völker* including Germans) – their fear is inevitable.

We shall try to show how this view is based on one and perhaps two profound misconceptions with unfortunate consequences both for Germany itself and for Europe. Our challenge, note, is *not* to the ethno-cultural, homogeneous concept of *Volk* as such. It is, instead, to the view which insists that the *only* way to think of a demos, bestowing legitimate rule-making and democratic authority on a polity, is in these *Volkish* terms. We also challenge the concomitant notion that the *only* way to think of a polity, enjoying legitimate rule-making and democratic authority, is in statal terms. Finally, we challenge the implicit view in the decision that the only way to imagine the Union is in some statal form: State, confederation of states, federal state. Noteworthy is not only the 'enslavement' to the notion of

State, but also, as we shall see, the inability to contemplate an entity with a simultaneous multiple identity. Polycentric thinking is, apparently, unacceptable.

We shall construct the critique step-by-step, beginning with Demos-as-*Volk* first. We want to raise three possible objections to the Court's version of the No Demos thesis and its implications.

The first objection has two strands. One, less compelling, would argue that the No Demos thesis simply misreads the European anthropological map. That, in fact, there is a European sense of social cohesion, shared identity and collective self which, in turn, results in (and deserves) loyalty, and which bestows thus potential authority and democratic legitimacy on European institutions. In short, that there is, want it or not, a European people on the terms stipulated by the No Demos thesis, and that the only problem of democracy in the Community relates to the deficient processes, such as the weakness of the European Parliament, but not the deep structural absence of a demos. Though there is no common European language, that cannot in itself be a *conditio sine qua non*, as the case of Switzerland would illustrate. And there is a sufficient measure of shared history and cultural habits to sustain this construct. The problem is that this argument simply does not ring true. For most Europeans any sense of European identity defined in ethno-cultural or ethno-national terms would be extremely weak. We do not pursue this line of argument.

But there is one strand worth picking up from this first objection. One can argue that peoplehood and national identity have, at certain critical moments of transition, a far larger degree of artificiality, of social constructionism and even social engineering than the organic, *Volkish* view would concede. As such, they are far more fluid, potentially unstable and capable of change. Decidedly, they can be constructed as a conscious decision and not only be a reflection of an already pre-existing consciousness. Indeed, how could one ever imagine political unification taking place if it has strictly to follow the sense of peoplehood? In the creation of European states involving political unification, such as, yes, Germany and Italy, the act of formal unification preceded full and universal shift of consciousness. Although conceptually the nation is the condition for the state, historically, it has often been the state which constituted the nation by imposing a language and/or prioritising a dialect and/or privileging a certain historical narrative and/or creating symbols and myths. Often this would have to be the order in the process of unification. Think, say, of Prussia and Austria. Is it so fanciful to imagine a different historical path in which Prussia went its own way, privileging a particularised reading of its history, symbols, cultural habits and myths, and developing a sense of *Volk* and nation which would emphasise that which separates it from other

German-speaking nations and that Austria, in this would-be history, could just have become another part of a unified Germany?

We are, of course, taking no position here on the desirability or otherwise of European unification driven by the notion of nation and peoplehood. (As will transpire, we oppose it.) But we are arguing that to insist on the emergence of a pre-existing European Demos defined in ethno-cultural terms as a precondition for constitutional unification or, more minimally, a redrawing of political boundaries, is to ensure that this will never happen. The No Demos thesis which is presented by its advocates as rooted in empirical and objective observation barely conceals a pre-determined outcome.

The second objection is more central and is concerned with the notion of membership implicit in the No Demos thesis. Who are the members of the German polity? The answer would seem obvious: the German *Volk*, those who have German nationality. They are Germany's demos. Germany is the state of the Germans defined in the familiar ethno-national terms. By contrast, to say that there is no European demos is equivalent to saying that there is no European nation. We should immediately add that we agree: there is no European nation or *Volk* in the sense that these words are understood by the German Court and the constitutionalists on which it relies. But that is not the point. Is it mandated that demos in general and the European demos in particular be understood exclusively in the ethno-cultural homogeneous terms which the German Federal Constitutional Court has adopted in its own self-understanding? Can there not be other understandings of demos which might lead to different conceptualisations and potentialities for Europe?

We have, so far, studiously avoided using the concept of citizen and citizenship. Can we not define membership of a polity in civic, non-ethno-cultural terms? Can we not separate ethnos from demos? And can we not imagine a polity whose demos is defined, understood and accepted in civic, non-ethno-cultural terms, and would have legitimate rule-making democratic authority on that basis? To be sure, there is a German constitutional tradition from which the No Demos thesis arises which masks these possibilities since historically, at least from the time of the *Kaiserreich*, there has been such a strong current which insists on the unity of *Volk*-Nation-State-Citizenship. A German citizen is, save for some exceptions, a German national, primarily one who belongs to the *Volk*. Belonging to the *Volk* is normally the condition for citizenship. And, in turn, citizenship in this tradition can only be understood in statal terms. Here the very language reflects the conflation: the concept of state is built into the very term of citizenship. If there is citizenship, statehood is premised. If there is statehood, citizenship is premised. This is not simply a matter of constitutional and political theory. It finds its reflection in positive law. That is why naturalisation in Germany – other than through marriage, adoption and some other exceptions – is an act which implies not simply accepting civic obligations of citizenship and loyalty to the state, but of embracing German national identity understood in this thick cultural sense, a true cultural assimilation and a demand for an obliteration of other *Volkish* loyalties and identification. Thus, for example, emancipation of the Jews in Germany was premised on a consignment of Jewishness and Judaism to the realm of religion and a refusal to accept Jewish peoplehood. To be a German citizen, under this conception, you have to be part of the *Volk*. Germany is the state of the Germans. Likewise, until very recently, you may have been a third generation resident of Germany and be denied citizenship because you are unable or unwilling to become 'German' in a cultural and identification sense. With few exceptions, the law specifically denies naturalisation to residents who would wish to embrace the duties of citizenship but retain an alternative national identity. Multiple citizenship is permitted in peculiar circumstances, but is frowned upon. By contrast, if you are an ethnically defined German national, even if a third generation citizen and resident of some far-flung country, you would still be a member of the *Volk* and hence have a privileged position in applying for citizenship. On this view, the legal 'passport' of membership in the polity is citizenship; what defines you as a member of the polity with full political and civil rights and duties. But that, in turn, is conflated with nationality, with being a member of the *Volk* in the ethno-cultural sense. Since Demos is defined in national terms, the only Demos conceivable is one the members of which are citizen-nationals – hence the state.

We should point out again that Germany is not the only state in Europe or elsewhere whose membership philosophy is so conceived. In some measure that is the philosophy of the nation-state. But it does offer a rather extreme example of the conflation of State, *Volk*/Nation and Citizenship.

Be that as it may, this conflation is neither necessary conceptually, nor practiced universally, nor, perhaps, even desirable. There are quite a few states where, for example, mere birth in the state creates actual citizenship or an entitlement to citizenship without any pretence that one thus becomes a national in an ethno-cultural sense. There are states where citizenship, as a commitment to the constitutional values and the civic duties of the polity, are the condition of naturalisation, whereas nationality, in an ethno-cultural sense, is regarded, like religion, a matter of individual preference. There are states, like Germany, with a strong ethno-cultural identity which, nonetheless, allow citizenship not only to individuals with other nationalities who do not belong to the majority *Volk*, but to minorities with strong, even competing, ethno-cultural identities.

However, embedded in the decision of the Federal Constitutional Court is an understanding not only of German polity and demos but of Europe too, notably in its 'not yet' formulation. When the German Court tells us that there is not yet a European demos, it invites us implicitly to think of Europe, its future and its very telos in ethno-national terms. It implicitly construes Europe in some sort of 'pre-state' stage, as yet underdeveloped and hence lacking in its own legitimate rule-making and democratic authority. It is this (mis)understanding which produces the either-or zero sum relationship between Europe and member state. If demos is *Volk* and citizenship can only be conceived as 'state-citizenship' (*staat*sangehörigkeit), then European demos and citizenship can only come at the expense of the parallel German terms.

What is inconceivable in this view is a decoupling of nationality (understood in its *Volkish* ethno-cultural sense) and citizenship. Also inconceivable is a demos understood in non-organic civic terms, a coming together on the basis not of shared ethnos and/or organic culture, but a coming together on the basis of shared values, a shared understanding of rights and societal duties and shared rational, intellectual culture which transcend ethno-national differences. Equally inconceivable in this view is the notion of a polity enjoying rule making and democratic authority whose demos, and hence the polity itself, is not statal in character and is understood differently from the German self-understanding. Finally, and critically, what is also inconceivable on this view is that a member state like Germany may have its own understanding of demos for itself (for example its relatively extreme form of state=people=citizens) but be part of a broader polity with a different understanding of demos.

At the root of the No Demos thesis is ultimately a world view which is enslaved to the concepts of *Volk, Staat* and *Staatsangehöriger* and cannot perceive the Community or Union in anything other than those terms. This is another reason why the Union may appear so threatening, since the statal vision can only construe it in oppositional terms to the member state. But that is to impose on the Community or Union an external vision and not an attempt to understand (or define it) in its own unique terms.

Between State Citizenship and Union membership

How is it possible, it may be asked by those to whom *Volk* is the demos, and this demos is the basis for legitimate authority in a statal structure, to decouple peoplehood from citizenship other than in a formalistic and semantic sense? Do not *Volk* and nationality with their ethno-cultural grounding create in the individual member a sense of closeness, in the national community a sense of social cohesion, which are both necessary for the sense of duty and loyalty which are and should be conditions for citizenship?

There may be strength in this argument. The criticism of it is not that it is necessarily wrong, but that it is a world view which may be seen as more or less attractive. It is certainly far from compelling. We wish to look at it first at the level of individual states and then at the European level.

Note first at the statal level the impoverished view of the individual and human dignity involved in the *Volk*-state-citizenship equation. Is it really not possible for an individual to have very strong and deep cultural, religious and ethnic affiliations which differ from the dominant ethno-cultural group in a country, and yet in truth accept full rights and duties of citizenship and acquit oneself honourably? Looking at the societal side of this coin, is it necessary for the state to make such a deep claim on the soul of the individual, reminiscent of the days when Christianity was a condition for full membership of civic society and full citizenship rights, including citizenship duties?

The view that would decouple *Volk* from Demos and Demos from state, in whole or in part, does not require a denigration of the virtues of nationality – the belongingness, the social cohesion, the cultural and human richness which may be found in exploring and developing the national ethos. It simply questions whether nationality, in this ethno-cultural sense, must be the exclusive condition of full political and civic membership of the polity. Let us not mince words. To reject this construct as impossible and/or undesirable is to adopt a world-view which informs ethnic cleansing, though we are not suggesting of course, that the German Court and its Judges feel anything but abhorrence to that particular solution. Be all this as it may at the level of state and nation, conflating *Volk* with demos and demos with state is clearly unnecessary as a model for Europe. In fact such a model would deflect Europe from its supranational civilising telos and ethos. There is no reason for the European demos to be defined in terms identical to the demos of its member states or vice-versa.

Consider the Maastricht citizenship provisions: Article 8 declares that 'Citizenship of the Union is hereby established. Every person holding the nationality of a member state shall be a citizen of the Union [...]' The introduction of citizenship to the conceptual world of the Union could be seen as just another step in the drive towards a statal, unity vision of Europe, especially if citizenship is understood as being premised on statehood. But there is another more tantalising and radical way of understanding the provision, namely as the very conceptual decoupling of nationality/*Volk* from citizenship, and as the conception of a polity the membership of which is understood in civic rather than ethno-cultural terms. On this view, the Union belongs to and is composed of citizens who by definition do not share the same nationality. The substance of membership (and thus of the demos) is in a commitment to the shared values of the Union as expressed in its constituent documents, a commitment to the duties and rights of a civic society covering discrete areas of public life, a commitment to membership in a polity which privileges exactly the opposites of classic ethno-nationalism – those human features which transcend the differences of organic ethno-culturalism. What is special in this concept is that it invites individuals to see themselves as belonging simultaneously to two demoi, albeit based on different subjective factors of identification. I am a German national in the strong sense of ethno-cultural identification and sense of belongingness. I am simultaneously a European citizen in terms of my European transnational affinities to shared values which transcend the ethno-national diversity. So much so, that in the range of areas of public life I am willing to accept the legitimacy and authority of decisions adopted by my fellow European citizens, in the realisation that in these areas we have given preference to choices made by my outreaching demos, rather than by my inreaching demos.

The Treaties on this reading would have to be seen not only as an agreement among states (a Union of states) but as a 'social contract' among the nationals of those states – ratified in accordance with the constitutional requirements in all member states – that they will in the areas covered by the Treaty regard themselves as associating as citizens in this civic society. This would be fully consistent with, say, Habermas's notion of constitutional patriotism.[3] But we can go even further. In this polity, and to this demos, one cardinal value is precisely that there will not be a drive towards, or an acceptance of, an overarching ethno-cultural national identity displacing those of the member states. Nationals of the member states are European Citizens, not the other way around. Europe is 'not yet' a demos in the ethno-cultural sense and should never become one.

One should not get carried away with this construct. Note first that the Maastricht formula does not imply a full decoupling. Member states are free to define their own conditions of membership and these may continue to be defined in *Volkish* terms. (But then we know that the conditions of nationality and citizenship differ quite markedly from one member state to another.) Moreover, the gateway to European citizenship passes through member state nationality. More critically, even this construct of the European demos, like the *Volkish* construct, depends on a shift of consciousness. Individuals must think of themselves in this way before such a demos could have full legitimate democratic authority. The key for a shift in political boundaries is the sense of feeling that the boundaries surround one's own polity. We are not making the claim that this shift has already occurred. Nor are we making any claims about the translation of this vision into institutional and constitutional arrangements. We are making three claims. First, we do not know about public consciousness of a civic polity-based demos, because the question has to be framed in this way in order to get a meaningful response. Second, the shift will not happen if one insists that the only way to understand demos is in *Volkish* ways. Third, this understanding of demos makes the need for democratisation of Europe even more pressing. A demos which coheres around values must live those values.

There is one final issue which touches, perhaps, the deepest stratum of the No Demos thesis. It is one thing to say, as does Maastricht, that nationals of member states are citizens of the Union. But are not those nationals also citizens of their member state? Even if one accepts that one can decouple citizenship and nationality and that one can imagine a demos based on citizenship rather than on nationality, can one be a citizen of both polities? Can one be a member of not one but also a second demos? We have already noted the great aversion of this strand of German constitutionalism to multiple citizenship.

We address this question in two different ways. One is simply to point out the fairly widespread practice of states allowing double or even multiple citizenship with relative equanimity. For the most part, as a matter of civic duties and rights, this does not create many problems. This is so also in the Community. It is true that in time of war the holder of multiple citizenship may be in an untenable situation. But cannot even the European Union assume that war among its constituent member states is not only materially impossible but unthinkable? The sentiment against multiple citizenship is not rooted in practical considerations.

Instead, at a deeper level, the issue of double citizenship evokes the spectre of double loyalty. The view which denies the status of demos to Europe may derive from a resistance to the idea of double loyalty. The resistance to double loyalty could be rooted in the fear that some shallow, nondescript unauthentic and artificial 'Euro-culture' would come to replace the deep, well articulated, authentic and genuine national version of the same. It could also be rooted in the belief that double loyalty must mean that either one or both loyalties have to be compromised.

On the first point, we do not believe that any of the European ethno-cultural identities is so weak or fragile as to be threatened by the spectre of a simultaneous civic loyalty to Europe. We have already argued that the opposite is also likely. Unable to rest on the formal structures of the state, national culture and identity has to find truly authentic expressions to enlist loyalty which can bring about real internally found generation. What is more, the existential condition of fractured self, of living in two or more worlds, can result not in a blunting of one's cultural achievement but in its sharpening and deepening. Can anyone who has read Heine, Kafka or Canetti doubt this? (It might, in fact, be threatened far more by the simple economic Europe of the Single Market. One cannot overestimate the profound impact of the market on low and high culture.)

But what about the political aversion to double loyalty? This, paradoxically, is most problematic, especially in a polity which cherishes ethno-cultural homogeneity as a condition of membership. It is hard to see why, other than for some mystical or truly 'blood is thicker than water' rationale, a British citizen who thinks of her or himself as British (and who forever will speak with an English accent) but who is settled in, say, Germany, and wishes to assume all the duties and rights of German citizenship, could not be trusted in today's Europe loyally to do so. Moreover, we have already seen that European citizenship would have a very different meaning from German citizenship. The two identities would not be competing directly 'on the same turf'. The aversion to double loyalty, like the aversion to multiple citizenship itself, does not seem to be rooted primarily in practical considerations. It rests in a normative view which wants national self-identity to rest very deep in the soul, in a place hitherto occupied by religion. The imagery of this position is occasionally evocative of those sentiments. Religion, with greater legitimacy, occupies itself with these deeper recesses of the human spirit, and consequently makes these claims for exclusiveness. The mixing of state loyalty and religion risks, in our view, idolatry from a religious perspective, and can be highly dangerous from a political one. Historically, it seems as if *Volk* and State did indeed come to occupy these deepest parts of the human spirit to the point of being accepted *über alles* with terrifying consequences. It is not that the very idea of *Volk* and State was murderous nor even evil, though our preference is for multiple loyalties, even demoi within the polity. It is the primordial position which *Volk* and State occupied, instilling uncritical citizenship which allowed evil, even murderous, designs to be executed by dulling critical faculties, legitimating extreme positions, subduing transcendent human values and debasing one of the common strands of the three monotheistic religions that human beings, all of them, were created in the image of God.

How then do we achieve 'critical citizenship'? The European construct we have put forward, which allows for a European civic, value-driven demos co-existing side by side with a national ethno-cultural one (for those nation-states which want it), could be seen as a rather moderate contribution to this noble goal. Maybe in the realm of the political, the special virtue of contemporaneous membership in a national ethno-cultural demos, and in a supranational civic, value-driven demos, is in the effect which such double membership may have on taming the great appeal, even craving, for belonging in this world which nationalism continues to offer but which can so easily degenerate into intolerance and xenophobia. Maybe the national in-reaching ethno-cultural demos and the out-reaching supranational civic demos, by continuously keeping each other in check, offer a model of critical citizenship. Maybe we should celebrate, rather than reject with aversion, the politically fractured self and double identity which dual membership involves, which can be seen as conditioning us not to consider any polity claiming our loyalty to be *über alles*. Maybe this understanding of Europe makes it appear alluring to some, threatening to others. In any event, if there is to be a European demos, it should, we argue, be constructed in this, rather than the ethno-cultural mode.

EUROPEAN DEMOCRACY – INTERNATIONAL, SUPRANATIONAL, INFRANATIONAL

A description and analysis of European governance will depend today in large measure on the literature you chose to study. Three approaches have become prominent – for convenience we have called them international (intergovernmental), supranational, and infranational. There is an inevitable correlation between the disciplinary background of the literatures and their respective focus on governance. The international approach, typified by the work of Andrew Moravscik, has its intellectual roots and sensibilities in international relations. The supranational approach, typified by the work of Weiler and others, has its roots and sensibilities in public law and comparative constitutionalism. The infranational approach, typified by the work of Giandomenico Majone and his Florence associates, stems from a background in domestic policy studies and the regulatory state. This is not, however, a case of disciplinary entrenchment. All approaches are mindful of the need to weave together the political and social, the legal and economic. The three approaches are aware of the others but choose to 'privilege' what, given the disciplinary background, seems most important to explain and understand in Union governance. More importantly, the approaches, in our view, reflect a reality. In some crucial spheres Union governance is international; in other spheres it is supranational; in yet others it is infranational. How the Single European Act was negotiated is not simply an example of the IR approach; it is an example of the Community at a high international or intergovernmental moment. Instances of supranational decision-making would be the adoption of the big framework harmonisation directives such as Banking or Video Rental Rights or, at a lower level, the Tobacco Labeling Directive and, no less interestingly, the rejection of the Tobacco Advertising Directive. The infranational approach is characterised by the relative unimportance of the national element in the decision making. Technical expertise, economic and social interests, administrative turf battles shape the process and outcome rather than 'national interest'. Infranational decision-making is typified by the miasma of, say, health and safety standard setting, telecommunications harmonisation policy, international trade rules-of-origin.

It is not, then, that the observational standpoint and the sensibility of the observer defines the phenomenon. There are three approaches, but also three modes of governance. Likewise, it would be facile, based on the above examples, to conclude that intergovernmental deals with 'important' issues, supranational with 'middle range' issues and infranational with trivia. Huge diplomatic effort may be invested in this or that provision of, say, the SEA; enormous resources may be invested in shepherding a harmonisation measure through the ever more complex Commission-Council-Parliament procedures; and yet the reality of important aspects of the Single Market may have a lot more to do with the details of implementation, with the actual standards set by committees and the like.

As Table 1 shows, for the international approach, states are the key players and Governments the principal actors. As a mode of governance, the Union, on this perspective is seen as an inter-national arena or regime in which governments (primarily the executive) are the privileged power holders. The Union is principally a context, a framework within which states/governments interact. In the supranational approach states are privileged players, but the Community/Union is not only or primarily a framework but a principal player as well. The privileged actors are state governments and Community institutions. State governments here are understood to include the legislative and judicial branches though not necessarily with equal weight. But here, too, the executive branch is the key state player. The Commission, Council and increasingly the European Parliament, are critical actors and fora of decision making. The infranational approach downplays both the Community and the member states as principal players and likewise the role of primary state and community institutions. In that it is distinct from the international and supranational. It is like the international approach in that Union is primarily a context, a framework within which actors interact. The actors however tend to be, both at Union and member state levels, administrations, departments, private and public associations, certain, mainly corporate, interest groups.

TABLE 1
INTERNATIONALISM, SUPRANATIONALISM AND INFRANATIONALISM –
STATIC (STRUCTURAL) ELEMENTS

Arena	International	Supranational	Infranational
Disciplinary Background of Observers	International Relations	Law (typically public law)	Policy Studies; Sociology
Typical Issues of Governance	Fundamental system rules; Issues with immediate political and electoral resonance; International "High-Politics"; Issues *dehors* Treaty	The primary legislative agenda of the Community; Enabling-legislation; Princpal Harmonization measures	Implementing and executive measures; standard setting;
Principal Players	member states	Union/Community & member states	[Union/Community is policy making context]
Principal Actors	Governments (Cabinets-Executive Branch)	Governments, Community Institutions: Commission, Council, Parliament	Second level organs of governance (Com. Directorate, Committee, Govt. departments etc.); Certain corporate and social-industrial NGOs.
Level of Institutionalisation	Low to Medium	High	Medium to Low
Mode of Political Process	Diplomatic negotiation	Legislative process bargaining	Adminstrative process, "networking
Type/style of Intercourse	Informal procedures; low level of process rules	Formal procedures; high level of process rules	Infromal procedures; low level of process rules
Visibility/ Transparency	High actor and event visibility. Low transparency of process	Medium to low actor and event visibility and medium to low transparency of process	Low actor and event visibility and low transparency of process

In the international mode the focus is on negotiation, intergovernmental bargaining and diplomacy. There is a relatively low level of institutionalisation, and a premium on informal and unstructured interaction. Formal sovereign equality (including a formal veto) and the loose reflexes of international law prevail which, of course, should not be understood as leading to full equalisation of power among the actors. The materia is often – though clearly not always – constitutional (in a non-technical sense). The *modus operandi* of the supranational mode is more structured, formal and rule bound. Bargaining and negotiation are far more akin to a domestic legislative process of coalition building, vote counting and rule manipulation. The materia is, frequently, primary legislation. Infranationalism is mostly about regulatory governance and management.

There is a medium to low level of institutionalisation, and informal networking between 'government' and corporate players abound. The international mode is characterised typically by high actor visibility and medium to low process visibility. Supranationalism is characterised by medium (aspiring to high!) actor visibility and medium to low process visibility. Infranationalism has both low actor and process visibility.

Internationalism, Supranationalism and Infranationalism – Dynamic Elements

The inter-supra-infra trichotomy enables us to build a better picture of the disbursement of power and accountability in the Union. Critical in building this picture is to understand not only the different modes of empowerment of various actors according to the mode of governance, but also the fluidity and hence dynamics of allocation of issues to the different forms of decision-making. The stakes as to arena, *where* (in this scheme) issues get decided, is as important as *what* gets decided, since the where determines the what. For the lawyers among readers, the ERTA decision or Opinion 1/76[4] was not about content but about forum and mode of decision-making: a bid by the Commission to transfer the treaty negotiation from the international to supranational arena. The Maastricht three-pillar structure is also about arena, and the various positions of the European Parliament in the ongoing Community debate should be partly understood as bids about mode rather than content of policy-making. Since the SEA, which saw the strengthening of both the legal framework of supranational decision-making and the relative empowerment of the Commission and Parliament, we have seen considerable political battles concerning fora rather than outcome. Comitology becomes a live issue in exactly the same period.

The static model already suggested 'inbuilt' empowerment of certain actors: state government in the international mode, state government and Community institutions in the supranational mode, administrations (national and Community) and certain corporate actors in the infranational mode. But this is only a starting point. Examine the three modes from the perspective of non-governmental public and private actors. Actors which have privileged access to national government (e.g., government political parties) could have an interest in international decision making. An opposition party may, by contrast, press for supranational decision-making, if the Community balance of power favours its position. A coalition of member states may pressage transfer of an issue in the supranational arena where majorities have more weight and are more legitimate. A minority or individual member state may press for transfer to the international arena where the specific gravity of each member state is higher.

Control and accountability are also critical variables in understanding the implication of the three modes. The international mode will favour domestic arenas of accountability (national parliaments, national press). The supranational mode suffers from all the defects which the Standard Version tends to highlight. Infranationalism has an all-round low level of accountability. By contrast, judicial review tends to be more substantive in the supranational arena, procedural in the infranational arena and scant in the international arena. When judicial review is perceived as a threat we may expect to find arena battles. All this suggests the need for a differentiated approach in understanding the democratic problems of European integration.

MODELS OF DEMOCRACY

Whatever insight the study of the three arenas may eventually yield regarding the disbursement and accountability of power, it will not, in and of itself, point to 'democratic' deficiencies or solutions. One key problem is that democratic theory and democratic sensibilities have developed almost exclusively in statal contexts. One enterprise would be to fashion a tailor-made democratic theory for the Community. We are far less ambitious. We wish to use off-the-peg democratic wares. But the discussion of demos and of governance illustrates the care with which we must handle the transferability of statal concepts to the European context. What is needed, perhaps, are different garments for the different arenas and modes of Union governance. We shall only explore possible 'fits' between various democratic models and Union modes of governance with a view to a better understanding of the problems of democratic governance in the Union.

International (Intergovernmental) Governance and the Consociational Model

Consociational theory emerged to fill a gap in traditional democratic theory. One of the main tasks of democratic theory was to explain the functionality and stability of pluralistic democratic political systems, given that by definition such systems would be divided by competing political forces. The classical explanation given by democratic theory to this basic paradox of functional stability in a competitive pluralistic society was by reference to the notion of cut-crossing cleavages which lead both to stability and functionality. By contrast when social cleavages reinforce each other (catholic-protestant; poor-rich; urban-agrarian), when the social policy is deeply fragmented, society becomes conflict-laden, which leads in turn (while democracy is preserved) to immobilism in policy-making and erosion of stability.

Yet historically, several smaller countries in Europe – Holland, Austria, Switzerland and Belgium up to a point – were socially 'cleavaged' in just that way, and yet managed to display in certain periods the functionality and stability of the centripetal explanation until the 1960s. (Daalder, a Dutchman, and one of the fathers of consociational theory, recalls how he was told by a leading political scientist: 'You know, your country theoretically cannot exist'.)[5] Consociational theory tries to explain the functionality and stability of these countries. Its basic explanatory device has been the behaviour of political elites which control/lead the fragmented social segments.

Crucial to consociational theory is the existence of sharply segmented societal sectors. Consociational theory is not interested in the reasons for segmentation (the content of the cleavages) but in their empirical existence. At this level, the model seems to correspond to the international dimension of Union governance: a transnational polity sharply segmented by its member states and indeed displaying the expected characteristics of immobilism, yet somehow creating structures which manage to transcend these immobilistic tendencies. Of course, the very creation of *structures and institutions* for the international mode, like the two non-Community Maastricht pillars, like the European Council, may be said to indicate a higher level of commonality than consociationalism is designed to accommodate. We think the commonality is in the desire to have a common policy but substantive policy fragmentation is acute in relation to several of the contexts in which the International mode operates. Indeed, *the very lack of substantive commonality is what pushed the member states to insist on this form of governance in this area.*

The essential characteristic of consociational democracy is not so much any particular institutional arrangement as the deliberate joint effort by the elites to render the system functional and stable. The key element is what Dahrendorf has termed a cartel of elites.[6] Consociational theorists seek to show how, in all successful consociational democracies, normal traditional political fora were bypassed, and substituted by fora in which the leaders of all social segments participated, and compacts were arrived at, disregarding the principle of majority rule and using instead consensual politics. Competitive features are removed and cooperation sought. Worth noting is that the alternative fora might in themselves become institutionalised and rather formal. Typically, consociationalism works on the basis of consensus, package deals and other features characteristic of elite bargaining. The elites, representing their respective segments, realise that the game is not zero-sum nor is it a winner take all.

The two basic requirements for success, according to consociational theory, would be that elites share a commitment to the maintenance of the system and to the improvement of its cohesion, functionality and stability; and that elites understand the perils of political fragmentation. Elites must also be able to 'deliver' their constituents (and compliance) to deals thus struck. This of course begs some questions. In traditional consociational theory this commitment will come out of the loyalty of elites to their country and society. Our claim is that the formal extension in Maastricht of Union governance to areas hitherto dealt with informally, or at best within European Political Cooperation, demonstrates a degree of commitment to the European polity which, however, is not matched by a sufficient degree of trust in supranational governance, hence consociationalism as a model.

But consociational theorists suggest it is possible in addition to identify several further features which will be conducive to the success of consociationalism. These include the length of time a consociational democracy has been in operation; the existence of external threats to the polity; the existence of a multiple balance of power; a relatively low total load on the decision-making apparatus. We think all these features are characteristic of the Union international mode of governance, too.

So far we have concentrated on the behaviour of the elites themselves. Consociational theory stipulates two further conditions for successful functioning: the elites must be able to carry their own segments along; there should be widespread approval of the principle of government by elite cartel. In looking at past practice there do seem to be several points of contact between the consociational model and the international practice of the Union: the existence of a structure composed of highly sharp segments (the member states) which display a tendency to immobilism (which classical theory would predict) but which manage nonetheless to score a measure of functionality and stability (which consociational theory tries to explain). The key factor of consociationalism elite behaviour (in our case governments) also seems confirmed in the international mode.

The advantage of consociationalism seems to be the achievement of stability in the face of a high degree of social fragmentation which normal pluralist models cannot achieve. There are, naturally, implications for self-understanding of democracy in the polity. The democratic justification of consociationalism begins from the acceptance of deep and permanent fragmentation in the polity. Even in traditional constitutional pluralist democracies there is an acceptance that certain 'high stake' decisions, such as constitutional amendments, require 'super majorities' or other mechanisms which would be more inclusive of minorities. Consociationalism rejects the democratic legitimacy of permanent minorityship which is possible, even likely, for a fragmented polity operating a pluralist, majoritarian election and voting system.

Consociationalism seems, thus, to enhance legitimacy in its inclusiveness and the broadening of ultimate consent to government. Theoretically, there is a strong case to be made for a consociational type of inclusiveness also in relation to at least certain areas of Union governance. If the international mode is, in fact, consociational, this would be a justification not from an efficiency and stability perspective but from a normative representational one as well.

The democratic problems of consociationalism, and hence of the Union, when operating in the International mode are no less grave. First, the democratic gaze must shift to the constituent units of the consociational model, the member states. It will often be discovered that some elites, within the consociational cartel of elites, have very deficient internal democratic structures of control and accountability. Even a facile comparison among the structures which exist within the various member states to control their governments is sufficient to illustrate this point. Even more troubling, consociationalism might actually act as a retardant to internal democratisation, because the 'external' context both empowers the representing elite (executive branch of government) and may even create a mobilising ethos of the 'national interest' which justifies sacrificing calls for transparency and accountability. These calls can be, and usually are, presented as 'weakening' the ability of the elite to represent effectively in the external context.

Second, consociational power-sharing is favourable to 'status' social forces, those whose elites participate in the cartel. It excludes social forces which are not so recognised. 'New' minorities are typically disfavoured by consociational regimes. The corollary of this in the Union would be 'new' minorities within the member states whose voices are not vindicated by the government and are those doubly disfavoured both at national and Union levels. Consociationalism can be seen as weakening true representative and responsive government.

Finally, consociational politics typically favour the social status quo and, while mediating the problems of deeply fragmented societies, also are instrumental in maintaining those very fragments. This can be highly problematic for some conceptions of European integration. Given that the consociational fragments in this context are the member states themselves, the international mode understood in consociational terms is not only about ensuring the inclusion of all member state voices in certain critical areas but in actually sustaining the member states and their governments as such and, for example, retarding the formation of transnational coalitions of interests who, in the areas of the international mode, would and could have no impact in a process which privileged states and their governments.

Supranationalism, Pluralism and Competitive Elitism

The supranational mode of governance is the closest to a state model and thus, paradoxically perhaps, we shall say little about it. It can be analysed most profitably in our views, either with insights from the Weberian or Schumpeterian competitive elites model of democracy, or, aspirationally at least, to a statal, federal version of pluralist democracy. The Standard Version we presented captures most of its actual or potential shortcomings.

Infranationalism and the Neo-Corporatist Model of Governance and Democracy

It is not our claim that Infranationalism is the Union variety of neo-corporatism but they share some common features and hence the conjunction of both may help us identify some of the democratic problems with infranationalism.

Classical neo-corporatism identified a privileging of government, industry and labour in an attempt to avoid a confrontational mode of governance and reach a politics of accommodation which would resolve economic problems in both periods of expansion and stagnation. The focus was on macroeconomic policy as defining the central public choices confronting the polity. Neo-corporatism believed in management, distrusted to some extent markets, and favoured stability and predictability. It is not surprising that its political instincts also favoured governance through negotiation with highly organised interests having representational monopoly. In some respect neo-corporatism is a technocratic version of consociationalism. Neo-corporatism does not replace parliament and other institutions and processes of pluralist democratic government, but simply side-steps them in reaching the fundamental public choices of the polity. Inevitably there is an erosion in the substantive power and status of parliamentary bodies' parties and the like. Corporatism of pre-World War II was aimed at undermining those aspects of pluralist democracy in the name of efficiency and stability. Its postwar neo-corporatist version did not have that objective but had some similar institutional frameworks.

The infranational arena is no neo-corporatist model. Its reach extends well beyond macro-economic policy and the concerns of managing the business cycles which dominated politics of the 1960s and 1970s. It is decidedly not a tripartite relationship between government, business and labour, but it has some evocatively similar features:

1. The underlying ethos of Infranationalism is managerial and technocratic, the belief that rational regulatory solutions can be found

by employment of expertise.

2. There is an underlying premise which puts a premium on stability and growth and is suspicious of strongly redistributive policies and, more generally, on ideology and 'politics'.

3. Infranationalism strongly encourages representational monopolies and the creation of structures which will channel organised functional interests into the policy-making and management procedures.

4. Infranationalism, because of its managerial, functional and technocratic bias, operates outside parliamentary channels, outside party politics. There is nothing sinister or conspiratorial in infranationalism, but its processes typically lack transparency and may have low procedural and legal guarantees. It seeks its legitimation in results rather than process.

As we would expect, in some respects infranationalism overcomes some of the problems of the international mode. It is both an expression of, and instrumental in, the decline of the state and its main organs as the principal vehicle for vindicating interest in the European polity. Infranationalism is about transnational interest groups, governance without (state) government, empowerment beyond national boundaries and the like. But it suffers too from many of the problems of neo-corporatism and some problems of its own. We would mention in particular the following:

(a) The technocratic and managerial solutions often mask ideological choices which are not debated and subject to public scrutiny beyond the immediate interests related to the regulatory or management area.

(b) Participation in the process is limited to those privileged by the process; fragmented and diffuse interests, other public voices are often excluded.

(c) As in the consociational model, the process itself might distort power relationships and democracy within the groups represented in the process.

(d) The process itself not only lacks transparency but also is typically of low procedural formality, thus not ensuring real equality of voice of those who actually do take part in the process. Judicial review is scanty and tends to insist on basic rights to be heard, rather than fairness of outcome.

(e) In general, the classical instruments of control and public accountability are ill-suited to the practices of infranationalism. They are little affected by elections, change in government and the new instruments introduced by Maastricht.

FUNDAMENTAL RIGHTS AND FUNDAMENTAL BOUNDARIES

Let us start with truism. Although the principle of universal suffrage and majoritarianism informs all modern systems of democratic governance, it is not an absolute principle. Modern democracies, taking their cue principally from the American rather than British democratic tradition, increasingly acknowledge a higher law – typically a constitution – which binds even the legislature. In an increasing number of modern democracies the higher law is backed up by courts and a system of judicial review which give it teeth. Within this constitutional ethos, judicial protection of fundamental human rights has a central place. Constitutionalism, despite its counter-majoritarian effect, is regarded as a complementary principle to majoritarianism rather than its negation. One formulation which describes the complex relationship between the two is the notion of protection against a tyranny of the majority. We will not enter into the complex theoretical discussion of rights and their relationship to democracy. The appeal of rights, whatever the theoretical justification, has two roots. The first of these regards fundamental rights as an expression of a vision of humanity which vests the deepest values in the individual which may not be compromised by anyone. Probably one of the oldest and most influential sources of this vision is to be found in the Pentateuch: 'And God created man in His own image, in the image of God created He him.' (Gen.I:27). With this trademark, what legislator has the authority to transgress the essential humanity of the species? Naturally, there are secular, humanist parallels aplenty. The other root for the great appeal of rights, and part of the justification of their counter-majoritarian semblance, looks to them as an instrument for putting constraints on power. Modern democracy emerges, after all, also as a rejection of absolutism, and absolutism is not the prerogative of kings and emperors. .

Similar sentiments inform the great appeal of fundamental boundaries in non-unitary systems, federal states and the European Union. We use the term Fundamental Boundaries as a way of conceptualising in a normative sense the principle of enumerated powers or limited competences of the central authorities in these systems. The appeal of fundamental boundaries rests in two parallel roots. First, as an expression of a vision of humanity which vests the deepest values in individual communities existing within larger polities which, thus, may not be transgressed. The vision of humanity derives from an acknowledgement of the social nature of humankind, as a counterbalance to the potential atomism of fundamental rights – 'And the Lord God said: It is not good that man should be alone' – (Gen. II:18), and from the realisation that smaller social units can suffer parallel oppression to individuals by stronger societal forces. That enumeration is also said to work as a bulwark against aggregation of power is its second appeal.

We are unaware of any federal system which does not claim to give expression to these notions. But there are as many variants as there are systems. Comparative analysis can be particularly alluring here. In Europe there has been a practical eruption of the hitherto dormant question of Community 'competences and powers', a question and debate which has found its code in the deliciously vague word and concept of subsidiarity. This is inevitably connected to the continued preoccupation with governance structures and processes, balance between Community and member state, and the democracy and legitimacy of the Community.

What accounts for this eruption? The student of comparative federalism discovers a constant feature in practically all federative experiences: a tendency, which differs only in degree, towards controversial concentration of legislative and executive power in the centre/general power at the expense of constituent units. This is apparently so independently of the mechanism for allocation of jurisdiction/competences/powers between centre and periphery. Differences, where they occur, are dependent more on the ethos and political culture of polities rather than on mechanical devices.

The Community has both shared and differed from this general experience. It has *shared* it in that the Community, especially in the 1970s, has seen a weakening of any workable and enforceable mechanism for allocation of jurisdiction/competences/powers between Community and its member states. It has occurred by a combination of two factors.

(a) Profligate legislative practices especially, for example, in the usage of Article 235.

(b) A bifurcated jurisprudence of the Court, which on the one hand extensively interpreted the reach of the jurisdiction/competences/ powers granted to the Community, and on the other hand has taken a self-limiting approach towards the expansion of Community jurisdiction/competence/powers when exercised by the political organs.

To make the above statement is not tantamount to criticising the Community, its political organs and the Court. This is a question of values. It is a sustainable thesis, which we share, that this process was overall beneficial, in its historical context, to the evolution and well-being of Community, member states and its citizens and residents. But this process was also a ticking constitutional time bomb which one day might threaten the evolution and stability of the Community. Sooner or later, 'Supreme' courts in the member states would realise that the 'Socio-legal Contract', announced by the Court in its major constitutionalising decisions, namely that 'the Community constitutes a new legal order... for the benefit of which the states have limited their sovereign rights, *albeit within limited fields*' (emphasis added) has been shattered, that although they (the 'Supreme' courts) have accepted the principles of the new legal order – supremacy and direct effect – the fields do not seem any more to be limited, and that in the absence of Community legislative or legal checks it will fall on them to draw the jurisdictional lines of the Community and its member states.[7]

The interesting thing about the Community experience, and this is where it *does not share the experience of other federative polities*, is that, despite the massive *legislative* expansion of Community jurisdiction/competences/powers, there had not been any political challenge or crisis on this issue from the member states. (The challenges and dissatisfaction occurred on some of the occasions when competences mutated as a result of a Court decision such as in the *ERTA* case or *Rubber* Opinion).[8]

How is this so? The answer is simple and obvious and resides in the pre-Single European Act decision-making process. Unlike federal states, the governments of the member states themselves (jointly and severally) could control absolutely the *legislative* expansion of jurisdiction/competences/powers. Nothing that was done could be done without the assent of all national capitals. This fact diffused any sense of threat and crisis on the part of governments.

This era has now passed with the shift to majority voting, and the seeds – indeed the buds – of crisis are with us. Not only is there an imminent danger that one of the national courts will take the position predicted (and this might happen sooner rather than later, with the decision pending before the Federal Constitutional Court in Germany, concerning the Television Without Frontiers Directive), but the member states have become aware that in a process that does not give them a *de jure* or *de facto* veto, the question of jurisdictional lines has become crucial.

Our own concern is that if something is not done so that the European Court of Justice is seen to be the obvious body for resolving this kind of prospective dispute, some national supreme courts will 'rebel' very much as the Italian and German Constitutional Courts 'rebelled' in the 1960s and early 1970s on the issue of protection of fundamental human rights, when it was not clear that the European Court was going to act in this matter in a vigorous manner. We are well aware that in theory the Court already has jurisdiction to resolve this kind of issue under Article 173 and 177(b) (lack of competences), but since to date no Commission or Council measure has been struck down for pure and simple lack of competences our assessment is that this existing provision in itself will not satisfy the fears of the member states.

The German Constitutional Court rejected the ECJ's claim to exclusive judicial *Kompetenz-Kompetenz,* and claimed that the limits to Community legislative powers was as much a matter of German constitutional law as it was a matter of Community law.[9] As such, the German Constitutional Court regards itself as competent, indeed, as mandated, by the German Constitution to monitor the jurisdictional limits of the Community legislative process. Formally, the decision constitutes a flagrant act of defiance vis-à-vis the European Court of Justice, in direct contradiction with its jurisprudence on the power of national courts to declare Community law invalid. It flies in the face, *inter alia*, of the third paragraph of Article 177. It is also untenable in a legal functionalist sense. There would be as many fundamental boundaries to the Community as there are member states. And how can the same Community measure be considered intra-vires in one member state and ultra-vires in another?

How should one evaluate this development in legal-political terms? We want to use some of dynamics of the Cold War as a device for evaluating the judicial *Kompetenz-Kompetenz* aspect of the Maastricht Decision of the German Constitutional Court. On this reading, it is not a declaration of war, but the commencement of a cold war with its paradoxical guarantee of co-existence, following the infamous MAD logic: Mutual Assured Destruction. For the German Court actually to declare a Community norm unconstitutional, rather than simply threaten to do so, would be an extremely hazardous move, so hazardous as to make its usage unlikely. The use of a tactical nuclear weapon always was considered to carry the risk of creating a nuclear domino effect. If other member state courts followed the German lead, or if other member states legislatures or governments were to suspend implementation of the norm on some reciprocity rationale, a veritable constitutional crisis in the Community could become a reality – the legal equivalent of the Empty Chair political boycott in the 1960s. It would be hard for the German government to remedy the situation especially if the German Court decision enjoyed general popularity. Would the German Constitutional Court be willing to face the responsibility of dealing such a blow (rather than a threat of a blow) to European integration?

The logic of the Cold War is that one has to assume the worst and to arm as if the other side would contemplate a first strike. The European Court of Justice would, thus, have to be watching over its shoulder the whole time, trying to anticipate any potential move by the German Constitutional Court. It could be argued that this situation is not unhealthy because the German move of the 1990s, in relation to competences, resembles their prior move in relation to human rights, and that it was only that move which forced the European Court to take human rights seriously. Thus, the current move will force the Court to take competences seriously.

This view has some merit, but we find it unpersuasive for two reasons.

First, there is no 'non-proliferation treaty' in the Community structure. MAD works well, perhaps, in a situation of two superpowers. But there must be a real fear that other member state Courts will follow the German lead in rejecting the exclusive judicial *Kompetenz-Kompetenz* of the ECJ. The more courts that adopt the weapon, the greater the chances that it will be used.

Second, courts are not the principal Community players. The German Government and governments whose Courts will follow the German lead, will surely be tempted to play that card in negotiation. 'We really cannot compromise on this point, since our Court will strike it down...'

For reasons which space does not allow to elaborate, we do not think that a solution to this problem can be found by a simple drawing up of a new list of competences for the Community. Instead, we believe that a long term solution requires a change of ethos. Institutions can play a role in this. We would propose the creation of a Constitutional Council for the Community, modelled in some ways on its French namesake. The Constitutional Council would have jurisdiction only over issues of competences (including subsidiarity) and would decide cases submitted to it after a law was adopted, but before coming into force. It could be seized by any Community institution, any member state or by the European Parliament acting on a majority of its members. Its President would be the President of the European Court of Justice and its members would be sitting members of the constitutional courts or their equivalents in the member states. Within the Constitutional Council no single member state would have a veto power. The composition would also underscore that the question of competences is fundamentally also one of national constitutional norms but still subject to a Union solution by a Union institution.

We cannot elaborate here some of the technical aspects of the proposal. Its principal merit, if it has any, is that it gives expression to the fundamental boundary concern without, however, compromising the constitutional integrity of the Community, as did the German Maastricht decision. Since, from a material point of view, the question of boundaries has an inbuilt indeterminacy, the critical issue becomes not what are the boundaries but who decides. The composition of the proposed Constitutional Council removes the issue, on the one hand, from the purely political arena; on the other hand, it creates a body which, on this issue, would, we expect, enjoy a far greater measure of public confidence than the ECJ itself.

NOTES

We thank Zenon Benkowski, Neil McCormick, Andrew Scott, Simon Bulmer and the Edinburgh Seminar on Legal Theory and European Integration for helpful comments on an earlier draft as well as Anne Marie Slaughter and other participants of the Harvard Seminar on Advanced Issues in the Law and Policy of European Integration. The usual disclaimer applies.

1. See, e.g., P. Kirchhof, 'Der deutsche Staat im Prozeß der europäischen integration', in Josef

Isensee and Paul Kirchhof (eds.), *Handbuch des Staatsrechts der Bundesrepublik Deutschland*, Vol.VII: Normativität und Schutz der Verfassung – Internationale Beziehungen, Heidelberg 1992, p.855; P. Kirchhof, 'Europäische Einigung und der Verfassungsstaat der Bundesrepublik Deutschland', in Josef Isensee (ed.), *Europa als politische Idee und als rechtliche Form* (Berlin, 1993), p.63. On the 'Schmittian connection' see Weiler, 'The State über alles', in Festschrift Everling (*Nomos,* 1995)
2. See A. Carty, Alfred Verdross and Othmar Spann, 'German Romantic Nationalism, National Socialism and International Law', *European Journal of International Law*, (forthcoming).
3. J. Habermas, 'Staatsbürgerschaft und nationale Identität (1990)', in Jürgen Habermas, *Faktizität und Geltung, Beiträge zur Diskurstheorie des Rechts und des demokratischen Rechtsstaats* (Frankfurt/M., 1992), pp.632–60.
4. Case 22/70, Commission v. Council (ERTA case), [1971] ECR 263 Opinion 1/76, [1977] ECR 741.
5. H. Daalder, 'The Consociational Democracy Theme', *World Politics* 26/4, (1974), p.606.
6. Ralf Dahrendorf, *Society and Democracy in Germany* (Garden City 1967), p.276.
7. For a full discussion of constitutional cases and literature on new legal order, see Weiler, 'The Transformation of Europe', 100 *Yale Law Journal* 2403 (1991).
8. Case 22/70, Commission v. Council (ERTA case), [1971] ECR 263; Opinion 1/78, International Agreement on Natural Rubber, [1979] ECR 2871.
9. Decision of the *Bundesverfassungsgericht*, BVerfGE 89, 155, at 188 (1993).

FURTHER READING

G. Soledad (ed.), *European Identity and the Search for Legitimacy* (London: Pinter 1993).

E. Meehan, *Citizenship and the European Community* (London, Newbury Park CA.: Sage 1993).

A. von Bogdandy, *Die Europäische Option* (Baden-Baden: Nomos 1993).

J. Weiler, 'The State 'über alles' – Demos, Telos and the German Maastricht Decision' in O. Due et al. (eds.), *Festschrift for U. Everling* (Baden-Baden: Nomos, forthcoming 1995)

Ph. Schmitter, 'Representation and the Euro-Polity', in T. Ellwen, J.J. Hesse, D. Grimm, G.F. Schuppent (eds.) *Jahrbuch zur Staat und Verwaltungswissenschaft*, Vol.6 55, (1992/93).

Political Parties, Popular Legitimacy and Public Privilege

PETER MAIR

The challenge facing the established party democracies and the apparent growth in popular disenchantment with parties is not a function of party decline as such. Rather, it can be associated with a contradictory development in which parties at one and the same time become less relevant as representative agencies (in terms of both their purposive role and their position on the ground) while achieving more status and privileges in their role as public-office holders.

When the nobles had real power as well as privileges, when they governed and administered, their rights could be at once greater and less open to attack... True, the nobles enjoyed invidious privileges and rights that weighed heavily on the commoner, but in return for this they kept order, administered justice, saw to the execution of laws, came to the rescue of the oppressed, and watched over the interests of all. The more these functions passed out of the hands of the nobility, the more uncalled-for did their privileges appear – until at last their mere existence seemed a meaningless anachronism.[1]

Two major waves of democratisation have marked the beginning and the end of twentieth century European political history. In the first 20 years, democratisation involved the opening up of the political process to more and more formerly excluded citizens, and the granting of the vote to the propertyless and to at least some women. Most recently, in the last 20 years, and beginning with the transformations in Greece and Portugal, we have witnessed the widespread collapse of authoritarian regimes, and their replacement by multi-party democracies. The experiences were far from identical, of course: in the one period, democratisation was carried by means of enfranchisement and incorporation, and, in the other, it was effected by means of regime change, a contrast which has also forced other differences to become apparent, most noticeably in terms of the sheer pace and controllability of the democratisation process itself. For whereas the democratisation process which took place in most of the European countries in the first 20 years of the century was relatively gradual and managed, the most recent experiences of democratisation in southern Europe, and most especially in post-communist Europe, have proved both rapid and abrupt.

But despite such crucial differences, there nevertheless remains one major similarity between both processes: that is, both waves of democratisation have emphasised, if not required, the agency of political parties. In the first wave, and in the early part of the century, democratisation was accompanied by the development and the essential triumph of the mass party, which, in Pizzorno's terms, 'emerge[d] both to strengthen and control the access of the new masses into the political system'.[2] These were parties which, necessarily so, were strongly rooted in civil society; which emphasised engagement and involvement; and which at the same time were hierarchical and disciplined. These were parties which came from and belonged to civil society, and which sought to express and then implement the interests of their constituency within public policy. In the most recent wave of democratisation, too, the role of party has been central, although now, more than half-a-century on, there is little to suggest that this emphasis on party will promote the emergence of mass parties as such, in that the parties which are developing in both southern and eastern Europe tend to be typified by loose organisational structures, by small if not non-existent memberships, and by an absence of any pronounced ties to civil society. But although far removed from the styles and structures associated with the traditional mass party, the role of party in building these new democracies has nevertheless proved crucial, with the importance of party being seen even in the manner in which these new democracies are defined. For in situations where democratisation has resulted from a change of regime rather than from a process of enfranchisement, we see democracy itself being defined not in terms of the rights of citizens, but rather in terms of the existence of a plurality of parties, which compete against one another in free elections.

In modern democracies, therefore, whether these are long-established democracies or newly-created democracies, politics is about party politics; to put it another way, the twentieth century is not only the century of democratisation, and hence of democracy, but it is also the century of *party democracy*. As the century closes, however, it has become increasingly clear that many of the long-established party democracies in particular are beginning to show distinctly unhealthy symptoms. For despite, or as I will suggest, perhaps even *because of*, the importance of party in our modern democracies, party democracy itself has become an increasingly troubled form of democracy.

For more than a decade now, a major theme within both academic and journalistic discourse has taken 'the decline of party' as more or less a matter of conventional wisdom. Parties are *passé*, it is often argued, and even if it may have been precipitate to have written them off as a result of the challenge of neo-corporatism, a supposedly enduring phenomenon which appears itself to have experienced an untimely demise, it is now the assault from the ground, in the form of changing citizen preferences, which is finally proving to be the catalyst of change. There are two related elements within this new transformative process. On the one hand, the citizenry is seen to have become fragmented and individualised, and preferences have become 'particularised'[3] in a manner which is largely anathema to the aggregative instincts of traditional party politics. On the other hand, competing channels of representation have opened up in the form of new social movements and 'alternative organisations'[4] which are often believed to link citizens to the decision-making process in a manner which is at once more effective and more satisfactory.

Both elements are seen to imply that parties, at least as we know them, become increasingly marginalised and ineffective, with the result that, in time, they may simply wither away. This is not seen as necessarily problematic. Indeed, were parties to decline and then eventually disappear, this might even be seen by some observers as a potentially healthy process, in which an increasingly outdated *Jurassic Park*-style politics would be replaced by involvement in other 'political' activities which would be closer to the citizens' interests, and in which these citizens could play a more direct and responsible role. Such a development would therefore imply the development of a more self-sufficient citizenry, and this could only be good for democracy. The decline of parties, in short, could be seen to reflect an inevitable change, a change that is certainly not worse, and is perhaps even better; a change, that is, to a healthier, more participant and more self-controlled style of democracy.

But although there may be a certain truth in these assumptions about party decline, it is nevertheless only a partial truth, in that parties are viewed from one perspective only, that is, from the perspective of their relations with civil society. As a result, these assumptions tend to overlook the extraordinary capacity of parties to see off challenges and so ensure their own survival.[5] Even beyond that, however, the assumption that the declining popular relevance of political parties may eventually lead to their passing in quite an unproblematic way is also very questionable. As I will suggest, the difficulty with this latter assumption is that it misses the essential contradiction between an apparent weakening of the role of parties as representative agencies, on the one hand, and an apparent strengthening of their role as public-office holders, on the other. It is, in this sense, a contradiction between the relevance (or its absence) of parties, on the one hand, and their visibility on the other; or, more sharply, between the legitimacy (or its absence) of parties, on the one hand, and their privileged position on the other. It is the existence of this particular contradiction which may well pose much more severe problems than are implied by any simple hypothesis of 'party decline'. Before returning to this question, however, I will first briefly review some of the evidence regarding the role of parties as representative agencies, which includes the position of parties 'on the ground' and their relevance as 'purposive' actors, and some of the evidence regarding their position as public office holders.

PARTIES AS REPRESENTATIVE AGENCIES

Parties on the ground

The most easy and oft-cited evidence of the erosion of parties in modern European democracies is usually drawn, first, from the perspective of ordinary voters and citizens, with the most obvious symptom of this malaise being seen in the already ample but still growing evidence of popular disenchantment and even distrust of parties and of the political class more generally. Indeed, this sense of disenchantment has become so pervasive and endemic that there is now a whole new terminology in which it can be expressed. Whatever the terms, however, it is an attitude which is more than evident from opinion surveys throughout Europe. It can be seen in Norway, for example, where almost half the respondents to a survey in 1989 agreed that politicians basically did not know what they were talking about; or in France, where more than two-thirds of respondents to a survey in 1991 felt that politicians were not very interested in their problems; or in Austria, where a survey in 1989 reported that more than two-thirds of respondents expressed agreement with the proposition that politicians were essentially 'corrupt and bribable'; or in Germany, where a 1991 survey reported that only a quarter of those questioned expressed confidence in the political parties, and that almost two-thirds believed that politicians lined their own pockets; or in the United Kingdom, where a 1994 survey reported that almost two-thirds of respondents regarded the Conservative party as 'sleazy and disreputable'.[6]

Second, and perhaps unsurprisingly, these sorts of attitudes have sometimes translated into a loosening sense of party attachment or party identification. It must be emphasised, however, that this particular trend is far from universal, and in some cases the sense of party belonging among voters does not appear to have been eroded. Nevertheless, there are at least five countries where a decline is certainly apparent. In Austria, for example, those reporting any sense of identification with political parties, whether this be a strong or a weak identification, fell from some 75 per cent of voters in 1969 to 59 per cent in 1990; in West Germany, a similar measure evidenced a decline from 82 per cent in 1972 to less than 75 per cent in 1987, while in Ireland the proportion fell from just over 72 per cent in 1981 to just 40 per cent in 1989. In Sweden, those reporting a strong sense of party identification fell from 52 per cent of voters in 1960 to 27 per cent in 1988, and in the UK the proportion of those with a strong sense of identification with either Labour or the Conservatives fell from some 22 per cent in 1964 to just seven per cent in 1987.[7]

The third symptom of this malaise, the one which may perhaps prove most worrying for the parties, is reflected in trends in party membership. At one level, the changes here may not seem particularly marked and the sense of decay is not particularly pronounced. Six of the eleven countries for which comparable data from the 1960s onwards are available, for example, record an actual increase in the total numbers of party members between the early 1960s and the beginning of the 1990s (the countries are Belgium, Finland, France, Germany, Norway and Sweden), with only five recording a decline in the total numbers of members across the same period (Austria, Denmark, Italy, the Netherlands, and the UK).[8] At another level, however, and more crucially, the change is quite marked, in that this period has also witnessed a massive growth in the size of European electorates (see also Table 1 below), and the major problem associated with levels of party membership is that they have failed to keep pace with this expansion. In other words, while the total numbers of members may sometimes have remained the same, or even increased, the *relative* membership/electorate ratio has more often than not declined, thus indicating a reduced organisational presence within the society. In fact, only two of the eleven countries for which comparable data are available, Belgium and Germany, have registered an increase in the share of the electorate who maintain a party membership (increasing from 7.8 per cent to 9.2 per cent of the electorate in the case of Belgium, and from 2.7 per cent to 4.2 per cent in the case of West Germany), while a third country, France, has evinced a more or less stable (albeit low) membership-electorate ratio over time. All other countries, by contrast, have registered a sharp decline in their relative membership levels, ranging from the remarkable Danish fall from more than 21 per cent of the electorate in the early 1960s to just less than seven per cent of the electorate in the late 1980s, to the more muted fall of less than one per cent in Sweden across the same period.

TABLE 1
VOTING TURNOUT IN WESTERN EUROPE, 1960s AND 1990s

| Country | Early 1960s: | | | Early 1990s: | | |
	Year	Turnout N ('000)	%	Year	Turnout N ('000)	%
Austria	1962	4424.7	94.2	1990	4848.7	86.1
Belgium	1961	5573.9	92.3	1991	6624.0	92.7
Denmark	1960	2439.9	85.8	1990	3265.2	82.8
Finland[a]	1962	2310.1	85.1	1991	2777.0	72.1
France	1962	18918.2	68.7	1993	35222.1	68.9
Germany[b]	1961	32849.6	87.7	1990	37830.0	78.6
Ireland	1961	1179.7	70.6	1992	1751.4	68.5
Italy	1963	31766.1	92.9	1992	41404.4	87.3
N'ands[c]	1963	6420.0	95.1	1994	8966.2	78.3
Norway	1961	1850.5	79.1	1993	2472.6	75.8
Sweden	1960	4271.6	85.9	1991	5562.9	86.7
UK	1964	27698.2	77.2	1992	33653.8	77.8

	Early 1960s:	Early 1990s:
Total N. Votes ('000):	139,702.5	184,378.3
Mean turnout (%):	84.6	79.6
Excluding N'lands:	83.6	79.8

Notes: a The percentage turnout in 1991 excludes the votes of Finnish citizens living abroad,
who were given the right to vote in 1975 and who currently participate in very small
numbers.
b The 1990 figure refers only to West Germany.
c Compulsory voting in the Netherlands, or, more correctly, compulsory attendance at
the ballot box, was abolished in 1970.

Sources: T.T. Mackie and Richard Rose, *The International Almanac of Electoral History*
(Basingstoke: Macmillan, 3rd ed., 1991); Ruud Koole and Peter Mair (eds.), *Political
Data Yearbook*, Vols 1, 2 and 3, special issues of the *European Journal of Political
Research* 22/4 (1992) 24/4 (1993) and 26/4 (1994).

This near universal decline in party membership as a share of the
electorate clearly indicates that the parties' relative hold on the electorate is
being weakened, and this, together with the other evidence cited above,
further reinforces the sense of erosion in the position of the party on the
ground, and hence a weakening of the capacity of parties to act as
representative agencies. What is striking to note, however, is that this sense
of erosion is not really immediately discernible at the level of rates of
turnout in national elections, even though, in this particular context, patterns
of turnout are difficult to interpret. On the one hand, it might be possible to
cite long-term trends in the levels of voting turnout, in the expectation that
a weakening of the position of the party on the ground would be reflected

in a declining propensity to vote. There is little sign of this in reality, however: levels of turnout at national elections still remain reasonably high, and precisely because the size of the electorate has grown so substantially, the sheer numbers of those voting has also grown. Indeed, despite a modest decline in average turnout levels from just less than 84 per cent to just less than 80 per cent across most of western Europe between the early 1960s and the early 1990s, the actual numbers of those voting in national elections increased by almost one-third – from some 140 million in the early 1960s to more than 184 million in the early 1990s (see Table 1). These figures therefore offer little or no evidence of disenchantment or malaise. On the other hand, it also seems to be the case that a small but nonetheless increasing proportion of these voters in a variety of different countries are now expressing a preference for 'new-politics' parties of the left and the right, many of which mobilise as 'anti-party parties' in opposition to the established order (discussed below). Thus while an increased vote for these parties might be taken to indicate rising anti-party sentiment, and hence malaise, it may also result in an increase (or, at least, not a decrease) in voter turnout, and this, in turn, may be read as evidence of the maintenance of trust and legitimacy. In this particular context, therefore, it is difficult to reach any hard and fast conclusions about potential disenchantment with parties from turnout figures alone.

Parties as purposive actors

From one perspective, then, it can be argued that parties are increasingly unable to *engage* voters and to win their affective commitment. From another perspective, and especially within the boundaries of traditional politics, it might be argued that they are also increasingly unable to convince voters of their relevance in purposive terms. Part of the problem here lies in the changing international circumstances within which national states, and hence national governments and the parties which occupy these governments, attempt to guide and control domestic policy-making. In one sense, all of the European economies are now open economies, and all are becoming 'semi-sovereign',[9] in that they are now subject to a set of constraints and persuasions that lie quite outside their own direct control. The freedom of manoeuvre of national states and national governments is therefore severely constricted, and the scope for partisan discretion is correspondingly curtailed. This has two immediate effects on the capacity of parties in government to act as representative agencies. In the first place, the responses of national governments to political and economic problems increasingly tend to be influenced by international as well as local pressures, and hence they cannot always respond to domestic demands in a way which fully satisfies the local interests on which they depend for their legitimacy and authority. Second, and perhaps more importantly, the increasing complexity of the global economy leads to severe problems for the monitoring and control of the policy-making process, and hence undermines the capacity for effective and authoritative action.[10] The result is that governments, and hence the parties in those governments, often find themselves increasingly unable to cope, and increasingly unable to convince sceptical voters of the merits of their partisan purpose.

Indeed, a partisan purpose is itself more difficult to discern. All 'established' parties in western Europe, with one or two notable exceptions, have now been in government at one time or another in the past 15 or 20 years; all have had their hands on power – whether exclusively or in concert with others; and all have operated within the limits imposed by the post-1973 international economic environment. Faced with burgeoning economic and social problems, many of which in any case lie outside the control of national governments, none of these parties can now plausibly claim to provide a panacea. Moreover, as Richard Rose has pointed out, since much of contemporary policy-making is simply policy-making by inertia, in which governments tinker at the margins of programmes which they have largely inherited,[11] none of these parties might prove capable of even the plausible promise of something new and different, at least in a purposive sense. Given that some of the most exacting scholarship in political science in the early 1980s found it difficult to determine conclusively whether parties had made a difference,[12] it would then hardly be surprising to find that ordinary voters might also have despaired of a partisan intent.

Nor is this process likely to be ameliorated by the increasing integration of states into the European Union. Quite the contrary. In the first place, despite the growing evidence of popular scepticism about the benefits of further integration, almost all mainstream parties in almost all Western European countries are more or less in agreement on the need to pursue the European project, with the challenge to this overarching consensus coming principally from either fringe parties on the left and right, or from maverick elements within the established parties. Here, too, differences within the mainstream have been blurred to almost non-existence. Second, as noted above, the Europeanisation of policy-making will further constrict the discretion available to national governments and hence to the parties in those national governments, and will further curtail their room for manoeuvre, thus accentuating the apparent decline in their authority. Finally, precisely because decision-making within Europe itself is not seen to be mediated by party – decisions are taken primarily by either the representatives of national governments acting behind closed doors in the various councils of ministers, or by commissioners who formally eschew a representative role, or even, and more marginally so, by a European Parliament which is organized by parliamentary groups standing at one remote remove from the parties as organized at national level – this is likely to undermine even further the relevance of party in representative terms. .

TABLE 2
DISTANCE ON A LEFT-RIGHT SCALE BETWEEN MAJOR PARTY OF THE LEFT AND MAJOR
PARTY OF THE CENTRE RIGHT, 1983 AND 1993

Country	Parties	Distance in 1983	Distance in 1993a	% Change
Austria	SPÖ-ÖVP	2.8	1.7	-39.3
Belgium	PS/SP-PSC/CVP	3.4	2.0	-41.2
Denmark	SD-Con	3.5	3.6	+2.9
Finland	SD-Nat.Coal	4.2	3.3	-21.4
France	PS-RR	5.6	Q4.2	-25.0
Germany	SPD-CDU	3.4	2.9	-14.7
Ireland	Lab-FF	2.7	1.9	-29.6
Italy	PCI/PDS-DC	3.8	4.2	+10.5
N'lands	PvdA-CDA	3.1	2.3	-25.9
Norway	Lab-Con	4.7	4.3	-8.5
Spain	PSOE-PP/AP	4.8	3.9	-18.8
Sweden	SD-Con	4.8	4.7	-2.1
UK	Lab-Con	5.5	3.6	-34.6

Notes: a The 1993 figures have been adjusted to allow a comparison between the 1993 index, which is based on a 10-point scale (1-10), and the 1983 index, which is based on an 11-point scale.

Source: 1983: Francis G. Castles and Peter Mair, 'Left-Right Political Scales: Some "Expert" Judgments', *European Journal of Political Research* 12/1 (1984), pp.73–88; 1993: John Huber and Ronald Inglehart, 'Expert Interpretations of Party Space and Party Location in 42 Societies', *Party Politics* 1/1 (1995), pp.73–111.

The decline of a partisan purpose and the blurring of differences between traditional parties can also be seen at a variety of other levels. In the first place, and most directly, it can be seen in the declining distance which separates these parties in left-right terms. Within the last decade, for example, as two comparable 'expert' surveys indicate (see Table 2), the gap which separates the traditional major party on the left from that on the centre-right has declined in 11 of the 13 European countries for which the comparable data are available. In some cases, the increasing proximity of the traditional opponents is particularly marked, as in Belgium, for example, where the gap has been reduced by more than 41 per cent, Austria, where it has been reduced by almost 40 per cent, and the UK, where it has been reduced by almost 35 per cent. Elsewhere, as in Norway and Sweden, for example, the reduction has proved more muted. It is only in Denmark and Italy (notwithstanding the transformation of the PCI into the PDS), on the other hand, that the relative distances between the traditional protagonists have widened in the last ten years (by 3 per cent and 11 per cent respectively).

Second, and more impressionistically, the blurring of differences between the traditional parties can be seen in the gradual broadening of the range of coalition alternatives, and the development of a pattern of promiscuity in the formation of governments which seems to belie any sense of substantive and enduring inter-party conflicts. In West Germany, for example, over the past 30 years, all possible two-party coalitions between the three main parties have proved possible both in principle and in practice; in the Netherlands, each of the three main parties has by now coalesced with each of the others at various stages during the last ten years, with virtually all possible permutations and combinations of governing parties (including a government without the CDA) coming to office at one stage or another; in Italy, the formerly dominant Christian Democrats proved willing to work with both the PSI and, albeit less formally, the PCI (and the PDS); in Ireland, Labour has now had recent experience of joining governments with both Fianna Fáil and Fine Gael, while, most recently, even Fine Gael itself has proved willing to take on the Democratic Left as a coalition ally; in Austria in the last ten years the SPÖ has formed governments with both the FPÖ and the ÖVP; in Belgium, the Socialists, Liberals and Christians have all recently worked with one another, and also, on occasion, with the Volksunie and the Rassemblement Walloon; even in Sweden, where a sharp two-bloc pattern of competition has long been established, the run-up to the 1994 election witnessed a lengthy discussion of a possible coalition between the Social Democrats and the Liberals.

Finally, it is possible to add to these factors a variety of different elements which together suggest that individual parties may now find it increasingly difficult to maintain a separate identity. In the past, which, to be sure, may well be a largely mythical past, the dominant image of party was that of a more or less 'closed community'. Parties, in this supposed golden age, enjoyed very distinct identities. Each, to a greater or lesser extent, had its own 'natural' constituency, whether defined in terms of class, religion, occupation, or region, the core of which identified with and belonged to the particular party concerned and would rarely, if ever, consider voting for an alternative. Each party also controlled its own organisational resources, whether these be drawn mainly from ordinary supporters, from registered members, or from particular donors. Each more or less maintained its network of communications, in the form of its own internal party press or a sympathetic but ostensibly autonomous 'public' newspaper. Each had its own distinctive programme and ideology which was geared to the needs of its own specific constituency. And each hoped, at best, to be able to form its own government, or, at worst, to form a coalition with another party or parties whose interests either approximated to, or at least did not substantially conflict with, its own interest.

In contemporary politics, on the other hand, this sense of separateness is less and less apparent, with the situation now being characterised more accurately as one in which all of these aspects are now shared between the different parties.[13] One of the factors involved here derives from the familiar arguments concerning the erosion of collective identities within civil society – the blurring or even erosion of traditional boundaries based on class and religion, the changing patterns of social stratification, and the emergence of a greater emphasis on individualistic or particularistic identities – one consequence of which is that parties are losing a distinct electoral profile and are now more likely to find themselves sharing the same electoral market.[14] A second element relates to party organizational change, and the marked convergence between party organisational styles both within and across national boundaries, whether this be seen in terms of organisational structures *tout court*, or in terms of the techniques of political communication, or in terms of the nature of organisational resources. Most major parties have now abandoned their own independent means of communication, for example, and now prefer to rely on winning space and attention in the shared national media, whether public or private. In most countries, parties have also come to rely much less heavily on their own distinctive organisational resources, and lean increasingly on their shares of the same font of resources that is provided in the form of state subventions and public subsidies. Indeed, there is ample evidence to suggest that organisational distinctions between parties are gradually becoming a thing of the past and that shared experiences are now increasingly commonplace, not least as a result of the need to conform to the new party laws which have often accompanied the introduction of public subventions.[15] The third element, as noted above, is that parties are increasingly constrained by the same set of policy parameters and, at least within the mainstream, find themselves sharing the same policy priorities, often within the context of increasingly promiscuous coalition cabinets. In this sense also, as was probably already beginning to be the case with the emergence of the catch-all party, substantive programmatic and purposive differences become more difficult to discern.

All of this clearly has implications for the capacity of individual parties to maintain a distinct identity, and hence also a distinct purpose. Differences between (mainstream) parties are less easily identified, especially by voters, and ostensible protagonists may often be lumped together as constituent elements of a more or less undifferentiated political class,[16] thus helping to render these traditional parties vulnerable to the sort of 'anti-party system' assault which proved so effective in the North American campaigns since 1992 of Ross Perot and Preston Manning, and which is also often echoed within the contemporary European polities.[17] That said, however vulnerable they might become, neither the blurring of differences nor the waning of partisan purpose would seem sufficient in themselves to generate a sense of resentment against parties and against the so-called political class; indeed, at most, these are likely to lead only to indifference and apathy. Conversely, resentment can play a role when this seeming decline in the relevance of parties on the ground is accompanied by a growth in their status and their privileges as holders of public office.

PARTIES AS PUBLIC OFFICE HOLDERS

The echoes of the 'party decline' thesis should already be evident. The position of party on the ground is now weakening, and the more purposive role of party is being constrained and curtailed. Parties, in apparent decline, risk losing their capacity to engage the electorate in any meaningful sense. Yet, as noted above, this is only part of the picture, for there is in fact another aspect of party, the party as public office holder, in which it is important to emphasise that the weight of the argument runs quite counter to that implicit in any discussion of parties as representative agencies. Indeed, in this case, the evidence suggests that, far from being in decline, and far from being *passé*, parties are now much stronger than ever before, and have access to far greater resources. A number of factors are involved here.[18]

In the first place, parties are more 'powerful', or at least more parties have more access to power, in the sense that, as noted, more and more of them are gaining access to government. Indeed, one of the most neglected developments in the world of party politics in western Europe over the past 20 years has been the fact that almost every substantial party has now enjoyed at least one period in government and at least one stab at the exercise of public power. There are exceptions, of course, but these simply reinforce the point, since almost all of these exceptions are either 'new politics' parties of the left or the new parties of the far right. If we take as the crude criterion of relevance the winning of at least five per cent of the vote in a recent election, then the list of 'relevant' parties in western Europe which have never governed at least once in the past 20 years reads almost like an encyclopaedia of the new political fringe: in Belgium, the Vlaams Blok and the Ecology parties; in Denmark, the Progress Party and Socialist People's Party; in Finland, the Greens; in France, the Ecologists and the National Front; in Germany, the Greens; in Luxembourg, the Greens and the Communists; in Norway, the Socialist Left and the Progress Party; in Sweden, the Greens and New Democracy, and in Switzerland, the Greens and the Auto-partei. Indeed, in Austria, Ireland and the Netherlands, there is no single party which has recently won five per cent and yet which, at the same time, has been persistently excluded from office. Among the long-established European democracies, this leaves just the United Kingdom, where, despite the Lib-Lab pact of the late 1970s, the mainstream Liberal Party/Liberal Democrats (also in the form of the Alliance in 1983 and 1987) have been persistently excluded; and Italy, where the increasingly conventional PCI, and its even more conventional successor, the PDS, were, and are, kept at arm's length from national government. Almost all mainstream parties in western Europe are also therefore parties of public office, if only sporadically so in some cases, and this clearly is a source of strength, status and privilege.

Second, and despite their regular complaints about the risks of bankruptcy, most European parties now have more money at their disposal than ever before. Indeed, with the exception of Italy, where figures on party finances clearly must be regarded with some scepticism, parties in *all* other European countries for which comparable data are available have reported a substantial growth in party income in *real terms* over the past two decades. Thus the Danish parties, for example, despite having lost the vast bulk of their membership, now generate 50 per cent more income than was the case 20 years ago; in Ireland, party income has more than doubled in the same period; in Austria, it has increased almost fourfold. Even in the Netherlands, where party finances have always been exceptionally 'modest',[19] the parties are now 40 per cent richer in real terms than was the case 20 years ago.

Third, the evidence of growing party resources can also be seen in terms of the increased numbers of party staff and personnel. Thus, almost without exception, parties are now significantly better staffed than was the case 20 years ago, with the numbers of professional party bureaucrats increasing by more than twofold in Denmark, for example, by more than threefold in Germany, and by more than fourfold in Ireland. Much of this increase can be accounted for by the growth in the staff employed by parties in parliament, and, with one or two exceptions, the growth of parliamentary party staff has consistently outstripped that of central office staff, sometimes by a ratio of more than ten to one. Finally, albeit less easily specified, it also seems to be the case that parties have gained increasing access to patronage resources, which offers yet another source of strength. While the evidence here is necessarily sketchy and is sometimes nebulous, there is nevertheless a degree of consistency which suggests that party patronage is becoming an increasingly prevalent (or at least noticeable) phenomenon. The most obvious illustration is of course provided by the Italian case, but there is also other, less dramatic evidence of patronage which can be seen in countries such as Austria, Belgium, Finland, France, Germany, Ireland, Spain and the United Kingdom. In each of these countries, it would seem, support for, and/or membership of a party, is capable of being translated into the receipt of public appointments or publicly-funded benefits.[20]

The picture here looks very different from that elaborated earlier. In place of party decline, we now see growing party strength and party status. The distinction is clear: while parties on the ground may be in decline, the public face of party, and especially the party in public office, is becoming stronger and is enjoying an enhanced profile. In other words, we see a shift in the balance of party in Europe, a shift which is not unlike that which has already been frequently noted in the USA.

From one perspective, of course, this shift can simply be seen as part of a long-term and almost autonomous process of party adaptation in which parties have moved from civil society to the state, and in which their eroding linkages with civil society have been compensated for by an ever closer linkage with the state.[21] This new linkage is obvious as far as access to government is concerned, which is now a virtually standard experience for most west European parties. Linkages with the state go much further than this, of course. Much of the extra staff whom parties have at their disposal, for instance, as noted, are in the employ of the *parliamentary* parties. Moreover, much of the new party sources of income also derive, either directly or indirectly, from the state and from the subventions to the parties which have been introduced in almost every European country during the past 20 years, and which in many cases now count for by far the largest single share of party revenues. The importance of linkage to the state is also highlighted by the patronage question, which depends almost entirely on access to public resources, as well as by the increased importance of party laws, in that there is now an increasing amount of legal regulation of party life in western Europe which not only protects the parties but also helps to determine how they organise and behave. The access which parties enjoy in terms of the state-regulated broadcasting networks should also be noted here, and offers a further illustration of the way in which parties become entwined in state-directed activities.

From another perspective, however, this movement from civil society to the state can be seen as part of a strategy by which the parties consciously attempt to ensure their own survival. The state, in this sense, is not some 'neutral' or 'external' agency which comes to the aid of the parties; rather, the state *is* the parties, or the parties *are* the state, in that it is the parties themselves that are drawing up and then implementing the laws and proposals from which they benefit. It is the parties that are deciding that more personnel resources should be allocated to their organisations, and it is the parties (sometimes, literally, in the dead of night)[22] that are deciding on the introduction and eventual amounts of public subsidies. Above all, it is the parties that are privileging themselves by means of public resources which are made available through the state.

So, in terms of party as public office holder, the picture is therefore not only one of increased strength and increased resources, which already stands in sharp contrast to the development of party as representative agency; but it is also, and perhaps more importantly, one of increased *public privilege*. These are parties which are privileged in terms of appointments, which are privileged in terms of resources, money, and status, and which are privileged in terms of access to public networks of communication, privileges which all derive from their linkage to the state and from their position as the holders of public office.

POPULAR LEGITIMACY AND PUBLIC PRIVILEGE

This is the source of the contradiction which now lies at the heart of the world of party politics in many of the established democracies. On the ground, and in terms of their representative role, parties appear to be less relevant and to be losing some of their key functions. In public office, on the other hand, and in terms of their linkage to the state, they appear to be more privileged than ever. Indeed, if we think of the classic functions of party,[23] then it might be concluded that while some of these functions have been undermined (such as the articulation of interests and the aggregation of demands, and perhaps also the formulation of public policy), other functions have acquired an increased importance and visibility (such as the recruitment of political leaders and, above all, the organisation of government).

But this does not necessarily reflect a shift towards a new balance or a new equilibrium; on the contrary, it suggests that there may be an absence of balance, and an absence of equilibrium, which, in the extreme case, might well act to undermine the legitimacy of party government itself. To put it another way, what can be seen here, albeit in a very embryonic and often muted form, may be precisely the same imbalance between popular irrelevance and public privilege that was famously cited by de Tocqueville as contributing to the downfall of the nobility of the French *Ancien Régime*, and which is quoted at the beginning of this paper. On the one hand, the parties as public office holders, like de Tocqueville's nobles, are clearly privileged – indeed, with time, they tend to have become even more privileged. On the other hand, as was suggested earlier here, they now appear to lack real representative weight or purpose, and this, too, has become more evident with time. In other words, their status has increased while their popular relevance has tended to become eroded.

This is not to suggest, however, that contemporary parties, like de Tocqueville's nobles, now risk becoming 'meaningless anachronisms'. On the contrary: given the importance of parties in terms of the recruitment of leaders and the organisation of government, it is almost impossible to conceive of a parliamentary polity which can really evade the principle of party. Nevertheless, the problem clearly exists, for whatever the importance of party as an organising principle in government and in the state, de Tocqueville was clearly correct in pointing to the dangers involved in combining (enhanced) *public* privilege, on the one hand, with declining *popular* purpose, or relevance, on the other.

It is this particular combination which lies at the root of the feelings of popular political distrust. This is also probably one of the most important factors underlying the emergence, albeit not always on a major scale, of anti-party sentiment and anti-party parties,[24] with the evidence of public privilege helping to translate potential indifference into potential resentment and hence into even greater vulnerability. The disenchantment with parties and even the resentment against parties should therefore not simply be read as a symptom of party decline *per se*; indeed, were parties to be wholly in decline, as public-office holders as well as representative agencies, then the sense of discontent might well evaporate. Rather, the problem appears to lie in a set of contradictory developments, in which parties are at once less able but more visible, less relevant but more privileged.

NOTES

1. Alexis de Tocqueville, *The Ancien Régime and the French Revolution*, trans. Stuart Gilbert (Glasgow: Collins/Fontana, 1966), p.60.
2. Alesandro Pizzorno, 'Interests and Parties in Pluralism', in Suzanne Berger (ed.), *Organizing Interests in Western Europe: Pluralism, Corporatism, and the Transformation of Politics* (Cambridge: Cambridge CUP, 1981), p.272.
3. See Cees van der Eijk, Mark Franklin, Tom Mackie and Henry Valen, 'Cleavages, Conflict Resolution and Democracy', in Mark Franklin *et al.*, *Electoral Change: Responses to Social and Attitudinal Structures in Western Countries* (Cambridge: CUP, 1991), pp.406–31.
4. Kay Lawson and Peter Merkl (eds.), *When Parties Fail: Emerging Alternative Organizations* (Princeton: Princeton UP, 1988).
5. See Richard S. Katz and Peter Mair, 'Changing Models of Party Organization and Party Democracy: the Emergence of the Cartel Party', *Party Politics* 1/1 (1995), pp.5–28.
6. The sources are as follows: Jorgen Goul Andersen and Tor Bjorklund, 'Structural Changes and New Cleavages: the Progress Parties in Denmark and Norway', *Acta Sociologica* 33/3 (1990), p.203; Colette Ysmal, 'France', in Ruud Koole and Peter Mair (eds.), *Political Data*

Yearbook, Vol 1, sp. issue of *European Journal of Political Research* 22/4 (1992), p.407; Wolfgang C. Müller, 'The Development of Austrian Party Organizations in the Postwar Period', in Richard S. Katz and Peter Mair (eds.), *How Parties Organize: Change and Adaptation in Party Organizations in Western Democracies* (London: Sage, 1994), p.52; Hans-Joachim Veen, Norbert Lepszy and Peter Mnich, *The Republikaner Party in Germany: Right-Wing Menace or Protest Catchall?* (Westport, CT: Praeger/*Washington Papers* No.162), 1993, p.45; *Daily Telegraph*, 10 Oct. 1994. In the case of the UK, this sort of critical attitude has also begun to pervade the otherwise rather staid establishment press: thus a recent editorial in *The Independent* asserted that the ruling Conservatives 'have been profoundly corrupted' (12 Jan. 1994), while even the *Daily Telegraph* was driven to complain of the quality of the contemporary Conservative MPs, arguing that 'in the place of the old knights of the shire is a host of frankly inadequate men and women who, far from entering Parliament in any spirit of public service, are driven solely by the pursuit of self-advancement' (*Independent*, 15 Jan. 1994).

7. The figures come from Richard S. Katz and Peter Mair (eds.), *Party Organizations: A Data Handbook on Party Organizations in Western Democracies, 1960–90* (London: Sage, 1992), pp.39, 330, 398, 633–4, 789–90, 846. See also Hermann Schmitt, 'On Party Attachment in Western Europe and the Utility of Eurobarometer Data', *West European Politics* 12/2 (April 1989), pp.122–39.

8. For figures on France, see Colette Ysmal, *Les Partis politiques sous la Ve République* (Paris: Monchrestien, 1989), p.163, and for figures on all other countries cited see Richard S. Katz and Peter Mair (eds.), *Party Organizations: A Data Handbook on Party Organizations in Western Democracies, 1960–90* (London: Sage, 1992) and Richard S. Katz and Peter Mair (eds.), *How Parties Organize: Change and Adaptation in Party Organizations in Western Democracies* (London: Sage, 1994).

9. For the original reference, see Peter J. Katzenstein, *Policy and Politics in West Germany: The Growth of a Semi-Sovereign State* (Philadelphia, PA: Temple UP, 1987).

10. See Richard Stubbs and Geoffrey R.D. Underhill, 'Introduction: State Policies and Global Changes', in Richard Stubbs and Geoffrey R.D. Underhill (eds.), *Political Economy and the Changing Global Order* (Basingstoke: Macmillan, 1994), pp.421–5. It should be emphasised that this argument does not necessarily imply that all governments which are subject to these international pressures end up by pursuing more or less the same policies or that they are all converging towards a particular (neo-liberal) consensus. Indeed, this suggestion is already contested by scholars who point to evidence of cross-national *divergence* in policy directions and outcomes (see, e.g., Fritz Scharpf, *Crisis and Choice in European Social Democracy* (Ithaca, NY: Cornell UP, 1988) and Geoff Garrett, 'Capital Mobility, Trade and the Politics of Economic Policy', *International Organizations*, forthcoming). Rather, the argument is that *within* any given country, and almost regardless of whether or not it is diverging from its neighbours and competitors, the range of policy options is being constrained, with the result that *national* partisan differences become muted and *national* partisan policies converge.

11. See, e.g., Richard Rose, 'Inheritance Before Choice in Public Policy', *Journal of Theoretical Politics* 2/3 (1990), pp.263–91.

12. See, e.g., Francis G. Castles (ed.), *The Impact of Parties* (London: Sage, 1982), and Richard Rose, *Do Parties Make a Difference?* (Chatham, NJ: Chatham House, 2nd ed., 1984).

13. See also the discussion of cartel parties in Katz and Mair, 'Changing Models of Party Organization' (note 5).

14. See Mark Franklin *et al.*, *Electoral Change: Responses to Social and Attitudinal Structures in Western Countries* (Cambridge: Cambridge UP, 1991).

15. See Katz and Mair, *How Parties Organize* (note 8).

16. See also Klaus von Beyme, *Die politische Klasse im Parteienstaat* (Frankfurt am Main: Suhrkamp, 1993).

17. Ibid, pp.195–209; Hans-Georg Betz, *Radical Right-Wing Populism in Western Europe* (Basingstoke: Macmillan, 1994), pp.37–67.

18. The data on party finance, staffing, and so on, which are cited in the following paragraphs are drawn from Katz and Mair, *Party Organizations: a Data Handbook* and *How Parties Organize* (note 8), and the argument draws on and summarises some of the discussion in my

chapter 'Party Organizations; From Civil Society to the State' in the latter volume, pp.1–22.
19. See Ruud A. Koole, 'The "Modesty" of Dutch Party Finance', in H.E. Alexander (ed.), *Comparative Political Finance in the 1980s* (Cambridge: CUP, 1989), pp.200–19.
20. See, for some examples, the various country chapters in Katz and Mair, *How Parties Organize* (note 8).
21. See Katz and Mair, 'Changing Models' (note 5).
22. See Müller, 'Development of Austrian Party Organizations' (note 6), p.54.
23. See, e.g., Anthony King, 'Political Parties in Western Democracies: Some Sceptical Reflections', *Polity* 2/2 (1969), pp.111–41.
24. For two recent discussions of anti-party sentiment see Thomas Poguntke, 'Explorations into a Minefield: Anti-Party Sentiment – Conceptual Thoughts and Empirical Evidence', and Susan Scarrow, 'The Consequences of Anti-Party Sentiment: Anti-Party Arguments as Instruments of Change', both papers presented to the Joint Sessions of the European Consortium for Political Research, Madrid, 1994. See also Betz, *Radical Right-Wing Populism* (note 17), and Piero Ignazi, *L'Estrema Destra in Europa* (Bologna: Il Mulino, 1994).

The Reshaping of National Party Systems

RUDY ANDEWEG

The problem with political representation within the European Union lies less with the much discussed 'democratic deficit' than with the lack of a party system that offers a meaningful choice to the voters and reflects this choice in the European Parliament. The current transnational political groups in the European Parliament are unstable and heterogeneous alliances of national parties. These national parties fight European elections on national issues. The potential alternatives to the further institutionalisation of the transnational party system include a truly European party system or a split-level party system. These alternatives would benefit from the introduction of a uniform electoral system other than the currently most widely used PR with nation-wide districts. Paradoxically, it would be advantageous for the established national parties to withdraw from the European arena, which would insulate them from the growing risk of spillover from the vagaries of Euro-elections.

Political Parties at the European level are an important factor for integration within the Union. They contribute to forming a European awareness and to expressing the political will of the citizens of the Union.

Article 138a of the Maastricht Treaty

THE 'DEMOCRATIC DEFICIT': THE WRONG DIAGNOSIS

Rather than the shifts in the overall party balance, it was the turnout in the fourth direct elections to the European Parliament that has attracted most attention and comments from Europe's political class and press. In combination with at most meagre majorities in national referendums on 'Maastricht', the low and consistently declining turnout in the European elections is seen as boding ill for the legitimacy of European integration in general, and the European Parliament in particular. This lack of legitimacy is often hypothesised to result from a 'democratic deficit'; as more and more powers are transferred from national capitals to 'Brussels', the oversight over these powers by national parliaments is not replaced by the scrutiny of the much weaker European Parliament. Especially since the abolition of the unanimity rule for some decisions in the European Council in the Single European Act (1986), national ministers cannot always be held accountable in their national parliaments for decisions taken at the European level. Voters are hypothesised to perceive this 'democratic deficit' and to refuse to vote for the powerless European Parliament. The diagnosis of the democratic deficit is shared by Euro-sceptics and Euro-enthusiasts alike: while some advocated abstention in the 1994 Euro-elections as a democratic duty, others have interpreted the low turnout as a signal that the European Parliament's position within the European Union should be strengthened if further decline in voter participation is to be avoided.

The diagnosis is flawed, or at best incomplete. It is a strawman to contrast a 'weak and remote' European Parliament with 'strong and nearby' national parliaments. According to a 1994 Eurobarometer survey, in all member-states, satisfaction with the functioning of European democracy may be low (48 per cent dissatisfied, 40 per cent satisfied), but not lower than satisfaction with the way the national democracies work (on average 53 per cent dissatisfied, 43 per cent satisfied). While in some countries satisfaction with national democracy is higher than with European democracy (especially in Denmark, the Netherlands and Luxembourg), in other countries European democracy outperforms national democracy (Spain and Italy).[1] On the whole, the differences between national and European democratic satisfaction are so small that they cannot account for the huge differences in turnout between national and Euro-elections. On the individual level, Niedermayer has compared perception of the European Parliament's powers with the intention to vote in the Euro-elections: 'among those who do know of the EP's limited power, the intended electoral participation is not systematically lower than among those who perceive the EP as very powerful. On the contrary: with respect to both points in time, in three-quarters of the member states those knowing of the EP's limited power are more likely to turn out and vote'.[2]

Moreover, the powers of the European Parliament have increased considerably since the first direct elections to the European Parliament in 1979. To the original consultation procedure and later budgetary role, the Single European Act of 1986 added a cooperation procedure (that is to say, amendment rights) and an assent procedure for certain international agreements, and the Maastricht Treaty added a codecision procedure in 1993. It is a science in itself to ascertain which parliamentary rights apply to which policy area or type of decision, but there is no gainsaying the gradual strengthening of the European Parliament. If the diagnosis of a democratic deficit were correct, a slow increase in turnout would have accompanied the increase in parliamentary powers instead of the steady decline in turn-out (from 63 per cent in 1979 to 56.5 per cent in 1994) that actually took place.

This is not to say that there is no democratic deficit, or that it is a mistake to advocate a strengthening of the European Parliament, but to point out that such a strengthening in itself is unlikely to deliver democratic legitimacy and high voter participation. The diagnosis of the democratic deficit is flawed because elections do not produce legitimacy directly. Legitimacy is merely a by-product of elections as an instrument of representation. Where elections do function as an instrument of political representation, they will confer legitimacy on the elected assembly, even if it is not very powerful. Where elections are prevented from performing this function, legitimacy will not develop, regardless of the elected assembly's powers. The remainder of this paper will argue that the Euro-elections do not function as an instrument of representation, that the political parties prevent it from performing this role, that a different party system could solve the crisis of representation, and that it will be in the current parties' self-interest to allow such a different party system to develop.

THE ABSENCE OF A EUROPEAN PARTY SYSTEM

For citizens to be able to choose in elections, they must be offered a choice. The menu from which voters may choose is the party system. But for this choice to be meaningful, and for elections to serve as an instrument of political representation, the party system in the parliamentary arena must reflect the party system in the electoral arena. It is this crucial link that is missing in the context of the Euro-elections.

At first sight the demands of representation appear to be met. In each member state the voters are presented with a choice between national political parties, and these national parties then join forces with their ideological counterparts from other member states in transnational parties. Such transnational political groupings were able to build on long-established international organisations for each of the dominant *'familles spirituelles'*: Communist, Socialist, Christian Democrat, and Liberal. On a European level, the Christian-Democrats were probably the first to create a transnational organisation, the *Nouvelles Equipes Internationales*. Soon after the first European 'parliament' was established in 1952, the Assembly of the European Coal and Steel Community, delegates from each ideological current joined in separate parliamentary groups: 23 June 1953 is the official date of foundation for the Socialist, Christian Democratic, and Liberal groups. When direct elections to the European Parliament were introduced, the continuation of the 'transnational' party system was a foregone conclusion. It was expected that direct elections would strengthen the transnational parties, and to some extent such an institutionalisation has taken place. The main parliamentary parties in the European Parliament have developed extra-parliamentary parties on the European level: the Party of European Socialists (PES), the European Liberal Democrats and Reformists (ELDR), and the (Christian Democrat) European Peoples' Party (EPP). These parties now publish European election manifestos. The parliamentary parties have their own funds, their own staffs, and they have even introduced 'Le Whip'.[3] Recently, the practice has evolved to hold party 'summits' on the eve of European Council meetings, bringing together heads of government, national party leaders, the chairpersons of the European parliamentary party, and the Commissioners of that particular party.[4] The EPP is already organised as a supranational party, with at least the nominal possibility of direct individual membership,[5] and with an organisational structure that 'resembles an ordinary party'.[6] In other parties a development in this direction is visible. In July 1991 the Socialist parliamentary party called on the extra-parliamentary federation to create a truly European Socialist Party.[7]

Despite such developments, the transnational parties are still weak. With the possible exception of the EPP, they lack the organisational structure to link them to the grass roots, their recently expanded staffs are small (PES: 13, EPP: 10, ELDR: 6), and they are poorly financed. Most importantly: the transnational parties are not involved in the nomination of candidates. Only in the ELDR are the national parties required to communicate their list of candidates to the transnational Executive Committee.[8]

Instability

That the transnational parties are weakly organised, however, is not important in itself. For their role in structuring political representation it is much more significant that they are unstable and heterogeneous. The instability of the European transnational party system is the result of the fact that in each new parliament some parties change their transnational alliance, sometimes resulting in the disappearance of old and emergence of new party alliances: 'In fact, inter-group realignments accounted for 91 seat changes between 1984 and 1989 (17 per cent of the total), as opposed to 40 (7.7 percent of the total) which were the consequence of elections'.[9] The clearest example is the European Democratic Alliance (EDA), originally founded as the European Conservative Group in 1973. In the 1984 Parliament it was the third largest parliamentary party (66 members). In 1989 the Spanish *Partido Popular* defected to the EPP. When the British Conservatives followed this example, the party all but disappeared. The Communist transnational group split into United European Left and Left Unity when it could no longer reconcile its Italian and French member parties; in 1994 Left Unity disappeared when the Italian Communists joined the socialist PES. On the extreme Right, the Italian MSI left European Right when the German *Republikaner* joined this group (because of differences of opinion about Süd-Tirol/Alto-Adige), but later in the 1989 Parliament, the *Republikaner* left the group as well. This instability points to a low degree of institutionalisation of the transnational party system, but in terms of representation it would be less problematic if voters would know in advance of which transnational group the party of their choice would become a member. Prior to the 1994 elections, Italian voters may have expected *Forza Italia* to join the Christian-Democratic EPP: junior foreign minister Livio Caputo said so, and Berlusconi visited Chancellor Kohl to apply for membership.[10] However, *Forza Italia* passed the 27-member threshold to form its own European parliamentary group, and became a separate 'transnational' party: *Forza Europa*. Dutch voters for D66 were similarly left in the dark as to whether their deputies would join the liberal ELDR.

Heterogeneity

The three main transnational parties are more stable, but each of them contains some odd bedfellows.

The socialist PES is perhaps most homogeneous in ideological terms, but it has always contained two competing Italian parties: PSI and PSDI in the past, and after the 1994 elections the PSI/*Alleanza Democratica* and the formerly communist *Partito Democratico della Sinistra*, causing PSDI to leave. The Christian-Democratic EPP has included national parties in its parliamentary party which are outside its extra-parliamentary party, because they do not share its Christian-Democratic ideology: the Spanish *Partido Popular* and the British and Danish Conservatives. The EPP's Italian branch now consists of *Partito Populare Italiano* (the former DCI), the *Sudtiroler Volkspartei*, and *Patto Segni*, but the Irish *Fianna Fáil*, which wants to join, is prevented from doing so by a veto from its national competitor *Fine Gael*. The Liberals include the Portugese *Partido Social Democrata* (and in the previous parliament also the Spanish *Centro Democratico y Social*). From both Denmark and the Netherlands, competing national parties have joined the ELDR parliamentary party: *Venstre* and *Radikale Censtre*, and VVD and D66. Among the smaller parties, ENS (Europe of the National States), a new transnational party, combines not only the two Danish anti-EC parties with the French *Majorité pour l'Autre Europe* (which seems logical), but also the combined list of the three Dutch Orthodox Protestant parties (which

TABLE 1
THE TRANSNATIONAL PARTY SYSTEM IN THE 1994 EUROPEAN PARLIAMENT

	PES	EPP	ELDR	EUL	FE	EDA	GREENS	ERA	EN	OTHER
Belgium	SP/PS	CVP/PSC/ SZP	VLD/PRL FDF	—	—	—	Agalev/ Ecolo	VU	—	VB; FN
Denmark	SocialDem	Kons. Folkeparti	Venstre; Rad.Ven-stre	—	—	—	Social. Folkeparti	—	Junibev.; Folkebev.	—
France	PS	UDF/RPR	UDF/RPR	PC	—	UDF/RPR	—	Energie Rad.	Autre Europe	FN
Germany	SPD	CDU; CSU	—	—	—	—	Grünen	—	—	—
Greece	PASOK	ND	—	KKE; SYN	—	POLA	—	—	—	—
Ireland	Labour	Fine Gael	Indep.	—	—	Fianna Fail	Green Party	—	—	—
Italy	PSI; PDS	PPI; Patto Segni; Südtirol VP	PRI; Lega Nord	Rif.Comm.	Forza Europa	—	Verdi; la Rete	Panella	—	PSDI; All.Naz. (MSI)
Luxemburg	LSAP	CSV	DP	—	—	—	Dei Greng	—	—	—
The Netherlands	PvdA	CDA	VVD; D66	—	—	—	Groen Links	—	SGP/ GPV/ RPF	—
Portugal	PS	PSD	PSD	CDU	—	CDS	—	—	—	—
Spain	PSOE	Part.Pop.; Conv.i. Unio; Coal.Nac.	Conv. i. Unio	Izq. Unida	—	—	—	—	—	—
United Kingdom	Labour; SDLP	Conservative; Ulster Union	Lib.Dem.	—	—	—	—	SNP	—	Dem. Unionists

seems less self-evident, even though these parties are somewhat sceptical about further European integration).

Traditionally, French national parties have most difficulties in dovetailing with transnational parties. In 1989 the Giscard d'Estaing list (UDF-RPR) competed with the Simone Veil list for the centre-right vote, but after the elections deputies elected on both lists left to join various parliamentary parties. Moreover, Giscard himself switched from the Liberals to the Christian-Democrats in the middle of the 1989–94 parliamentary period. In 1994 the 28 MEPs elected on the joint UDF/RPR ticket again spread out over three transnational parties: EPP (13), ELDR (1), and EDA (14). This lack of cohesion is also displayed by some Iberian parties.

From this overview it appears that the transnational parties may have a core of national parties sharing a common ideological heritage, but that their political identity is obfuscated by the inclusion of parties, and parts of parties, that do not belong to the same political family. This could be accepted, even welcomed, in terms of political representation, if these transnational parties, despite or because of their ideological heterogeneity, were cohesive with regard to the main issues on the European Parliament's agenda. This agenda is dominated by constitutional issues: 'The progress of the Community, the extension of the competence and efficiency of the EC institutions, and the strengthening of the EP are the focus of MEPs activities.'[11] However, on these issues the transnational parties appear to be at least as divided as in regard to ideology. The PES and EPP parties are generally considered as the majority coalition in favour of further integration,[12] but the socialist group contains Euro-sceptical British and Danish socialists, and the Christian Democrats have embraced the British Conservatives.

Despite the obvious heterogeneity of the transnational parties, one study of the first two directly elected European Parliament found considerable party cohesion in MEP voting behaviour, leading to the conclusion 'that, on the whole, European Parliament Groups are formations uniting national parties which have great political and ideological affinity and a pronounced similarity in their social foundations.'[13] This cohesion, I suspect, is at least partly an artefact, caused by the selection of data. Attina used roll-call votes, but the usual way to vote in the European Parliament is either electronically or by show of hands. 'Roll-call votes tend to be called by Political Groups for three main reasons; firstly to put that Group's position on an issue firmly on the record; secondly to embarrass another Group by forcing the latter to take a special stance on an issue; and thirdly to keep a check on their own members' participation in a vote, and voting stance.'[14] Any analysis of such roll-calls would seem to be biased to find party cohesion. Studies of MEPs' attitudes have generally found much lower levels of party cohesion.[15]

National Party Delegations

The most homogeneous units within the European Parliament are the national party delegations: 'They will often take a collective decision and try to act as a block in Group discussions. On important issues, Groups will try to negotiate compromises among their national delegations before taking a decision. When Groups fail to vote cohesively, it is usually because one or more national delegations have decided to opt out of a Group position.'[16] These national party delegations are at least as integrated into their national party organisation as they are into the transnational parties. It is to their national party organisation that MEPs have to look for renomination. MEPs are sometimes incorporated into national party bodies, like the British Labour MEPs into the Labour Party's electoral college, which is responsible for electing the national party leader. As the then Conservative spokesman on European Affairs, Douglas Hurd, argued in 1978:

> it is essential that they [the MEPs] and their staffs should be meshed into their political parties at home at all levels, from the leadership through the parliamentary party, the voluntary organizations, to the constituencies. Indeed, it will be in their own interests to keep this close connexion. They will rely on it for their election, for their constituency operations after the election, and for their re-election later.[17]

In that sense it may be better to speak of a 79 (national) party system than of a nine (transnational) party system in the European Parliament. Do these 79 national parties provide the missing link between the citizens' choices in the electoral arena and the MEPs' choices in the parliamentary arena? The parties certainly do not play this role overtly. Indeed, every study of each of the four direct elections so far has concluded that (with the exception of Denmark) the parties have primarily campaigned on domestic issues, and that the citizens of Europe have cast their vote on the basis of national, rather than European considerations. The Eurobarometer survey found that 37 per cent of the voters in the 1994 Euro-election reported that their vote was influenced by European issues, compared to 55 per cent claiming to be influenced by national issues. Only in the Netherlands did European issues outweigh national issues (53 per cent to 38 per cent).[18] These figures probably overstate the Europeanness of the elections, because it is not specified what constitutes a 'European' issue (is environmental pollution a national or a European issue?). The conclusion about the first direct elections in 1979, that 'The "European" elections are simultaneous national elections in each of the EC-member nations'[19] still applies.

Despite the 'domestication' of the European elections, the national parties may still represent their voters' views on Europe: the manifest national party systems may be latent European party systems. This is the assertion of a study by Van der Eijk and Franklin in a study comparing European citizens' perceptions of their national parties' positions on the EC and their own attitudes towards European integration. The comparison is hazardous as the two variables are measured in different studies, and operationalised in different ways, but the authors nevertheless conclude 'clearly that only a few parties take positions which are clearly out of line with the average position of their voters. The parties involved are the orthodox-Protestant combination in the Netherlands, the Workers Party in Ireland, the Italian MSI and the Greens in Germany, the Netherlands, Ireland and, to a somewhat lesser extent, Luxembourg'.[20] However, based on the author's own data, I come to a rather different conclusion.

TABLE 2
RANKORDERING NATIONAL PARTIES' AND PARTY-VOTERS' POSITIONS
ON EUROPEAN INTEGRATION

		Pro European Integration Anti
Belgium	parties	CVS-PS-PRL-PVV-PSC-SP-Ecol-FDF-VU
	party-voters	PSC-CVP-PVV-PRL/SP-Ecol-PS-VU-FDF
Denmark	parties	Venstre/Kons-CD-Fremskrit-Socdem-Rad-SFP
	part voters	Venstre-Kons-CD-Fremskrit-Rad-Socdem-SFP
France	parties	PS, MRG-UDF, RPR-Ecol-PCF-FN
	party voters	UDF, RPR-PS, MRG-Ecol-PCF-FN
Germany	parties	CDU, CSU-FPD-SPD-Grunen-Republikaner
	party voters	CDU, CSU/Grunen-SPD-FDP-Republikaner
Greece	parties	ND-PASOK-Left All
	party voters	ND-PASOK-Left All
Ireland	parties	Fianna Fail-Fine Gael-Progr.Dem-Labour-Green-Workers
	party voters	Progr.Dem-Fine Gael-Fianna Fail-Labour-Green-Workers
Italy	parties	DC-Verdi-PSI-PLI, PRI-PSDI-PCI-DP-MSI
	party voters	PSDI-DP-DC-MSI-PSI-Verdi-PLI, PRI-PCI
Luxembourg	parties	CSV, PCS-DP, PD-LSAP, POSL-Ecol
	party voters	DP, PD-CSV, PCS-LSAP, POSL-Ecol
Netherlands	parties	VVD-CDA-PvdA-D66-Green-SGP, GVP, RPF
	party voters	D66-VVD-CDA-PvdA-SGP, GPV, RPF-Green
Portugal	parties	PSD-PS-CDS-PPM-MDP, CDE-CDU-UDP
	party voters	PSD-CDS-PS-PPM-CDU-MDP, CDE-UDP
Spain	parties	PSOE-CDS-AP, PDP, PL-CIU, PNV-IU, PSUC-HB, EE, ERC
	party voters	CIU, PNV-AP, PDP, PL-PSOE-CDS-IU, PSUC-HB, EE, ERC
UK:	GB parties	Conservative-Social Lib Dem-SPD-Labour
	party voters	Social Lib Dem-Labour-SDP-Conservative
UK:	NI parties	All.-SDLP-Ulster U-Other U-Workers-Dem. U.-Sinn F.
	party voters	All.-SDLP-Other U.-Workers-Ulster U.-Sinn F.-Dem U.

Source: C. Van der Eijk and M. Franklin, 'European Community Politics and Electoral Representation: evidence from the 1989 European Elections Study', *European Journal of Political Research* 19 (1991), pp.111–123, (parties = average voter perception of party position on European integration; party voters = average position on European integration of a party's voters).

For the methodological reasons mentioned above (different surveys, different operationalisations of EC attitudes) it would seem misleading to calculate the exact distance between (average) voter and the perceived party positions, but the data do allow a comparison of the rankorderings of the (averaged perception of the) party positions with rankorderings of the average positions of the party voters. Table 2 shows that only in Greece is the ordering of the party positions and of the party-voters' positions the same: New Democracy is most pro-Europe and the Left Alliance is least pro-Europe. In all other countries there are small (Luxembourg, Denmark, Portugal, France, Ireland) or large (Belgium, Northern Ireland, the Netherlands, Italy, Great Britain, Spain, Germany) incongruencies between the rankordering of the parties and of the parties' voters when it comes to European integration.

The conclusion must be that neither the transnational party system, nor the 12 national party systems provide the link between voter choice and MEP behaviour that is crucial for democratic representation in the European Union. This, rather than the 'democratic deficit', is the correct diagnosis of the European legitimacy crisis.

IN SEARCH OF A EUROPEAN PARTY SYSTEM

Unfortunately for advocates of a democratic European Union, this diagnosis leads to a pessimistic prognosis. However hard it may be, the 'democratic deficit' can be remedied by institutional reform, but a party system is much more difficult to engineer, especially when it is rooted in 15 long-standing national party systems. In the context of this paper we can only speculate about a few alternative scenarios for the future development of the European party system.

Scenario I: The Transnational Party System

The most likely prospect is for the further institutionalisation and entrenchment of the current transnational party system. Assuming the logic of 'political spillover', each step in the strengthening of the supranational institutions eventually results in a strengthening of the transnational parties. This was the widespread assumption on the eve of the first direct elections: '... it may be said with little hesitation that direct elections ought to witness a new historical departure for Euro-Parliamentary activity involving a qualitative change in the status and functioning of the transnational groups'.[21] One of the reasons behind this expectation was that most elected deputies would become full-time MEPs. As Pridham and Pridham predicted in 1979: 'Undoubtedly, the relatively full time nature of the groups will increase their socialising effects. This could well lead to an increased group identification and a corresponding increase in group loyalty, so facilitating the achievement of a common group viewpoint and promoting group cohesion.'[22] The rules and procedures of the European Parliament also stimulated the existing party groups to strengthen their organization through the threshold for recognition as a Group, and through the allocation of funds, speaking time, and patronage.

The most recent steps in strengthening the institutions of the European Union, and especially the Single European Act, are once again expected to provide a new impetus for the institutionalisation of the transnational party system. Ladrech relates recent programmatic and organisational developments in the transnational Socialist party directly to the intensified pace of European integration since 1985.[23] One might even go further and speculate that, as European-level decision-making replaces national decision-making, the transnational party system will become a supranational party system, with European parties having branches in each member-state, rather than being confederations of autonomous national parties.

However, other observers point out that further European integration could just as well provide incentives for the national parties to increase their hold over their MEPs. Currently, the solution for the problem of the 'democratic deficit' is often sought in integration of MEPs in the national policy-making process, for example through Joint Committees of a nation's MEPs and MPs, as suggested by the British Prime Minister.[24] The widening of the European Union and the concomitant need to absorb parties with weak links to the main ideological families will also work against the institutionalisation of the transnational party system. Bardi concludes: '... the formation of genuine "Euro-parties" is thus rather unlikely' and 'the obstacles to the transnationalization of the European party system appear to be stronger than the incentives'.[25]

Whether the transnational party system continues in its present state or will become more institutionalised, however, makes little difference for the problem of representation: the transnational party system, reflecting national cleavages, cannot present citizens with a choice that is relevant for European decision-making. Bogdanor has compared the effect of the transnational party system to the Swiss situation, in which citizens have no choice because all parties are represented in government according to a fixed formula, regardless of the election outcome. Expecting no change in the European party system, and further following the logic of the Swiss model, he recommends the introduction of elements of direct democracy into the European Union's machinery of government.[26]

Scenario II: A Truly European Party System

We may contrast the continuation of the transnational party system with a scenario in which the current party system is replaced by a truly European party system, consisting of supranational parties presenting the voters with a relevant European choice. Party systems must simplify the variety of choices into more or less coherent packages, differentiating the parties on the basis of some overriding social or ideological cleavage. The current transnational party system vaguely reflects the class and religious cleavages dominating the party systems of the six founding members. However, there are also signs of the older urban-rural cleavage hidden in the European Parliament. This is how Steed interpreted the 1983–84 budgetary crisis, and he continued:

> in theory one could envisage a real debate at Community level along this classic cleavage. If groups were free to seek alliances in the absence of constraints of nationality and present party, one could also envisage the numerically weaker farming interest seeking links with elements in the heterogeneous urban majority, and, with several such elements having more important demands than that of their mild consumer-interest in lower prices, succeeding.[27]

A second latent cleavage that could give rise to a truly European party system is based on constitutional issues.[28] Analogous to the development of the American party system on the basis of the Federalist/Anti-Federalist cleavage, European parties could develop hostility towards the European Union, press for further European integration, or advocate the intermediate 'states rights' position: a confederal Europe. According to Bogdanor, 'A party system of this type would seem to be the most rational for allowing the expression of electoral opinion on the future of the Community.'[29]

These two cleavages need not be seen as rivals. They may coincide when parties would align themselves on both dimensions in the same order. Outside the current European Union, evidence for such a combination of the two latent cleavages can be found in Norway. In his classic study of the 1972 referendum on EC membership in Norway, Valen argued that the EC issue had a disruptive effect on the national party system. In addition to the class and religious cleavages, opposition versus support of EC membership constituted a new cleavage. This new cleavage was in fact a revival of the old urban-rural and centre-periphery conflicts.[30]

There are no indications that the urban/rural or federalist/anti-federalist cleavages, alone or in combination, are already seriously threatening the current transnational party system, but they are not without potential. In Denmark a strong anti-EC party (*Folkebevaegelsen mod EF-Unionen*) does not contest national elections, but is quite successful in all Euro-elections. In 1994 it had to share the anti-EU vote with the more moderate *Junibevaegelsen*, an outgrowth of the anti-Maastricht campaign in the 1992 referendum. In 1994 the Danish example was followed in France, where several Euro-sceptical lists provided a choice for anti-European voters who could not bring themselves to vote Communist or *Front National*, such as *Autre Politique* (led by former Defence Minister Jean-Pierre Chevènement, the leader of the *Socialisme et République* [formerly CERES] faction of the Socialist Party), *Majorité pour l'autre Europe* (led by Philippe de Villiers, a UDF deputy in the *Assemblée Nationale*, and by Sir James Goldsmith), and 'Sarajevo' (led by Bernard-Henri Lévy). Only *Majorité pour l'autre Europe* passed the electoral threshold (with 12.3 per cent of the vote it won 13 seats), but 'Anti-Maastricht lists got almost 40 per cent of the vote'.[31] Given these successes, and given the proven ability of the Danish *Folkebevaegelsen* to survive despite its abstention from national elections, it is not unlikely that the Danish and French examples will find followers in other member states in future Euro-elections. This would be the first step towards a European party system.

Further potential for such a party system can be found in the curious phenomenon of 'intergroups' inside the European Parliament. Intergroups consist of members from different transnational parties who share a common interest in a particular issue. Originally, they were officially recognised by the European Parliament and provided with certain facilities, but such support was no longer forthcoming when the number of intergroups expanded: in the 1989 Parliament 51 intergroups existed. Some of these intergroups are more like social clubs (such as the Mountain Intergroup) or represent rather narrow interests (the TGV Intergroup, presumably competing with the Wings of Europe Intergroup, or the Hunting Intergroup v. the powerful Animal Welfare Intergroup). However, some intergroups represent broader interests or political positions and they may attract MEPs because 'The Political Groups tend to be very heterogeneous and a member may sometimes find that he or she has more in common with certain members in other groups.'[32] One of the best organised intergroups is the Kangaroo Group, dedicated to the abolition of barriers obstructing the free movement of goods, services and people within the European Union. It is funded by industry, has its own leadership and staff, organises weekly luncheon meetings and an annual conference, and publishes the bimonthly Kangaroo News and *Kangaruh Nachrichten*. It has enlisted MEPs from all major transnational parties. Another prominent intergroup is the Crocodile Club, now officially named Federalist Intergroup for European Union, which title neatly summarises the group's purpose. It was set up in 1986 and has attracted more than 150 members. It holds monthly meetings, has its own rules of procedure, leadership and staff (mostly volunteers from the Federalist Youth Movement), commissions opinion polls, and tries to forge links with like-minded MPs in national parliaments. In addition to the Land Use and Food Policy intergroup and the Rural Areas inter group, one might see seeds of a European party system in such cross-party organisations.

Scenario III: A Split-Level Party System

A third speculative scenario would see the arrival of anti-EU parties and the proliferation of intergroups as challenges to the transnational party system, to which it will seek to adapt. It may take the wind out of its potential competitors' sails by absorbing the urban/rural or federalist/anti-federalist cleavages. The transnational parties would assume a political identity based on these cleavages, rather than on the class and religious cleavages that define the national party systems. In our first scenario, the transnational parties fight the Euro-elections on the same grounds as the national parties fight domestic elections; in the second scenario, different parties would fight the two elections; in this third scenario the transnational parties fight the Euro-elections under the same labels as national elections, but on different grounds. This scenario is akin to the American model, in which Republicans and Democrats contest elections at all levels, but where the Democratic party in particular fights the presidential elections on different grounds than within-state elections, at least in the South. Voters are aware of this and often 'split their ticket' accordingly, that is to say, they vote for different parties in the different electoral arenas. The resulting 'split-level alignment' is often mentioned to explain why the pre-1994 Democratic majority in Congress did not translate into a Democratic monopoly on the presidency.

Both a truly European party system and a split-level alignment would be considerable improvements over the current transnational party system in terms of political representation. The French and especially the Danish examples show that a combination of the second and third scenario is the most likely alternative to the transnational party system. In Denmark, the anti-EU choice is presented by specific Euro-parties, while the federalist and states-rights positions are represented by national parties: Conservatives, *Venstre* (Liberal), Centre Democrats and Christian People's Party on the one hand, and Social-Democrats, *Radikale Venstre*, and *Fremskridtspartiet* on the other hand.[33] These national parties attract different voters in European elections than in national elections. One poll showed 20 per cent vote switching between two European elections, five years apart, and 30 per cent vote switching between the Euro-election and the national election held in the same year.[34] In 1984 Borre concluded that 'the continued strength of the People's Movement and the weakness of the Social Democrats in the context of EP elections seem to indicate that there still exist two rather different party systems, one for national elections and one for European elections. The latter has not disintegrated in spite of the lapse of five years containing three national elections'. And in 1989

> The outcome of the election reaffirmed the peculiar Danish Euro-party system, a voting pattern in European elections that deviates remarkably from voting behaviour in national elections. After the first two European elections the Euro-party system left no trace on Danish domestic politics, and there is no reason to assume it will be otherwise after the election of 1989'.[35]

Comparison of the 1990 national election outcome with the 1994 Euro-election outcome does not indicate a change in this respect, although Thomsen did detect leakage from the national party system in the 1994 elections.[36]

Party System and Electoral System

There are few constitutional instruments available for manipulation of the party system in a direction that would transform it into a relevant choice. One such instrument is legislation to outlaw non-democratic parties, as exists in Germany, but preventing democratic national parties from fighting Euro-elections is a step unlikely to find much support. Another instrument would be to tinker with the electoral system. Electoral system reform is on the European agenda anyway, as the Maastricht Treaty reaffirmed the long-existing obligation to develop a uniform electoral system for Euro-elections. Currently there are 13 different electoral systems for the election of MEPs from the 12 member states (Northern Ireland and Great Britain have different systems). Some, but not all, countries have artificially high electoral thresholds (Germany, France), some but not all do not allow preferential voting (Spain, France, Germany), some but not all have compulsory voting (Belgium, Luxembourg, Greece, Italy to some extent), some but not all divide the country into electoral districts (Ireland, Belgium, Italy, Great Britain). The date of the election varies from country to country, and not even the principle of 'one man, one vote' is honoured (Luxembourg having a seat for every 65,000 inhabitants, Germany for every 820,000 inhabitants). The most notorious difference is between the first-past-the-post or plurality system in Great Britain and the varieties of proportional representation on the Continent (with the single transferable vote in the Irish Republic as an intermediate system).

The lack of a uniform electoral system is sometimes seen as an obstacle for the further development of the transnational party system: 'The failure of the transnational parties to become the foci of the EC's voters' attention lay in part with the different electoral systems, polling days and campaign regulations in each Member State, making it hard for them to organize or develop cohesive, common electoral strategies.'[37] However, the experience of the first three directly-elected parliaments is that the variety of electoral systems has odd effects on the strength of some national party delegations (such as the British Liberal Democrats) and that an MP's style of representation is affected by being elected nationwide or from an electoral district,[38] but that the impact on the cohesiveness of the transnational parties is marginal.

Since 1979 several attempts have been made to find consensus on a uniform electoral system. The Patijn report, the Seitlinger report, the Bocklet report, and the De Gucht report all failed, primarily because the gap between plurality and PR-systems could not be bridged.[39] The search for a uniform system, or at least for further harmonisation is still on. What would be the effect of various proposals on the three scenarios outlined above?

Ever since Duverger and Sartori, the literature on the relationship between electoral and party systems concentrates more on the number than on the type of parties. Nevertheless, it seems clear that the current situation in which most member states use PR within a single nationwide district, favours national parties, and indirectly contributes to the continuation of the transnational party system. A uniform system of PR treating the whole European Union as a single 567-member district would be most favourable to the development of a truly European party system, but the absence of any form of territorial representation in such a huge polity would be unprecedented. If territorial representation is imperative, and if the two alternative scenarios are seen as worthy of promotion, the districts should not coincide but cut across national boundaries, or fragment the national territory. In that sense, the British electoral system may provide more opportunities for a truly European or split-level alignment, than the most widely practised nationwide PR.

THE INSULATION OF NATIONAL PARTY SYSTEMS

But why would national political parties, through the national governments and through the transnational parties, agree to institutional reforms that may weaken their own position? Strange as it may seem, it could be argued that a withdrawal from the European arena may be in the national parties' best interest. Outside Denmark, the national parties have so far treated the Euro-elections as quasi-domestic elections, nominating primarily national politicians, some of whom have no intention to accept a European mandate

(*Forza Italia*'s Berlusconi in 1994, or the Dutch VVD's Nijpels in 1984), others of whom rarely show up at the EP's sessions (many French MEPs), and campaigning largely on domestic issues. As the outcome of the Euro-elections does not have direct national consequences, these elections are treated by the parties as a kind of mid-term beauty contest. However, because the national parties regard the Euro-elections as second-rate elections, they have become what is known in the psephological literature as second-order elections. Like the national parties, the voters do not treat the Euro-elections seriously and behave differently: lower turnout, better prospects for small, new, and radical parties, and losses of governing parties,[40] the various effects depending on the timing of the Euro-election with regard to national elections.[41] The voters use the Euro-elections, if they vote at all, to send signals of protest, or vote expressively, rather than instrumentally. As a result, the Euro-elections are no longer the reliable test of mid-term popularity that the national parties apparently intended them to be.

What is worse from the perspective of the national parties, second-order elections with their 'irresponsible' voters may not be entirely without repercussions on the national party system. It is worth emphasising the word 'may' in this respect, because a longitudinal comparison of national and Euro-election results shows that spillover from the second-order to the first-order elections is far from automatic. Even when Euro-elections show a clear Europe-wide trend, its continuation in national elections is not guaranteed. Writing about the impressive gains made by Green parties in the 1989 European elections, Curtice concluded: ... the elections cannot be dismissed as a ritualistic irrelevance. They did register the existence of at least one important European-wide electoral trend. And in so doing they may leave a permanent mark on national electoral and party politics.'[42] That particular forecast proved mistaken, and the 'green tide' ebbed away in the 1994 Euro-elections.

With this caveat in mind, it cannot be denied that the national and transnational party systems are currently nested, and that in addition to the strong effects of national party systems on the transnational party system, an admittedly weaker effect in the opposite direction does exist. Failure of their parties in the Euro-elections did mark the end of the careers of national political leaders such as the German liberal Hans-Dietrich Genscher (although he was not even a candidate), the French socialist Michel Rocard, and three Italian party secretaries.[43] Success in the Euro-elections, helped by the different patterns of voting behaviour, or because of an electoral system that provides a slightly different opportunity structure from the one used in national elections, provides new challengers with legitimacy and resources that may help them breakthrough nationally (e.g., de Villiers' candidacy in 1995 for the French presidency).

One of the resources may be financial. Originally, the European Parliament also provided financial support to political parties. Even parties that failed to win a seat, but obtained at least five per cent of the vote in one member state, or at least one per cent in three member-states, were eligible for funds. The system was biased in favour of established parties, if only because parties not yet represented were reimbursed after the elections.[44] The French Greens challenged this use of budgetary item 3708 in the European Court of Justice, which decided that such subventions were *ultra vires*. They are now stopped in February of any Euro-election year, so that the funds cannot be used directly for campaigning.[45] However, success in the Euro-elections does entitle parties to national subventions in some countries. The clearest example is that of the German Greens. The 1979 Euro-elections were the first nationwide elections in which *Die Grünen* participated. Their 3.2 per cent of the vote fell below the German threshold for gaining seats in the European parliament, but it did attract considerable media attention and entitled the party to financial support under German law. This state subvention is not based on actual expenditure incurred, but on the number of votes won. 'Thus, although having spent only DM 300,000 on the European campaign in 1979 ... the German ecologists, *Sonstige Politische Vereinigung* (SPV) *Die Grünen* received more than 4.5 million DM, which, of course, substantially helped the structuring and rapid growth of the party the following year.'[46] However, even without access to such resources, a success in the European elections may be the breakthrough in the national arena. The 1984 European elections saw the take-off of the French *Front National*. Such a spectacular result bestows credibility and media attention on the new party (and provides parliamentary immunity for its leader!). It discredits the 'wasted vote' argument so often used by established parties to dissuade voters from actually casting their vote for new challengers.

The European elections may also affect the national party system in other ways. Close cooperation in the European arena may be a prelude to merger at home. When the Dutch Catholics asked the two main Protestant parties to join them in the *Nouvelles Equipes Internationales* in 1953, one Protestant leader still opposed the request 'as an invitation to participate in the papal striving for power'.[47] Travelling together and working together in the transnational Christian Democratic organisation is generally regarded as one of the factors contributing to the three parties merging into the CDA. However, it can also be the other way around. Contesting Euro-elections may also threaten national parties from within. They derive their cohesion from other conflicts than those over Europe, and their members and leaders may have different European preferences. If these differences are sufficiently pronounced, or when they are politicised as part of a leadership struggle within the party, they may threaten to split the party. This is what happened to the French PS in 1994 and is still threatening to happen to the British Conservatives.

So far, it should be reiterated, the breakthrough of new challengers, mergers, splits, and the downfall of national party leaders are still isolated examples of leakage of the current transnational party system to national party systems. However, such instances are likely to become more rather than less frequent in the years to come. There is now considerable evidence of a gradual weakening of the established parties' ties to civil society throughout western Europe. With only few exceptions, political parties are losing members,[48] and support is less loyal than it used to be:

> In an overall perspective, the proportion of EC citizens more or less attached to a particular party has been decreasing over the past decade by about ten percent, from below 70 per cent in the mid-1970s to below 60 per cent in the late 1980s. Accordingly, those not aligned with any party have become more numerous, and today constitute about 40 per cent of the EC electorate.[49]

The social cleavages that structured most national party systems into electoral alignments are becoming less relevant for party choice: 'Voters begin to choose'.[50] In short, Lipset and Rokkan's famous 'frozen' party systems have started to thaw. Parties may survive this end of the ice age by adapting to the new context,[51] but nowhere is their new vulnerability better illustrated than in recent Italian history. In the current era of party dealignment, the potential spillover of the vagaries of Euro-elections constitutes a real threat to established national parties. From that perspective, it would seem advantageous to such parties to follow the Danish example, and to insulate the national party system by allowing a truly European and/or split-level party system to take over the European arena.[52]

NOTES

1. European Commission, *Eurobarometer; Public Opinion in the European Union*, n.41, Brussels, July 1994, pp.1–3
2. O. Niedermayer, 'Turnout in the European Election', *Electoral Studies* 9 (1990), p.46. Low turnout may be caused by the lack of legitimacy of European integration in general, rather than of the European Parliament alone. Niedermayer finds more support for this hypothesis, but still concludes that: 'To use the actual turnout figures or the actual European turnout average and their variations over time as an indicator for the European citizens' perception of the EC, however, is misleading because the actual figures are considerably influenced by factors having nothing to do with the European Community' (ibid., p.49).
3. F. Jacobs, R. Corbett and M. Shackleton, *The European Parliament*, 2nd ed. (Harlow: Longman, 1992), pp.83–4.
4. Ibid., pp.86–7. Also S. Hix, 'European Integration and Party Behaviour: Party Adaption to

Extra-System challenges', paper presented to the workshop on Inter-Party Relationships in National and European Parliamentary Arenas, ECPR Joint Sessions of Workshops, Leyden Univ., 2–8 April 1993.

5. L. Bardi, 'Transnational Party Federations, European Party Groups and the Building of Europarties' in R.S. Katz and P. Mair (eds.), *How Parties Organize: Change and Adaptation in Party Organizations in Western Democracies* (London: Sage, 1994) p.361.

6. K.M. Johansson, 'Transnational Party Cooperation: the Case of the European People's Party', paper presented tot the workshop on Inter-Party Relationships in National and European Parliamentary Arenas, ECPR Joint Sessions of Workshops, Leyden Univ. 2–8 April 1993, p.7.

7. R. Ladrech, 'Social Democratic Parties and EC Integration: transnational party responses to Europe 1992', *European Journal of Political Research* [hereafter *EJPR*] 24 (1993), p.207.

8. Bardi, (note 5), pp.361–4.

9. Ibid., p.365.

10. *The Economist*, 4 June and 18 June 1994.

11. Attina (see Further Reading), p.559.

12. V.Bogdanor, 'Direct elections, representative democracy and European integration', *Electoral Studies* 8 (1989), pp.211–13.

13. Attina (note 11), p.576.

14. Jacobs *et al.*, (note 3), p.148.

15. Bardi (note 5), p.368.

16. Jacobs *et al.*, (note 3), p.82.

17. Quoted in G.Pridham and P.Pridham, *Towards Transnational Parties in the European Community* (London: Policy Studies Inst., 1979), p.2.

18. *Eurobarometer* (note 1), p.6.

19. K. Reif and H. Schmitt, 'Nine Second-Order National Elections – a conceptual framework for the analysis of European election results', *EJPR* 8 (1980), p.8.

20. C. Van Der Eijk and M. Franklin, 'European Community Politics and Electoral Representation: evidence from the 1989 European Elections Study', *EJPR* 19 (1991), p.124.

21. Pridham and Pridham, (note 17), p.10.

22. Ibid., p.9.

23. Ladrech (note 7).

24. John Major, 'Europe: a Future that Works', William and Mary Lecture, Leyden University, 7 Sept. 1994.

25. Bardi (note 5), pp.369, 370.

26. Bogdanor (note 12), pp.213–214.

27. M. Steed, 'Failure or Long-Haul? European Elections and European Integration', *Electoral Studies* 3 (1984), p.229.

28. Ibid., p.230.

29. Bogdanor (note 12), p.209.

30. H.Valen, 'National Conflict Structure and Foreign Politics: the impact of the EEC issue on perceived cleavages in Norwegian politics', *EJPR* 4 (1976), pp.47–82,

31. G. Grunberg, 'Notes on the 1994 elections to the European Parliament: France', *Electoral Studies* 13 (1994), p.8.

32. Jacobs *et al.*, (note 3), p.160.

33. Bogdanor (note 12), p.209.

34. O.Borre, 'Notes on the 1984 elections to the European Parliament: Denmark', *Electoral Studies* 3 (1984), pp.271–2.

35. T.Worre, 'Notes on the 1989 elections to the European Parliament: Denmark', *Electoral Studies* 8 (1989), p.244.

36. S.R.Thomsen, 'Notes on the 1994 elections to the European Parliament: Denmark', *Electoral Studies*, 13 (1994), pp.3–5.

37. J. Lodge and V. Herman, 'Direct Elections to the European Parliament: a supra-national perspective', *EJPR* 8 (1980), p.60.

38. S.Bowler and D.M.Farrell, 'Legislator shirking and voter monitoring: impact of European Parliament electoral systems upon legislator-voter relationships', *Journal of Common*

Market Studies 31/1 (1993).
39. See D. Millar, 'A Uniform Electoral Procedure for European Elections', *Electoral Studies* 9 (1990), pp.37–44; and Jacobs *et al.* (note 3), pp.12–28.
40. Reif and Schmitt (note 19).
41. K.Reif, 'National Electoral Cycles and the European Elections of 1979 and 1984', *Electoral Studies* 3 (1984), pp.244–55.
42. J.Curtice, 'The 1989 European Election: Protest or Green Tide?', *Electoral Studies* 8 (1989), p.217.
43. L.Lo Verso, 'Notes on the 1994 elections to the European Parliament: Italy', *Electoral Studies* 13 (1994), p.19.
44. O.Niedermayer, 'The Transnational Dimension of the Election', *Electoral Studies* 3 (1984), pp.238–9.
45. Jacobs *et al.* (note 3), pp.22–23.
46. V. Hoffmann-Martinot, 'Grüne and Verts, two faces of European Ecologism', *West European Politics* 14/4 (1991), p.72.
47. H.M. Ten Napel, 'Een Eigen Weg; de totstandkoming van het CDA (1952–1980)', doctoral diss., Leyden Univ., p.32.
48. R.S. Katz, P. Mair *et al.*, 'The Membership of Political Parties in European Democracies, 1960–1990', *EJPR* 22 (1992), pp.329–45.
49. H. Schmitt, 'On Party Attachment in Western Europe and the Utility of the Eurobarometer Data', *West European Politics* 12/2 (April 1989), p.125.
50. After the title of R.Rose and I.McAllister, *Voters Begin to Choose; from Closed-Class to Open Elections in Britain* (London: Sage, 1986).
51. S. Bartolini and P. Mair, *Identity, Competition and Electoral Availability* (Cambridge: CUP, 1990).
52. Cf. C.Van Der Eijk, 'De Noodzakelijke Terugtred van de Nationale Partijen: de electorale uitdaging' in G. Voerman (ed.), *Politiek Zonder Partijen?* (Amsterdam: Spinhuis, 1994), pp.33–53.

FURTHER READING

F. Attina, 'The Voting Behaviour of the European Parliament Members and the Problem of the Europarties', *European Journal of Political Research* 18 (1990), pp.557–79.

L. Bardi, 'Transnational Party Federations, European Parliamentary Party Groups and the Building of Europarties', in R.S. Katz and P. Mair (eds.), *How Parties Organize: Change and Adaptation in Party Organizations in Western Democracies* (London: Sage, 1994), pp.357–72.

F. Jacobs, R Corbett and M. Shackleton, *The European Parliament*, 2nd ed. (Harlow: Longman, 1992).

K. Reif and H. Schmitt 1980, 'Nine Second-Order National Elections – a conceptual framework for the analysis of European Election Results', *European Journal of Political Research* 8 (1980), pp.3–44.

C. Van der Eijk and M. Franklin, 'European Community Politics and Electoral Representation: Evidence from the 1989 European Elections Study', *European Journal of Political Research* 19 (1991), pp.105–27.

The Failure of National Parliaments?

DAVID JUDGE

National parliaments are commonly held to have 'failed' in their dealings with European institutions and in their impact upon the Community's legislative process. This article provides a 'revisionist' analysis to challenge this 'orthodoxy'. First, national parliaments have provided the legitimating frame within which the development of the European Community has been able to take place. Second, there has been no absolute, inexorable decline in the influence exerted by national parliaments in the EC policy process. If anything, events since the signing of the Treaty on European Union in December 1991 suggest that national parliaments have bargained increased powers of scrutiny over EC legislation. Third, it needs to be noted that there is a 'dual democratic deficit' within the European Union. The problem of the 'democratic deficit' is evident not solely in the accretion of decision-making power at the European level, but also in the fact that national parliaments within their own states exert limited control over their own national executives.

National parliaments have gradually lost substantial legislative functions to the European Community, now the European Union...Generally speaking, the national parliaments underestimated very much, for a long time, the impact of the EC's evolution on their political functions.[1]

Clearly, power has passed from national institutions to the institutions of the EC. That is a consequence of membership of the Community and has been exacerbated by the provisions of the Single European Act and the Treaty of European Union...National parliaments have been left behind in the rush. They have no formal role in the process of policy making, other than indirectly through national governments or in a sporadic and advisory form.[2]

These statements represent the orthodox assessment of national parliaments in the European Union, and could easily be reproduced in the nine different official languages within the Union itself. Manifestly, national parliaments are seen to have 'failed' in their dealings with European institutions and in their impact upon the Community's legislative process. Yet to say that they have limited direct impact upon EC policies, or that significant areas of policy which were formerly their own exclusive preserve are now parts of wider European competences, does not necessarily entail 'failure'. Rather there is a need for a more nuanced analysis of their role, one that takes into account both the broader debate about the role of legislatures generally, and the specific conceptions of the place of national legislatures within a developing Community. What is offered here, therefore, is a 'revisionist' analysis to offset, in part, the orthodoxy of the 'failure' of national parliaments.

This revision has three distinct elements. The first is that national parliaments have provided the legitimating frame within which the development of the EC has been able to take place. It remains true that 'democratic processes have hitherto only functioned within national borders',[3] and, hence, in the absence of a democratic *European* political culture, national parliaments have been crucial, and remarkably successful until the early 1990s at least, in providing *national* frames of legitimation within which *supranational* institutions and their policy initiatives have been accepted. This in itself is no mean achievement, but is often overlooked in discussions of the role of the national parliaments in the development of the EC.

The second way in which the orthodox assessment of 'failure' needs to be revised is in the assumption that there is a clear, inexorable decline in the influence exerted by national parliaments in the EC policy process. If anything, events since the signing of the Treaty on European Union by Heads of Government and States in December 1991 suggest that national parliaments have used the uncertainties surrounding ratification to bargain increased powers of scrutiny over EC legislation.

The third point of this 'revisionist' analysis is to note that there is a 'dual democratic deficit' within the European Union. The problem of the 'democratic deficit' is thus manifest not solely in the accretion of decision-making power at the *European* level – with the European parliament exerting only limited control over the Commission and the Council (the first dimension), but also in the fact that national parliaments *within their own states* exert limited control over their national executives (the second dimension). Their interconnection has been openly acknowledged by the Danish government: 'a considerable part of what is known as the democratic shortfall is attributable to the fact that apparently not all national parliaments have an adequate say in decisions at Community level.'[4] The 'problem' of the 'democratic deficit' is thus best conceived not at the

European 'level' but as a *universal problem* of how parliaments *sui generis* hold executives to account.

DUAL DEMOCRATIC DEFICIT

It is as well to remember at the start of a discussion on the 'failure' of national parliaments that most major Western European parliaments have conventionally been held to have had limited policy effect in the twentieth century.[5] Inevitably, to focus upon the policy impact of parliaments serves simply to confirm a perception of 'decline'.[6] Indeed, it is a truism in the study of legislatures that 'public policy has increasingly been initiated and formulated – in effect, "made" – elsewhere, usually by the executive'.[7] Thus, long before the advent of the European Community – and certainly long before the introduction of the Single European Act – national parliaments were perceived to have been 'failing' as 'legislatures'. All that the extension of decision-making competences at the European level did, therefore, was to exacerbate existing imbalances of policy influence between national executives and parliaments.

From the outset this imbalance was evident among the six founder member states of the European Community. The ECSC Treaty in 1951, and the EEC and EURATOM Treaties in 1957, made no direct reference to national parliaments. Logically, there was no need to include national parliaments in the new European institutional blueprint, as the dynamic agency of integration – the High Authority, later the Commission – was conceived as having a 'technocratic' and *supranational* development role; whereas, in contrast, the concerns of national parliaments were, by definition, 'political' and *national*. Perhaps, not surprisingly, therefore, Jean Monnet's 'ECSC strategy was to proceed in a piecemeal fashion, thereby not taking too many political risks by inflaming those jealously guarding national sovereignty'.[8] Initially, Monnet had not foreseen the need for any democratic controls over the High Authority,[9] but was later convinced that some democratic control should be inserted into the new ECSC institutional structure. The details of this democratic system were to be worked out later, within a developing consensus for further integration based upon the 'technocratic' success of the ECSC. If anything, the ECSC was to be a rough institutional sketch, drafted in freehand.[10] In practice, however, it came to serve as *the* institutional blueprint of the EC, with its omissions formalised in Treaty form, and with an inbuilt 'democratic deficit'.[11]

National parliaments were thus ascribed no direct role in the ECSC, or later in the EC decision-making process, nor did they expect, initially, to play such a role.[12] Any policy role that national parliaments expected to play was conceived in terms of exerting influence over their respective executives. From the outset, therefore, existing patterns of national legislative-executive relations came to imprint themselves upon the wider patterns of national parliamentary activity at the EC-level. And it is important to note that there was no single, uniform pattern, but rather six sets of indirect connections between national parliaments and 'Brussels'. Effectively, the influence of each parliament was mediated and structured by the constitutional and political relationships pertaining domestically with its own national government. How national parliaments responded to further European integration was largely 'predetermined' by their location at the interstices of national political controversies and concerns: by the conceptions of sovereignty within each state (whether sovereignty derived from parliament or the people, and hence where it was 'located' within the state); by party relationships (whether consensual or adversary); by the territorial organisation of the state (centralised vs decentralised/federal); and by the degree of commitment to effecting 'an ever closer union' within the European Community.

These differences were apparent among the six founder member states. At one extreme, in France, where the National Assembly's powers of initiative and scrutiny of the executive had been severely restricted under the new Republic's constitution in 1958,[13] no provision was made for consultation of the national parliament upon European Affairs, nor were scrutiny procedures for secondary legislation introduced.[14] In practice, for long spells under General de Gaulle, 'France's policy in the EEC context was a matter of presidential discretion and decision'.[15] At the other extreme, parliamentary procedures were rapidly developed in West Germany to enable the Bundestag, Bundesrat and Länder to exercise some legislative control over the national executive. Articles 2 and 3 of the 1957 Act of Accession required the federal government to inform both the Bundestag, and the Bundesrat, of the activities of the EC Council of Ministers, and of any proposals that were likely to affect German law. Specialised committees of the Bundestag and Bundesrat also, serially, scrutinised European legislative proposals. In practice, though, this scrutiny often amounted merely to 'passing most items on the nod and putting up formal "take note" motions to the plenary'.[16] The federal government was also required at six-monthly intervals to submit a formal report for debate by the respective 'European' committees in both chambers.[17]

In part, these arrangements reflected the German parliament's concern to assert its position through legislation,[18] and, in part, the constitutional position of the Länder. Indeed, regional concerns were given both institutional status and policy priority in West Germany, to the extent that the Länder, in ratifying the Treaties of Rome in 1957, secured a consultation procedure, via the Bundesrat. Within the context of an overriding commitment within the West German state to European integration, and the equally important practical stagnation of EC development in the 1960s, the German parliamentary system was able to modify its existing procedures to accommodate changes brought about by its membership of the EC.[19] More particularly, federal government ministers were expected to take into account the position taken by the Länder (via the Bundesrat) in their negotiations in the EC Council of Ministers. To reinforce their position a representative of the Länder was also present in the German delegation to the relevant meetings of the Council of Ministers. In these instances the national parliament was able to exercise 'binding parliamentary scrutiny'.[20]

In between the extremes displayed in Germany and France, the other founding EC states developed a variety of parliamentary procedures to cope with EC membership. Luxembourg, like France, did not establish a Committee on European Affairs, preferring instead to deal with EC legislation in the appropriate specialised committee. In Holland a Committee on European Affairs was established in the First Chamber, but it met only rarely, and then only to hear the reports of the prime minister on various EC meetings. Overall, therefore, its role was seen to be 'restricted'.[21] The Dutch parliament did, however, secure the general right to be informed of developments within the EC through inserting a clause in the ratification of the Rome Treaties which required the government to make an annual report on the application of the treaties. In Belgium the Chamber of Representatives established, in 1963, a European Affairs Committee whose primary task was to obtain information on the effects and application of EC legislation, and to scrutinise governmental reports upon the implementation of the Treaties. Proposals involving the approval of international treaties remained the responsibility of the Chamber's Committee on Foreign Affairs.[22] In Italy, a Senate Committee on European Affairs was established in 1968, alongside the specialised committee system, to deliver opinions on draft laws, as well as to consider, jointly with the Foreign Affairs Committee, government reports on the EC. The lower House preferred simply to process EC matters through its existing specialised subject committees.

Overall, therefore, no 'standard operating procedure' emerged for processing EC matters within the six founder member states. Significantly, the role of national parliaments in the EC policy process reflected both domestic political relationships – 'the extent [of] the effectiveness of each national parliament in controlling its government in Community affairs is dependent on how much control it can exert over the government in domestic affairs'[23] – and the extent to which national parliaments perceived a need to control their governments in pressing European integration. For those states in which a fundamental consensus existed around the cause of integration, the need for national parliamentary control of their respective executives in EC deliberations appeared, initially at least, less pressing than in those states more sceptical about the national advantage to be gained from closer cooperation. This distinction was made apparent in 1973 with the first enlargement of the Community, when two of the three new members, Denmark and the United Kingdom, entered with little enthusiasm for the integrationist rhetoric of the founder members and more robust parliamentary histories than any of the original six members.

Denmark

Upon entry into the EC the Danish parliament's (Folketing) Market Committee (Markedsudvalget) assumed responsibility for controlling the actions of Danish executives in their deliberations over EC policy and for ensuring some coordination of their actions. In effect, the Markedsudvalget assumed a power of 'co-decision' in EC affairs – a form of 'binding parliamentary scrutiny' – which, in large part, reflected the pre-existing institutional strength of the Folketing. The Danish constitution effectively ensured that the cabinet was responsible to the Folketing, to the extent that governments were required in practice to seek working majorities in parliament and in its committees. This tradition, of governments seeking broad cross-party agreements,[24] served to enhance the policy role of parliament, and also served to incorporate the opposition parties in the decision-making process through their participation in specialised parliamentary subject committees.

Equally, however, the rigid system of parliamentary control was interpreted by some 'as evidence of Danish lukewarmness towards the Community and a potentially dangerous source of obstruction'.[25] If, in the founder member states, the issue of democratic control of 'Brussels' was variously underestimated, left unaddressed, or merely regarded as a transitory problem capable of redress through the eventual transfer of sovereignty between national and EC parliamentary institutions, this was not the case in Denmark. There, the issues of democratic control and national parliamentary sovereignty were at the very heart of the political debate over membership of the EC.

The Act of Accession itself obliged the Danish government to keep the Folketing informed of EC policy developments. This it did by sending, every 14 days, information on Commission proposals to the Market Committee, with a summary of their legal and financial implications and a probable timetable for their adoption. The Committee also received a wide range of other, more general, EC documents. In considering these documents the Market Committee did not make written reports or adopt formal resolutions. Its decisions did, however, carry the full authority of the Folketing – with ministers politically obliged to follow the opinion of the Committee, or at least to obtain a 'negative clearance' in the sense of determining that there was no majority opposed to the government's position.[26] While accepting the requirement to have their actions in the Council of Ministers 'mandated' by the Folketing, Danish ministers were, of course, confronted with practical difficulties in ensuring that the will of their national parliament was secured in the complex and byzantine processes of policy-making within the EC.[27] Nevertheless, the Danish system of EC scrutiny and control was seen by many parliamentarians in other national legislatures as a 'model' to which to aspire.

United Kingdom

Shortly before the United Kingdom entered the European Community, a Select Committee, chaired by Sir John Foster and thereafter known as the Foster Committee, was appointed to consider possible procedures for dealing with the scrutiny of European secondary legislation in the House of Commons.[28] The Committee reminded parliament that it had entered a legislative process in which its direct approval for legislation was no longer required, and in which it was impossible for it to amend European legislation. Under Section 2(2) of the European Communities Act 1972, parliament's primary role was to scrutinise the secondary legislation needed to effect Community Directives. Indeed, the original aspiration of the Select Committee on European Secondary Legislation (created upon the recommendation of the Foster Committee) was to bring to the consideration of EC legislation the same level of scrutiny as provided for UK secondary legislation. The limited ambition of this objective is obvious, when it is remembered that the processing of secondary legislation has traditionally raised profound issues of executive accountability, and has generally demonstrated the supremacy of the executive over the legislature.[29]

Indeed, the crux of the matter is not so much the nature of the EC legislative process and the procedures for scrutiny, but rather the nature of domestic political and constitutional relationships between executives and parliament. Thus, in concluding that 'as the Council of Ministers was comprised of Ministers from Member States, the accountability of Ministers to parliament provided a route by which the House might maintain a degree of control and influence in the legislative processes of the Community',[30] the Foster Report simply reinforced the very doctrine – ministerial responsibility – that had traditionally undermined parliamentary scrutiny of executive actions.[31] As Kolinsky noted at the time: 'In Britain membership of the community accentuated the tendency to loosen control over the executive.'[32]

Yet, there was a paradox in all of this, as the procedures adopted by the House in 1974 allowed MPs to consider pre-legislative proposals for EC directives, while parliament remained systematically excluded from the pre-legislative stage of UK domestic legislation. The House was thus presented with the 'opportunity to participate in some policy areas at an earlier stage and possibly with more effectiveness than in most non-EC policy'.[33] However, as a general rule, where such participation strengthened ministerial bargaining positions in relation to their European counterparts in the Council of Ministers, it was welcomed;[34] where it offered no, or little, political support it was ignored.[35] Indeed, the very fluidity of Commission proposals at the pre-legislative stage, the unpredictable schedule of their consideration by the Council of Ministers, in combination with the range and increasing technical complexity of proposals, served to militate against effective scrutiny and hence, in theory, control of the actions of UK ministers by the UK parliament.

What stands out, therefore, is the replication and reinforcement of pre-existing power differentials between the UK parliament and the executive in the processing of EC legislation. The imbalance at the heart of the scrutiny system was evident in the conception of the primary role of the Select Committee on European Legislation as the 'sifting' of Community documents sent to the House by the government, and so to identify EC proposals with significant policy implications for the UK. Thereafter, it was the responsibility of the House itself to seek to influence UK ministers on these matters, Thus, the system was based upon two fundamental premises: first, that the Select Committee on European Legislation would receive the most important EC documents; and, second, that it would receive them in time to notify the House of *forthcoming* decisions in the Council. 'Since the United Kingdom parliament exercised no control over Community legislation other than through the voice and vote of United Kingdom Ministers in the Council of Ministers',[36] it was essential, therefore, that parliament was informed as to which proposals were under active consideration by UK ministers, and at a time when parliament's views could be expressed before a decision was reached in the Council of Ministers. On both counts the scrutiny system was inherently flawed.[37]

SINGLE EUROPEAN ACT AND THE TREATY ON EUROPEAN UNION

A basic precondition of effective scrutiny by national parliaments is that their views should be expressed before national ministers approve proposals in the Council of Ministers. Clearly, the 1980 Resolution of the UK House of Commons was intended to secure such prior approval. This Resolution stated that: 'No Minister of the Crown should give agreement to any proposal for European legislation which has been recommended by the Select Committee on European Legislation for consideration by the House, before the House has given it that consideration.'[38] Ministers were thus expected to place a 'scrutiny reserve' on documents coming before the Council upon which parliamentary scrutiny had not yet been completed. This arrangement was acquiesced to in the Council, despite no mention of it in the EC Treaties, in 'recognition of the fact that parliamentary control over European legislation has developed further in the United Kingdom than in most of the Community'.[39]

However, the 1980 Resolution of the House, and indeed the concept of 'scrutiny reserve', faced a serious constitutional and practical challenge with the introduction of the Single European Act on 1 July 1987. If the UK, as a condition of its Community membership had bound itself to accept the legislative authority of the Council of Ministers, only one of whose 12 members was accountable to the House of Commons, then the move to Qualified Majority Voting in the Council could be seen as 'weakening the power of UK ministers and [so] is felt equally by the United Kingdom Parliament'.[40] The SEA consequently 'placed constraints on the House's ability to scrutinize European legislation which [could] only be alleviated but not removed by changes in the practices of the House'.[41]

Similarly, in other member states, the significance of the SEA slowly dawned as national parliaments were increasingly asked, especially under the internal market provisions of the Act, to scrutinise a welter of legislation – often technical – in a short time. In these circumstances, 'the twin impressions grew of much being imposed by "Brussels" and of national parliaments being afforded little more than a fleeting glimpse of European legislation'.[42] National parliaments responded to the patent danger of their further residualisation by becoming more active on EC issues.[43] In 1985, for example, the Belgian Chamber of Representatives established an Advisory Committee on European Questions. In 1987 the West German Bundestag established a new Sub-Committee (Europe) of its Foreign Affairs Committee with responsibility for looking broadly at EC developments. In 1987, also, the Italian government introduced legislation requiring individual ministries to report on progress on EC policy initiatives within their area, and to coordinate the presentation of legislation to parliament, particularly on bills pertaining to the internal market. Reinforcement of these reforms came in 1989 with the simplification of the domestic Italian legislative process and the introduction of a fixed timetable for the annual passage of all outstanding EC legislation.[44]

In the UK, the House of Commons updated its 1980 Resolution to take account of the SEA's cooperation procedure, which now required legislative proposals covered by the procedure to be presented twice to the European parliament. In between 'readings', the Council was to adopt its 'common position' – effectively stating the terms under which it was willing to legislate. In this context, the cooperation procedure added a further complication to the scrutiny of EC legislation by national parliaments 'as, although a debate post-common position complies with the Government's obligations *vis-à-vis* the 1980 Resolution, it offers relatively limited and uncertain scope for the House to influence the content of the proposal'.[45] In October 1990, therefore, a revised Resolution was adopted,[46] which confirmed informal agreements reached in 1984 and 1989, extended the 1980 Resolution's coverage to agreements on 'common positions' in Council, and incorporated proposals which the Select Committee had not had an opportunity to scrutinise, or where it had not yet completed its scrutiny. The year 1990 also saw the creation of two new European Standing Committees that were intended to allow their members to question ministers and to debate EC proposals.[47]

As national parliaments increasingly recognised the importance of the changes wrought by the SEA, so, too, national (and sub-national) governments began to appreciate the potential incursion upon their own policy independence. In West Germany the Länder responded to the SEA by seeking and securing the right to more wide-ranging coordination with the federal ministers where their exclusive powers were affected by EC proposals.[48] In Italy two successive laws in 1987 and 1989 were introduced to provide parliament and ministries alike with a framework of rules necessary to process EC internal market legislation. However, perhaps, nowhere was this realisation more pronounced than in the UK.[49]

Road to the Treaty on European Union (TEU)

If the Single European Act served to focus attention upon the pace and speed of European integration within national parliaments (and national political elites), its passage also provided a 'clue' as to how national parliaments could insert themselves more forcefully into the EC policy process. The SEA reminded them of how treaty revision could be used to articulate the concerns of national parliaments. Manifestly, there was significant variation in anxiety levels about the residualisation of national parliaments in the 12 member states. In Italy, where there had traditionally been overwhelming support for European integration, and where there was 'a congruence between the style of politics and public policy-making to which Italians ha[d] become used over forty years, and the style of Community institutions and decision-taking procedures',[50] the position of the national legislature was not a major issue in the debate over the ratification of the SEA. In contrast, in the UK and Denmark there were serious intraparliamentary divisions and misgivings about the constitutional implications of the Single Act.

The real significance of the SEA for national parliaments rested ultimately, however, not in the negative effects of institutional change and enhanced competences of European institutions, but in the positive experience of actually having to approve change to the EC Treaties. Under the EEC Treaty, Article 236, amendments of the Treaties could only 'enter into force after being ratified by all Member States in accordance with their respective constitutional requirements'. In all 12 member states these 'requirements' encompassed parliamentary ratification. Hence, the SEA, as the first major treaty revision since 1957, highlighted the simple fact that it was national parliaments which, in the last instance, determined whether or not European integration was to proceed. Lessons were rapidly recalled from the process of ratification of the Treaty of Rome itself in 1957 – when some national parliaments inserted information requirements upon their national executive.

Certainly, the most reticent members and parties within national parliaments sought specific pledges from their national governments about increased opportunities to scrutinise EC legislation, and more generally used the ratification of the SEA as an occasion to voice their concerns about the direction of European integration. Several national governments were forced to concede procedural changes within domestic institutions to improve the transmission and quality of information provided on EC matters. In West Germany, for example, the Länder assented to the SEA only on the condition that the information exchange procedures instituted in 1979 were increased and formalised.[51] More importantly, after the SEA, there was a wider recognition on the part of national executives and of the European institutions themselves (admittedly for different reasons), of the need to involve national parliaments in discussions about the future development of the Community.

One result was the convocation in November 1990 in Rome of an *Assises*, using a traditional French term, of representatives from national parliaments and from the European parliament. The initial proposal for the *Assises* was contained in the Martin I Report[52] which recommended that a conference of parliamentarians should be held *before* national governments convened Intergovernmental Conferences to discuss further EC treaty amendment. Indeed, Corbett concluded that the *Assises* was a 'remarkable event' in that 'never before had the parliaments who would be called upon to ratify a Treaty met jointly to discuss its possible contents before their respective governments embarked on the negotiations'.[53] More specifically, the 1990 *Assises* adopted a resolution supporting 'enhanced cooperation between the national parliaments and the European parliament, through regular meetings of specialized committees, exchanges of information and by organising conferences of parliaments of the European Community when the discussion of guidelines of vital importance to the Community justifies it'.[54] Prompted in part by this resolution, the IGC on Political Union considered the role of national parliaments, and two Declarations were adopted and annexed to the Treaty on European Union.[55] One stated 'that it is important to encourage greater involvement of national parliaments in the activities of the European Union' and proceeded to call for greater exchange of information among parliaments, and for governments to ensure that their respective parliaments received EU documents in 'good time' for examination. The other Declaration invited the EP and national parliaments 'to meet as necessary as a Conference of Parliaments, or *Assises*'. While some commentators anticipate that such a conference will be convened before the 1996 IGC,[56] there is sufficient resistance within some member states – most notably in Holland, Denmark and the UK – to the convocation of future *Assises*, and sufficient reluctance within the European Parliament to see an institutionalisation of a 'Conference of Parliaments',[57] as to raise substantial doubts as to the prospects for future conferences.

Routinised, and established, interparliamentary cooperation does, however, take place in the Conference of European Affairs Committees of the National Parliaments and the European Parliament (CEAC). CEAC met originally in Paris in November 1989 and now meets twice a year in the countries holding the European Presidency. At its April 1994 meeting in Athens CEAC considered practical proposals designed to improve parliamentary scrutiny. One proposal, tabled by the EP, was for the Union's annual programme to be forwarded to national parliaments immediately after its adoption. It also suggested that progress on the legislative programme should be monitored and debated at the autumn meeting of CEAC. To assist this process the EP has formally committed itself to send to the national parliaments the programme as agreed by the Union's institutions. Moreover, the EP sends a progress report on the work of its own committees to the European Affairs committees in each parliament of member states.[58] Recently, the EP has established a computerised system designed to track the progress of legislative proposals and to record changes made therein. The information contained in this 'European Interinstitutional Legislative Observatory' (OEIL) will be made available to national parliaments. But, as Duff notes, there is an inherent limitation to what national parliaments can do in the EC, and this is delimited by the simple fact that 'they are not and cannot be part of the routine legislative process'.[59] Instead, 'their mundane duty is to hold national ministers to account for what they get up to in the Council'.[60]

National parliaments became convinced of the importance of this 'mundane role' during the ratification of the Treaty on European Union (TEU). In that period 'a broad consensus emerged among the parliaments of the need for each of them to exercise greater control over their own executive'.[61] This took tangible form in the revision and strengthening of scrutiny procedures within each national parliament between 1992 and 1994; with France providing, perhaps, the most dramatic illustration of the strengthening of scrutiny procedures exacted by a national parliament during the course of the ratification process. The National Assembly and the Senate secured a new Article (88-4) to the French constitution which states: 'The government shall submit to the National Assembly and the Senate all proposals for Community acts containing provisions of a legislative nature as soon as they are forwarded to the Council of the Communities. During or outside parliamentary sessions, parliamentary resolutions may be adopted under this Article'. Although these are non-binding resolutions, they provide the only example where the French parliament is authorised to adopt a resolution on its own initiative. In essence what this change entails is that Community policy is no longer designated as 'foreign policy' and hence the exclusive preserve of the executive. In recognition of this fact the French government pledged to inform parliament of progress at each legislative stage, and to take account of views expressed in parliament during its negotiations with other member governments. In July 1994 the French prime minister, Edouard Balladur, issued a circular to ministers and civil servants, stating that they should discover whether the National Assembly intended to pass resolutions on draft EU laws, and, if so, Ministers should then seek to place reserves on those matters in the Council. Moreover, on 6 October 1994 the EU Affairs Committee passed a unanimous resolution requesting that the French government should seek to delay a discussion of 'excessive budget deficits' in the Finance Council. The French government acceded to this request.[62] Significantly, however, the French government had refused earlier, in May 1994, to accept that legislative proposals based on the second and third pillars of the TEU (Common Foreign and Security policy, and Justice and Home Affairs) should be subject to the procedure laid down in Article 88-4.[63]

In Germany, ratification of the Maastricht Treaty was accompanied by a major revision of the Basic Law. Two new Articles (23 and 45) dealt specifically with parliamentary control of Community legislation. These changes were confirmed in October 1993 in a Constitutional Court ruling that the changes effected were compatible with the Basic Law. In outline, these changes required, first, the approval, by a two-thirds majority in both the Bundestag and Bundesrat, to any further transfer of powers to the European Union which affected the constitutional structure of Germany.

Second, the federal government is obliged to inform parliament 'comprehensively and at the earliest opportunity' about Community matters. Third, the Bundestag is to be given the opportunity to give its opinion before decisions are taken in Council, and the federal government is now obliged to take account of these opinions in the course of negotiations. Fourth, the position of the Länder was further strengthened in the requirement that, in policy areas which are the exclusive preserve of the Länder, the federal government should delegate to a representative of the Länder – appointed by the Bundesrat – the task of defending Germany's interests within the European institutions.

Constitutional changes were also made in Portugal in November 1992, to strengthen the role of the Assembly of the Republic with regard to the processing of European legislation. The Assembly was granted the power 'to monitor and assess', and the government was required to submit to it 'in good time' any information concerning Portugal's participation in the process of European integration.[64] These constitutional changes were consolidated, in May 1994, in new legislation specifying the procedures for the communication of information and the processes by which the Assembly was to be consulted. Provision was also made in this law for the parliamentary assessment of policy pursued by the Portuguese government within the Union.

In Greece and Ireland, the national parliaments responded to the TEU with procedural changes. The former, under Rule 32A, retroactively confirmed the creation of a Committee on European Community Affairs, and empowered the committee to call ministers before it to inform it of developments within the Council of Ministers. The latter created a new sub-committee of its Joint Foreign Affairs Committee, with a remit extending to the consideration of 'all EC matters'.

Not surprisingly, perhaps, the Danish Folketing pressed for enhanced powers of scrutiny and control over ministers during the protracted ratification of the TEU. Provisions were made for more debates on EU issues to be held in plenary, greater cooperation between the European Committee and other subject Committees, and for the establishment of an information and documentation section within the Folketing to inform the public of Community plans and legislation. In May 1994 the Danish parliament decided to extend its scrutiny of EU proposals to the very beginning of the legislative process rather than just before a decision was reached in Council.[65] Until the general election of September 1994, the political context in Denmark still remained favourable to parliamentary scrutiny, with the 'Government's basis for negotiation being accepted without amendment by the Common Market Committee in more than 95 per cent of cases'.[66] However, the changed party balance in the Folketing after the general election led to some internal speculation that the new Government was less sensitive to what the Committee (now called the European Union Committee) had to say.

In the UK, procedural change, in the form of the new European Standing Committees and in the form of the extended scrutiny reserve, preceded the ratification of the TEU. One example of the use of the scrutiny reserve was provided on 26 September 1994 in the Transport Council, when a reserve was placed on the draft railways directive.[67] However, too much significance should not be placed on scrutiny reserves, for as one experienced officer of the House explained:

> If a Government organises its business properly, they ought rarely to be needed. Their incidence does not show the effectiveness of the scrutiny process. One also has to take into account the cases when the Government writes to the Committee in advance to seek clearance when a vote is expected...or when a vote comes up and Ministers have to decide whether to vote in favour and convince the Committee afterwards, or impose a reserve. Nor is a reserve relevant if the Government votes against in the Council but it is outvoted under QMV (because the Resolution refers only to giving agreement).[68]

Of more significance, therefore, were the three paragraphs included in the European Communities (Amendment) Act 1993 – which incorporates the TEU into British law – which sought closer parliamentary scrutiny of the UK government's policies towards the third stage of economic and monetary union (EMU). Indeed, the incorporation of EMU in the Maastricht Treaty was of considerable concern to most national parliaments, and raised fundamental questions of democratic control. Particular worries arose over its provisions for the automatic achievement of EMU, once certain criteria had been met, and the degree of public accountability that could be expected of an independent European Central Bank.[69] In Britain, EMU was of specific importance, given the Conservative government's hesitancy and uncertainty about the automatic third stage of EMU.[70] An 'opt-out' clause was thus negotiated by the British prime minister, in the form of a protocol appended to the TEU, requiring the explicit consent of the UK parliament to the decision to proceed to stage three. The European Communities (Amendment) Act 1993 translated the intent of the protocol into British law. Significantly, during the political turbulence of its passage through parliament, this Act was amended to secure further parliamentary control over the movement to EMU than initially intended by the UK government. The latter is now obliged under the Act 'to report to Parliament on its proposals for the coordination of economic policies, its role in the European Council of Finance Ministers

(ECOFIN) in pursuit of the objectives of Article 2 of the Treaty and the work of the EMI in preparation for EMU'. In this context the Governor of the Bank of England is expected to make an annual report to parliament, and the government is required to seek approval for its assessment of the medium-term economic and budgetary position in relation to the goals incorporated in Article 2 of the TEU. The result was that parliament, or more precisely a fraction of the governing party, proved capable of securing long-term domestic constraints upon the European policies of the Conservative government.[71] Institutionally, the UK parliament was strengthened vis-á-vis the executive insofar as 'it went much further than any other parliament in specifying the shape of parliamentary control as part of the EMU process'.[72] Other parliaments, however, were not too far behind: in both Germany and Holland parliamentary approval of the move to the third stage of EMU was incorporated into the national laws adopting the TEU.[73] In Denmark, although the Edinburgh European Council agreed to Denmark's right not to participate in the third stage of EMU, the Folketing also managed to secure the commitment that its approval would have to be sought to any future revision of that specific agreement.

DUAL LEGITIMACY

National parliaments, as a result of the SEA and the TEU, have shown their willingness to limit the scope of the policy independence previously enjoyed by most national executives in the EC legislative process. Belatedly, national parliaments have come to recognise and to take seriously the 'second dimension' (see above) of the dual democratic deficit at the heart of the EU's decision-making process. The 1996 IGC will provide a further opportunity for national parliaments to 'monitor ongoing negotiations . . . and scrutinise the resulting treaty amendments with new-found intensity'.[74] Clearly, therefore, the position of national parliaments is not static within the EU's evolving institutional structure.

Equally, however, the problem of a 'dual democratic deficit' is paralleled by the issue of 'dual legitimacy' within the European Union.[75] As one of the Directors General of the European Parliament notes:

> one can maintain that the European Union is based on a system of dual legitimacy: the first legitimacy is based on the democratic institutions of member states and the fact that national parliaments have agreed to ratification of the EC Treaty and its amendments to the partial transfer of powers to the European Union and the exercise of power by the Community institutions according to these treaties. It is obvious that all Community institutions from the European Council to the Council

of Ministers, the Commission, the Court of Justice and parliament rely on the first basis of legitimacy . . . Gradually a second source of legitimacy has been building up, mainly based upon the direct elections to the European Parliament.[76]

The extent to which this second source has already developed, and can develop further, is an issue beyond the immediate concern of this paper.[77] What is of importance here, however, is to recall that the consent of all twelve member states' parliaments was necessary before any of them became members of the European Community. In this specific sense entry was 'authorised' by national parliaments. This was so, even in those countries where referendums were held. National parliaments were still an important part of the legitimation process, either insofar as the referendum was nominally 'consultative' (as in the UK, 1975), or in the fact that parliament was necessary for the enactment and final legitimation of the referendum result (as in Denmark, 1972). Indeed, the Danish constitution prescribes a referendum 'if the accession or the delegation of competences to a supranational institution is not ratified by a five-sixths majority of the parliament and government still seeks to pass the treaty legislation'.[78] In this provision parliamentary and 'popular' legitimation are combined. However, in all other member states, except Ireland, entry into the EC was secured without direct 'popular mandates'.

Having sanctioned entry into the EC, national parliaments continued to legitimise European integration variously by 'depoliticising' the issue of Europe for long periods, or at least containing the issue within a parliamentary frame. In some states, particularly the founder members, 'depoliticisation' reflected a fundamental consensus upon the desirability of integration. Thus, as Niblock noted, 'any review of national parliamentary activity during the 1960s reveals that in every Member State of the EEC there has prevailed a large measure of consensus between the executive and parliamentary branches regarding the objectives which the national government should espouse in Community politics'.[79] In other states, particularly in the UK, divisions over membership could be contained, in the decade 1975 to 1985, within parliamentary parties and bounded by parliamentary procedures and conventions. In an era of 'euro-sclerosis' intra-party and intra-parliamentary divisions could be subsumed within a common defence of national interests within a static Community. (There was always the potential, however, for these divisions to 'exit' the parliamentary arena – by dissident parliamentary elites attempting to mobilise the 'public' – should the dynamic of integration restart.) In still other states – Spain, Portugal and Greece – there was a reciprocal process of legitimation whereby, not only did national parliaments legitimise EC outputs, but membership of the EC served to bolster the domestic 'democratisation' processes within these states.[80]

Even in the 1990s, in the debates over Maastricht, discussion tended to be refracted through 12 national political prisms. It remains true that it is the national parliaments that constitute the 'democratic base' of the European Union. European institutions still seem remote to many citizens of the EU, and 'European' issues still tend to be seen through national lens. Thus, for example, Franklin et al conclude that in the three countries holding referendums on the TEU in 1992: 'what was supposed to be an exercise in public legitimation of foreign policy turned out to be largely an exercise in public legitimation (or in Denmark the reverse) of the makers of that policy'.[81] Equally, the key concepts that became entangled in the TEU and its ratification – subsidiarity, transparency and democratic legitimacy – while designed to address problems with the EU's legislative process, nonetheless, each stemmed primarily from the concerns and domestic political agendas of national governments.[82] If anything, the post-Maastricht EU is likely to remain one of intergovernmentalism, with national governments and elites seeking to 'repatriate' some areas of policy, curb supranational synergy within the Commission, and defuse the co-decision powers granted to the European Parliament.

In this 'new world' national parliaments may yet be presented with a double opportunity: first, at the European level, to hold national executives more closely to account for their actions in the Council of Ministers; and second, at the national level, to scrutinise directly the activities of governments in those policy areas successfully 'repatriated', if any. Equally, in these circumstances, national parliaments will continue to provide legitimation for the actions of national executives, and the latter will continue to 'trade' that general authorisation off against specific policy concessions within the EU's legislative process. In either case national parliaments will continue to provide the indispensable legitimation of national executives required for the mediated legitimation of EC policies. Whether, this form of mediated legitimacy will prove sufficient in the future; whether direct legitimation of EC legislation by the European parliament will develop; and what the necessary connection between the two – in logic or in practice – will prove to be, is beyond the scope of the present paper. To date, however, national parliaments have proved indispensable in providing the overarching frame of legitimation required to develop the European Union.

FAILING THE FUTURE

Definitive statements that 'there has been a major shift of political power upwards to the institutions of the Community' and that 'that shift has not been matched by a shift in democratic accountability, either at the level of the EP or through national parliaments'[83] need to be qualified by a recognition that there are no simple, uni-directional flows of power within the European Community. Intergovernmentalism is still entwined with supranationalism. In these circumstances the power of national executives may even be *reinforced* rather than weakened at a domestic level.[84] In turn, national parliaments may enhance their own scrutiny of the EC legislative process by exacting more information and establishing firmer procedural mechanisms to hold executives to account. The post-Maastricht world is likely to be characterised by national parliaments paying far closer attention to the actions of their respective governments in 'Brussels'. However, 'success' or 'failure' in this enterprise will have little to do with the structural design of the EU, and everything to do with the universal and historic problems confronting legislatures in relation to executives. In this specific sense they can be expected to continue to 'fail' in their contributions to policy 'making'.

The dual democratic deficit is destined to be a prominent part of the discussions preceding the 1996 IGC. There are those who believe that part of the solution to this 'deficit' rests in enhanced interparliamentary cooperation, and who discern a mutual compatibility between the roles of national parliaments and the European parliament.[85] Others are slightly more sceptical of both the probability and practical consequences of such cooperation.[86] Indeed, Shackleton observes that, in practice, the EP and national parliaments are not necessarily 'on the same side'[87] on the question of accountability at the European level. The ultimate paradox may yet prove to be, therefore, that national parliaments will 'fail' the cause of democratic accountability in the EU in the 1990s by doing precisely what they are supposed to do: holding national executives to account for their actions. The domestic 'success' of national parliaments – of increased informational flows and enhanced scrutiny of national executives – might yet contribute to a 'failure' of political will by national governments to promote the 'democratisation' of the Union's legislative process.

NOTES

Thanks are due, for their comments, to David Earnshaw, Jack Hayward, Robert Rogers, Mike Shackleton, Carsten Daugbjerg and the participants at the Conference on the 'Crisis of Representation in Europe', Oxford, Oct. 1994.

1. K. Neunreither, 'The Democratic Deficit of the European Union: Towards Closer Cooperation between the European Parliament and the National Parliaments', *Government*

and Opposition 29/3 (Summer, 1994), p.303.

2. P. Norton, 'National Parliaments and the European Union', Workshop of Parliamentary Scholars annd Parliamentarians, Berlin (19–20 Aug. 1994), p.14.
3. J. Habermas, 'Citizenship and National Identity', quoted in B. Laffan, 'Comment on Wallace', in S. Bulmer and A. Scott (eds.), *Economic and Political Integration in Europe* (Oxford: Blackwell, 1994), p.100.
4. Norton (note 2), p.3.
5. P. Norton, 'Legislatures in Perspective', *West European Politics* 13/3 (July 1990), p.146.
6. K.D. Bracher, 'Problems of Parliamentary Democracy in Europe', in S.R. Graubard (ed.), *A New Europe?* (Boston: Beacon Press, 1967).
7. P. Norton, 'Parliaments: A Framework for Analysis', *West European Politics* 13/3 (July 1990), p.3.
8. K. Featherstone, 'Jean Monnet and the "Democratic Deficit" in the European Union', *Journal of Common Market Studies* 32/2 (June 1994), p.158.
9. A. Milward, *The European Rescue of the Nation-State* (London: Routledge, 1992), p.336.
10. S. Gillingham, *Coal, Steel and the Rebirth of Europe, 1945–1955* (Cambridge: CUP, 1991), p.239.
11. Featherstone (note 8).
12. V. Herman, 'The European Parliament and the National Parliaments: Some Conclusions', in V. Herman and R. Van Schendelen, *The European Parliament and the National Parliaments* (Farnborough: Saxon House, 1979), p.267.
13. V. Wright, *The Government and Politics of France*, (3rd ed.) (London: Unwin Hyman, 1989), pp.133–42.
14. M. Kolinsky, 'Parliamentary Scrutiny of European Legislation', *Government and Opposition* 10/1 (Winter 1975), p.48.
15. M. Niblock, *The EEC: National Parliaments in Community Decision-Making* (London: Chatham House: PEP, 1971), p.10.
16. J. Fitzmaurice, 'The Danish System of Parliamentary Control over European Community Policy', in Herman and Van Schendelen, *European Parliament and the National Parliaments* (note 12), p.204.
17. D. Millar, 'Treatment of European Community Matters by Committees of the National Parliaments', in Herman and R. Van Schendelen (note 12), pp.190–1.
18. G. Smith, *Democracy in Western Germany* (London: Heinemann Educ. Books, 1979), p.139.
19. W.E. Paterson and D. Southern, *Governing Germany* (Oxford: Basil Blackwell, 1991), p.139.
20. EP Doc EN/DV/253/253692, *The European Parliament and the Parliaments of the Member States: Parliamentary Scrutiny and Arrangements for Cooperation*, Div. for Relations with Parliaments of the Member States, Directorate-Gen. for Committees and Delegations (Luxembourg: European Parliament, 1994), p.8.
21. Millar, (note 17), p.192.
22. Niblock, (note 15), pp.56–7.
23. Herman, (note 12), p.268.
24. Fitzmaurice (note 16), p.206.
25. Ibid., p.201.
26. N. Nugent, *The Government and Politics of the European Union* (London: Macmillan, 1994), p.419.
27. Fitzmaurice, (note 16), pp.215–6.
28. Second Report from the Select Committee on European Community Secondary Legislation, Session 1972–3, HC 463 (London: HMSO, 1973).
29. D. Judge, 'Parliament', in K. Boyle and S. Weir (eds.), *The Democratic Audit of the United Kingdom* (London: Routledge, 1995).
30. *The Scrutiny of European Legislation*, Select Committee on Procedure, Session 1988–89, HC 622-II (London: HMSO, 1989), p.104.
31. D. Judge, *The Parliamentary State* (London: Sage, 1993); T. Wright, *Citizens and Subjects: An Essay on British Politics* (London: Routledge, 1994).
32. Kolinsky (note 154), p.62.
33. H.N. Miller, 1977, 'The Influence of British Parliamentary Committees on European

Legislation, *Legislative Studies Quarterly* 2/1, (1977), p.46.
34. Biffen, HC 622-II, 1989, p.6.
35. E.g., Second Special Report from the Select Committee on European Legislation, Session 1985–6, HC 400 (London: HMSO, 1986), pp.v–vi.
36. *Single European Act and Parliamentary Scrutiny*, Select Committee on the European Communities, Session 1985–6, HL 149 (London: HMSO, 1986), p.7.
37. On the problem of obtaining information see St J.N. Bates, 'The Scrutiny of European Secondary Legislation at Westminster, *European Law Review* 1/1, (1976), pp.30–4; Miller (note 33), 1977, pp.50–1; Second Special Report from the Select Committee on European Legislation, Session 1985–6, HC 400 (London: HMSO, 1986), p.vii; St J.N. Bates, 'European Community Legislation before the House of Commons, *Statute Law Review* 12/2 (1991), pp.117–18; on the problem of timing see R. Wilson, 'Westminster and Brussels: The Relationship of Parliament to the EEC', *Public Administration* 63/2 (1985), p.238; *The Single European Act and Parliamentary Scrutiny*, First Special Report from the Select Committee on European Legislation, Session 1985–86, HC 264 (London: HMSO, 1986), p.11; HC 400, op cit, 1986, pp.xv–xvi.
38. CJ (1979–80), p.819.
39. HC 622-I, 1989, p.xvi.
40. HL 149, 1986, p.7.
41. HC 622-I, 1989, p.ix.
42. M. Westlake, 'The European Parliament, the National Parliaments and the 1996 Intergovernmental Conference', *Political Quarterly* 20/1 (1994), p.7.
43. Norton (note 2), pp.7–8.
44. D. Hine, 'Italy and Europe: The Italian Presidency and the Domestic Management of the European Community', in R. Leonardi and F. Anderlini, *Italian Politics: A Review,* Vol. 6, (1992), p.64.
45. HC 622-II, 1989, pp.106–7.
46. CJ (1989–90), p.646.
47. Bates, 1991 (note 37), *Review of European Standing Committees*, Select Committee on Procedure, Session 1991–92, HC 31 (London: HMSO).
48. S. Bulmer, 'The European Dimension', in G. Smith, W.E. Paterson, and P.H. Merkl (eds.), *Developments in West German Politics* (London: Macmillan, 1989), p.225.
49. D. Judge, 'Incomplete Sovereignty: The British House of Commons and the Internal Market in the European Communities', *Parliamentary Affairs* 41/4 (1988), pp.441–55; Judge 1993 (note 31), pp.184–92.
50. D. Hine, *Governing Italy: the Politics of Bargained Pluralism* (Oxford: Clarendon Press, 1993), p.286.
51. L.G. Feldman, 'Germany and the EC: Realism and Responsibility', *Annals of the American Academy*, Issue 531, (Jan. 1994), p.30.
52. EP OJ C 96, 14 March 1990.
53. R. Corbett, 'The Intergovernmental Conference on Political Union', *Journal of Common Market Studies* 30/3 (1992), p.274.
54. EP Doc EN/DV/253/253692, p.24.
55. Treaty on European Union, Office for Official Publications of the European Communities, Luxembourg (1992), pp.225–6.
56. Westlake (note 42), pp.2–3.
57. F. Jacobs, R. Corbett, and M. Shackleton, *The European Parliament* (London: Longman, 1992), p.258; Norton (note 2), pp.5–6.
58. EP Doc EN/DV/253/253692, op cit, p.32.
59. A. Duff, 'Building a Parliamentary Europe', *Government and Opposition* 29/2 (1994), p.163.
60. Ibid.
61. EP Doc EN/DV/253/253692, p.8.
62. D. Buchan, 'Paris Seeks to Alter EU Talks Agenda, *Financial Times*, 10 Oct. 1994.
63. EP Doc EN/DV/253/253692, p.15.
64. Ibid., p.19.
65. EP Doc EN/DV/253/253692, p.12.
66. P. Nedergaard, 'EF og det Demokratiske Spørgsmål: Den Danske Case', *Politica* 25/3

(1993), p.315.
67. Directive 9405/94, Proposals for a Directive on the Licensing of Railway Undertakings, and the Allocation of Railway Infrastructure Capacity and the Charging of Infrastructure Fees, 1785 Council Meeting Transport, Brussels, 26 Sept. 1994.
68. Private correspondence, 5 Dec. 1994.
69. M. Shackleton, 'Democratic Accountability in the European Union' in F. Brauwer, V. Lintner and M. Newman (eds.), *Economic Policy Making and the European Union* (London: Federal Trust, 1994), pp.91–4.
70. S. George, 'The Legislative Dimension', in S. George (ed.), *Britain and the European Community* (Oxford: Clarendon Press, 1993), p.183.
71. See D. Baker, A. Gamble, and S. Ludlam, 'The Parliamentary Siege of Maastricht 1993: Conservative Divisions and British Ratification', *Parliamentary Affairs* 47/1 (Jan. 1994), pp.37–60; B. Laffan, 'Developments in the Member States', in N. Nugent (eds.), *The European Union 1993: Annual Review of Activities* (Oxford: Blackwell, 1994), pp.110–11.
72. Shackleton (note 69), p.96.
73. Westlake (note 42), p.7.
74. Ibid., p.12.
75. J. Lodge, 'Democratic Legitimacy and European Union', *Public Policy and Administration* 6/1 (1991), pp.21–9.
76. Neunreither (note 1), p.312.
77. Lodge (note 75), pp.25–8; B. Boyce, 'The Democratic Deficit of the European Community', *Parliamentary Affairs* 46/4 (Autumn, 1993), pp.472–3; J. Lodge, 'EC Policy Making: Institutional Dynamics', in J. Lodge (ed.), *The European Community and the Challenge of the Future*, 2nd ed. (London: Pinter, 1993), pp.21–2.
78. Article 20; W. Luthardt, 'European Integration and Referendums: Analytical Considerations and Empirical Evidence' in A. W. Cafruny and G. G. Rosenthal, *The State of the European Community. Volume 2: The Maastricht Debates and Beyond* (Lynne Rienner, Colorado: Boulder, 1993), p.55.
79. Niblock (note 15), p.50.
80. G. Pridham, *Encouraging Democracy The International Context of Regime Transition in Southern Europe* (NY: St Martin's, 1991); Luthardt (note 78), p.58.
81. M. Franklin, M. Marsh, and C. Wlezien, 'Attitudes Toward Europe and Referendum Votes', *Electoral Studies* 13/2 (1994), p.119.
82. See Judge (note 49), pp.210–12; A. Scott, J. Peterson, and D. Millar, 'Subsidiarity: "A Europe of the Regions" v. the British Constitution', *Journal of Common Market Studies* 32/1 (1994), pp.61–5; J. Lodge, 'Transparency and Democratic Legitimacy', *Journal of Common Market Studies* 31/3 (1994), p.346.
83. Norton (note 2) p.15.
84. A. Moravcsik, 'Why the European Community Strengthens the State: Domestic Politics and International Cooperation', Paper presented at the Annual Meeting of the APSA, New York, 1–4 Sept. 1994, p.52.
85. Westlake (note 42), pp.10–11.
86. Shackleton (note 69), p.100; Norton (note 2), p.15.
87. Shackleton, ibid.

FURTHER READING

Of historical interest are V. Herman and R. Van Schendelen, *The European Parliament and the National Parliaments* (Farnborough: Saxon House, 1979); and M. Niblock, *The EEC: National Parliaments in Community Decision-Making* (London: Chatham House: PEP, 1971). On recent developments see EP Doc EN/DV/253/253692, *The European Parliament and the Parliaments of the Member States: Parliamentary Scrutiny and Arrangements for Cooperation,* Division for Relations with Parliaments of the Member States, Directorate-General for Committees and Delegations (Luxembourg: European Parliament, 1994). The special issue of *The Journal of Legislative Studies* 1/4 (Winter 1995) is devoted to National Parliaments and the European Union.

Referendum Outcomes and Trust in Government: Public Support For Europe in The Wake of Maastricht

MARK N. FRANKLIN, CEES VAN DER EIJK
and MICHAEL MARSH

The referenda conducted in France and Denmark in 1992 to ratify the Maastricht Treaty are often seen as giving evidence of 'true' attitudes towards Europe. In this paper we dispute this assumption, presenting evidence that shows referenda in Parliamentary systems with disciplined party governments to be subject to what we call a 'lockstep' phenomenon in which referendum outcomes become tied to the popularity of the government in power, even if the ostensible subject of the referendum has little to do with the reasons for government popularity (or lack of popularity). In the case of the Maastricht referenda in France and Denmark, the apparent unpopularity of the European project in fact appears to have been nothing of the kind, but instead to have reflected the unpopularity of ruling parties in both countries. A referendum conducted at about the same time in Ireland, where the government was more popular, achieved a handsome majority, as did the referendum conducted a year later in Denmark after a more popular government had taken office. The mechanisms involved are elucidated by means of survey data.

The referenda conducted in France and Denmark in 1992 to ratify the Treaty of European Union are often seen as giving evidence of the 'true' attitudes of voters in these countries towards Europe – attitudes apparently at odds with those obtained in opinion polls over the previous two decades which indicated considerable public support for the European project (see below).[1] Desmond Dinan, for example, has stated that

> The Danish referendum ... brought home the extent of popular alienation from Brussels... . As ... the distinction between domestic

affairs and Community affairs disappears, the public wants greater openness and involvement in Community decision-making.[2]

Butler and Ranney have pointed out that it is not uncommon for referenda to produce results apparently at odds with the findings of polls taken in the months before a referendum.[3] The rationale for assuming that referenda give a true picture while opinion polls do not, when elaborated at all, appears to be based on the notion that opinion polls relate to a sort of fuzzy idea (in 1992 an 'idea of Europe'); whereas referenda have to do with concrete steps needed for the idea to take on reality. According to this view, voters who in 1992 might have been favourably disposed towards the idea of Europe might nevertheless balk at the specific steps embodied in the Maastricht Treaty.

But this is not the only possible interpretation to place on the results of the Maastricht referenda in Denmark and France. Another possibility is that voters were not in fact giving vent to feelings about Europe but rather rendering a verdict on the general performance of their governments. According to this argument, referenda conducted in the context of national party politics, with the government of the day urging ratification of a treaty they have themselves negotiated, will inevitably be contaminated by popular feelings about the government. Popular governments will get votes in favour of referenda that they propose. Unpopular governments will be slapped on the wrist.

In this contribution we sift the evidence that might help us to distinguish between these two contrasting views of the meaning to be attached to the Maastricht referenda. We start by elaborating the case for treating the Maastricht referenda as definitive, but then proceed at much greater length to set out the evidence that supports the alternative view: first that deriving from a review of other referenda in Europe and elsewhere, and then evidence derived from a more careful perusal of the Maastricht results.

MAASTRICHT AS REALITY CHECK

The view has long been held that public opinion on Europe was favourable towards European integration, but did not see the issue as salient. Arguably, the consensus consisted largely of acquiescence on the part of those who took no great interest in European affairs and who had no real opinions on the subject of European Unification. Lindberg and Scheingold had suggested in 1970 that the 'permissive consensus' that has long characterised opinion on European integration might not withstand a major increase in the scope or capacity of the community.[4] This was echoed by Shepherd in a review of UK public opinion on the EC. He warned that 'conflict arising from positive integration could culminate in a crisis over political sovereignty'.[5]

Several points can be made about European unification in general, and the Maastrict Treaty in particular, which might provide an account of why public opinion apparently turned away from the idea of greater integration.[6] First of all, from the time of the Treaty of Rome European governments have moved forward with integration by treating 'Europe' as an aspect of foreign policy, to be made by national political leaders negotiating with one another behind closed doors, with the support of disciplined Parliamentary parties that would ratify the resulting deals. Public opinion was hardly involved. It could be argued that what happened with the Maastricht Treaty was that publicity arising from the various referendum campaigns led people to realise that the European project was developing in ways they had not been aware of, and, in many cases, were not prepared to support.

A second point is that governments have paradoxically contributed to their difficulty in 'selling' the European project by perpetuating the illusion of national sovereignty down the years. Governing parties have often tried to present themselves both as bringing home the bacon from the European cornucopia at the same time as defending the national interest against incursions from Brussels. The irony, however, is that in maintaining the illusion of national sovereignty beyond the point at which the truth could be hidden from voters, politicians in European countries may have come to appear impotent to affect events in Brussels. Observing this, many voters may have drawn the natural conclusion that if Brussels is out of control, then their country had better cut itself loose from Brussels. At the same time, because national parliamentary debate was often bypassed, opposition politicians – even those who agreed about the benefits of European unity – were given an incentive to take advantage of the disaffection of voters regarding Europe.

A third point is that integration, which initially involved the 'negative' activities of removing tangible barriers to trade, has now become more 'positive', involving the construction of joint policies in ever more salient areas. The Maastricht Treaty contained specific commitments to such policies, which would lead both to a larger and more visible role for European policy making as these policies came to have an increasingly visible impact on everyday life. While people could accept and even support the vague ideal of European Union, the concrete realities will have provoked opposition. Some will have been against the idea of a single currency, some against the idea of a central bank, some against a unitary defence policy, and so on. Of course different groups will also have been in favour of different components. In such a situation, politicians seeking agreement will carry out a log-rolling exercise, and develop a package which offsets the components groups do not like with others that they do like. This is how the Single European Act and the Maastricht Treaty were constructed, but the log-rolling all occurred at an elite level between groups that could understand how to balance costs against benefits.[7] Presenting such a solution for mass consumption is a different matter altogether. At a popular level it may well be that putting the elements of a package together involves the risk of losing support for the package as a whole. In this way, permissive consensus might give way to squabbling divisiveness.

When the implications of the Maastricht proposals became evident during the public debate over the treaty, many individuals may have decided that enough was enough. Arguably then, by the time of the Maastricht Treaty, permissive consensus had reached its limits, and the support registered in opinion polls for further integration was more apparent than real. Hence the size of anti-Maastricht votes in France and Denmark. If this were indeed what happened during the run-up to the Maastricht referenda, it would be an interesting example of popular attitudes on a complex topic adapting to changes in real world circumstances, and might testify to a greater sophistication in public opinion than many have found there.[8] Some recent studies have certainly suggested that the 'minimalist' view of the quality of public opinion is overdrawn and that public opinion can change in quite rational ways as circumstances change.[9]

But is this the proper interpretation to place on the outcomes of the Maastricht referenda? Two points are glossed over in the above account. Both are obvious but easily overlooked. The first is that, for all the talk of opposition to the European idea, while the Danes voted narrowly to reject the Maastricht Treaty in 1992, referendum votes were carried in France and Ireland in the same year, and, a year later (following amendments to the Treaty), in Denmark, too. The second even more obvious point is that these votes were not the first to be held in Europe. Referenda, and elections of all kinds, have been going on for a long time, and have been the object of extensive academic study. The finding that emerged from the first such studies, and which has been echoed by most of the others to varying degrees,[10] is that votes should not be taken at face value. Voters for a party do not necessarily support (or even know) what that party stands for, and the choice between Yes or No in a referendum may be made on the basis of many factors other than the substantive issue on the ballot paper.

MAASTRICHT AS IRRELEVANCE

As long ago as 1971, Ronald Inglehart suggested that while the sorts of questions asked about integration tapped deep-seated political values and orientations, any particular question, as put in a referendum, could, and quite probably would, be influenced also by short-term considerations.[11] Arguably, the voting in these referenda might be better understood as a response to the immediate circumstances of the situation, rather than as a manifestation of deep-seated views on European Union. Drawing on the experience of earlier referenda, the alternative view of the Maastricht experience that we want to put forward follows Inglehart in stressing the party political context of the vote.

It is clear from several studies that although referenda might be thought to allow for the unadulterated expression of the popular will, in practice they are prone, like elections, to the influence of political intermediaries.[12] A significant intermediary is party, and most studies have testified to the importance of party allegiance as a factor in people's choice in a referendum. The point emerges from the studies in various compendia about referenda.[13] Pierce and Valen expressed the point firmly in their comparative study of referenda in Britain and Norway on EC membership in the 1970s.[14]

Our findings about the centrality of partisanship, when taken in conjunction with the regularity with which that same factor shows up in other referendum studies, indicates that partisan attachments are almost certainly the primary factor in referendum voting. Partisan identification plays the same primary role in referenda that it does in general elections.

One of the striking features of the 1992 referenda on Maastricht, of course, was the fact that in all countries most parties called for a Yes vote. Nevertheless, the votes were close in France and Denmark. However, in many cases parties were in reality divided; and as Pierce *et al.* also point out: 'when parties divide, so do their followers'.[15] Parties have a strong impact only when they are united.

Our major point in the present article is that partisan attachments in parliamentary systems are inextricably entwined with government popularity, so that the outcome of a referendum has to be seen in connection with the position taken by the government. Particularly when public opinion is ill-informed and convictions are shallow, opinions can switch easily under the influence of salient factors. In a parliamentary regime nothing is more salient to voters than the standing of the government, and any government proposal is coloured by this fact. Once again, various studies testify to this, although less explicitly than is the case with respect to party allegiance.

While in the two countries which have most experience of referenda – Switzerland and the USA – referenda are generally proposed by citizens rather than governments (there are some exceptions to this in Switzerland), in most countries it is governments which are most clearly identified with the decision to hold a referendum and governments who almost invariably call for a 'yes' vote. As a consequence, the government is perhaps the real

object of many referenda, and while a popular government might expect to
see its referendum proposals approved, an unpopular government will often
see such proposals turned down.

These two factors – party allegiance and incumbent popularity – might
be expected to interact. Government parties have an added incentive to
preserve unity in a referendum campaign to the extent that the credibility of
the government is at stake. Opposition parties, on the other hand, may be
cross-pressured between their feelings on the issue itself and their
understandable desire to embarrass the government.

GOVERNMENT STANDING AND REFERENDUM OUTCOMES

In this section we will give several examples of referenda where we can
document the contaminating influence of government standing. These were
chosen purely on the basis of easy access to survey data that could be
analysed by us (or in one case had already been analysed elsewhere) to
determine the relationship between referendum outcomes, the popular
standing of governments that proposed them, and party preferences.

The first example shows the impact of party preference, and is
particularly interesting because it is the only one for which we have been
able to obtain panel data from two surveys, one conducted at the start of a
referendum campaign and one immediately following the vote. In 1979 the
British Labour government under James Callaghan redeemed a campaign
promise by proposing a referendum to the Scottish people that would
determine whether a Scottish Parliament would be established in Edinburgh
with legislative powers devolved from Westminster. As a sop to opponents
within his party, however, Callaghan had permitted a clause in the
referendum legislation to state that the result would not be considered
binding unless at least 40 per cent of registered voters were in favour. Faced
with this high hurdle, the referendum failed, but, from our perspective, the
interesting thing is, not whether it passed or failed, but the manner in which
opinion regarding the referendum evolved during the six-week campaign
that led up to it. By chance in this instance we have the advantage of a panel
study in which 200 respondents chosen to be representative of the electorate
of Glasgow were interviewed six weeks before the referendum and again
immediately after the referendum had taken place.

At the start of the campaign the Glaswegians were 3 to 2 in favour of
devolution for Scotland, with a moderate connection to party preference
($r=.386$). Six weeks later the balance had shifted radically towards a dead
heat, and the correlation with party preference had increased ($r=.464$). As
shown in Table 1, a regression analysis of referendum vote which tries to
predict it from initial position on the referendum and party preference finds

that initial position contributes less than party preference to the final position taken by voters. Evidently what had happened in the intervening six weeks is that the parties had made known their positions on devolution, and many voters had subordinated their own judgements to those of the parties they supported. The result was a referendum outcome that presaged the results of the General Election called a few weeks later. Even in Scotland, the unpopularity of the Labour government of James Callaghan overwhelmed voters' support for devolution.

TABLE 1

EFFECTS OF PARTY AND INITIAL REFERENDUM POSITION ON FINAL REFERENDUM VOTE, GLASGOW 1979 (N=113)

VARIABLE	B	BETA	SIGF
Party preferred	0.346	0.356	.000
Initial referendum position	0.309	0.278	.002
(CONSTANT)	0.072		.238
Variance explained	0.281		

Note: Referendum positions 1 = Yes, 0 = No; Party preferred 1 = Labour, Liberal, SNP; 0 = Conservative.

Adding up in different ways the terms of the equation whose components are given in Table 1 enables us to model the referendum votes of different types of voter. Those who were initially opposed and preferred the Tories were extremely unlikely to vote for the referendum (only seven per cent did so if the unreliable constant term is to be believed). Those who were initially in favour and supported Labour, Liberal or Scottish National Party eventually voted 72 per cent (almost 2:1) for devolution (the sum of all the coefficients in the B column). Those initially in favour who preferred the Conservatives were 35 per cent less likely to vote for devolution than those who preferred any of the other parties. In other analyses of the same data we find that those who switched from a pro-devolution to an anti-devolution stance had reasons for their vote other than their party preference, but since these reasons changed over the six-week campaign it seems likely that the reasons they gave for voting the way they did were the consequences of their partisanship rather than the cause.

The second example that shows the impact of party and government standing is from the Canadian 1992 referendum on the future of Quebec. In that case, we have evidence that those who voted against the referendum did so overwhelmingly because they opposed the Conservative government that had proposed it.[16] What the multivariate analyses show is that, net of party identification (together with opinions about various provisions of the referendum, region and other demographic variables, and measures of national community and regime support) levels of support for the federal Conservative government (as measured by the average thermometer scores for the party and prime minister) had sizeable and significant effects on referendum voting. Those supporting the government were more likely to vote 'yes'. Government support, in turn, was strongly affected by voters' perceptions of national and personal economic conditions. Several counterfactual scenarios indicated that, if the referendum had been held in a more favourable economic climate (with consequentially more support for the government proposing it), it would likely have passed in every region but Quebec.[17]

The third example is of the British 1975 referendum over the renegotiated terms of entry to the EC, and again shows the combined impact of party and government. The importance of this example is not that the government got a majority for staying in the EEC at a time when it stood high in the polls, but the fact that it managed to pull so many of those who had previously been anti-EEC into the 'yes' camp. This feature of the referendum outcome was noted by commentators at the time, who saw it as being due to a 'leadership effect'. Humphrey Taylor of Gallup Polls pointed out that 'the major public figures advocating EEC membership are relatively popular while those advocating leaving the EEC are relatively unpopular'.[18] The line-up of voters is, however, quite surprising, since it was the Tories who had originally negotiated British entry to the EC, and the Labour Party that had been most sceptical of entry. Opinion polls taken at the time of the October 1974 General Election show Labour supporters to have been most sceptical of the EC, with only 43 per cent believing Britain should stay in, and Tory supporters most united in support (76 per cent thought Britain should stay); yet opinion polls at the time of the referendum eight months later show that Labour supporters had been won round, with 58 per cent voting to stay in.[19] Sarlvik *et al*'s analysis of the survey evidence from the time concluded that voters had changed their views on the EEC in accordance with changes in the positions of their preferred parties, and that this shift was particularly decisive 'among voters whose party was in power'.[20] This is not particularly surprising, with the government of the day being a popular Labour government that claimed to have negotiated improved terms for Britain; but it is another instance that supports our general argument.[21]

The last example comes from the Irish divorce referendum of 1986. This was a very bitterly fought referendum, called in April and conducted in June. Fine Gael and Labour were in government, and the government was very unpopular. Only 25 per cent were satisfied with it in June. Fianna Fáil (unofficially) campaigned for a 'no', and the Progressive Democrats (PDs, who had yet to fight an election) were lukewarm (though ideologically they should have been in favour). Fine Gael was also increasingly divided. Only Labour mounted a solid campaign for a 'yes'. Comparing April and June it is clear that the swings against the referendum were strongest among the opposition parties; but, tellingly, the swings were virtually the same both for PD supporters (whose party mounted a lacklustre campaign) and supporters of Fianna Fáil (whose party was much more determined in its campaigning). So we must ask whether these swings were as much due to the efforts of the campaigners as to the unpopularity of the government, at a time when government popularity became linked to the divorce issue. Four months later, opinion among supporters of these two parties had bounced back more than half way to where it had been at the start of the referendum campaign, as though the uncoupling of the issue from party politics enabled people's true opinions to surface once again.[22]

TABLE 2
PERCENTAGE SUPPORT FOR THE 1986 IRISH DIVORCE REFERENDUM BY PARTY AND MONTH
OF SURVEY

	Feb.	Apr.	June	Oct.
Opposition parties				
Fianna Fáil	43	49	30	40
PD	62	68	50	60
Government parties				
Fine Gael	51	66	47	58
Lab	53	54	55	58

Source: Polls by Market Research Bureau of Ireland (MRBI), repr. in *Irish Political Studies*, Vol.2 (1987).

These examples illustrate the way parties have a critical impact on referendum behaviour. If the evolution of opinion that we observe in Scotland over the course of the referendum campaign also occurred in other cases and accounts for the findings we have reported, this would suggest that when governing parties propose a referendum in countries in which party government is the norm, a sort of 'lockstep' phenomenon comes into play in which voters tend (even on important matters) to see the referendum in terms of the standing of the party or parties that propose it, not the other way round.

The referendum lockstep seems to us to be a special case of a much more general phenomenon. As proposed by Reif and Schmitt and later by Reif writing alone,[23] the outcomes of elections depend greatly on the context in which they are held. What Reif calls 'first order' elections to the national parliament in European countries take precedence, and the standing of the parties in this primary arena are likely to colour and even determine results in other less salient arenas, such as European elections and local elections. What we are suggesting is that referenda proposed by governments in parliamentary regimes should be viewed as special cases of second order national elections in which the results should not necessarily be taken at face value because allowance must be made for the standing of governments in the first order arena. If this is the case with referenda in Canada, Britain and Ireland, then why not in France and Denmark?

THE MAASTRICHT REFERENDA AS PARTY VOTES

Unfortunately, in the case of the referenda conducted in 1992 as part of the ratification process for the Treaty of European Union, we have not been able to obtain panel data of the Glasgow type. In France and Ireland it does not exist; in Denmark the owners have not been willing to share it with us. However, published materials from Danish surveys raise real questions about whether Danes were voting about Europe rather than about domestic politics. Siune and Svensson report that those who were better informed about Europe were no more likely to bring their votes on the treaty into conformity with their attitudes than those who were less well informed.[24] This suggests that attitudes to Europe reflected domestic partisan preferences in Denmark rather than the other way around.[25]

TABLE 3
REFERENDUM SUPPORT BY GOVERNMENT SUPPORT IN DENMARK, FRANCE AND IRELAND

		Approved of Government	Disapproved of Government
DENMARK 1992*	YES %	84	32
	NO %	16	68
[N 468–889]			
FRANCE 1992**	YES %	79	35
	NO%	21	65
[N 9,301–801]			
IRELAND 1992***	YES%	82	43
	NO%	18	57
[N 391–346]			
DENMARK 1993*	YES %	57	65
	NO %	43	35
[N 381–917]			

Sources: MRBI June 15th; SOFRES Exit poll; Danish post-referendum study.
          * Supporter of governing party; ** Approved of Mitterrand; *** Approved government performance.

Moreover, the fact that we have published results from three countries on four occasions when the referendum fared very differently permits us to conduct something of a critical test of the proposition that referendum results follow government support. Table 3 demonstrates quite clearly that the referenda in Denmark, France and Ireland in 1992 turned out to a great extent to reflect the popularity of the government (or perhaps of the leader of that government). The table shows voting intention or reported vote in the referenda according to whether or not respondents thought their government was doing a good job. There is a striking similarity in the association between the two variables in the different countries. Even in Denmark, the overwhelming majority of those who approved of the government's performance in 1992 voted 'yes'.

For the 1992 referenda the percentages are the same to within five per cent in the other two countries. Among those unhappy with the performance of the government, a majority voted 'no', again with remarkable similarities between the percentages in each country. What was very different in the three countries was the degree of approval of the government in the first place. In Ireland, a new cabinet under a new prime minister was still enjoying a honeymoon of sorts with over half of all voters willing to make approving rather than disapproving noises about it to pollsters. Not so in France where, despite shuffling his pack of prime ministers, Mitterrand had become very unpopular. At the time of the French referendum, two out of three voters with an opinion disapproved of his performance. The Danish government too, with a relatively small parliamentary base, was out of public favour. When governments said 'trust us, and vote "yes"' it is not surprising that the referenda ran into difficulties in France and Denmark.[26]

At first glance the evidence from the 1993 Danish referendum shown in Table 3 seems to disprove our contention. In 1993 the Yes vote was actually higher among supporters of the opposition parties than among supporters of the government party. We have to remember, however, that the Maastricht Treaty had been negotiated by leaders of two parties which, by 1993, had become part of the opposition, giving those leaders especial (and unusual among opposition leaders) credibility in calling for a 'yes'. What is interesting is the changes in the positions of the supporters of the various parties between the two referenda. These are shown in Table 4 below.

Some of these figures must be treated with caution because they are based on quite small survey numbers – less than 100 each for the Radicals, Christian People's Party and Progress Party. Nevertheless, the largest increase in the 'yes' vote comes among the well-represented Social Democrats. In 1992 the party was out of government and, despite advocating a 'yes', mobilised only one in three of its supporters behind that recommendation. In 1993, now in government, it mobilised almost three out of every five. No other party showed anything like this sort of ability to shift its supporters from one camp to the other, not even the Socialist People's Party which had actually changed its recommendation from 'no' to 'yes'. It is true that the Danes had obtained concessions in the application of the treaty to Denmark, but one post referendum poll reported that of those Danes who voted in May 1993, only 17 per cent knew about the Edinburgh 'concessions' and only two per cent could name the four opt-out clauses.[27] Moreover, the Progress Party (which campaigned consistently for a 'no') actually proved to be more successful in 1993, despite the concessions, than in 1992.

TABLE 4
A COMPARISON OF VOTING IN THE 1992 AND 1993 DANISH REFERENDA BY PARTY

	% Yes	% Yes
Govt parties 1992		
Liberals	89	89
Conservatives	79	86
Govt party 1993		
Social Democrats	33	57
Opposition 1992/1993		
Radicals	64	69
Christian People's Party	55	48
Socialist People's Party	11	21
Progress Party	33	16

Sources: 1992 figures from Lars Bille, 'Denmark' in *European Journal of Political Research* 24/4 (1993), pp.411–18. 1993 figures supplied by Torben Worre.

A more persuasive explanation can be based on the movement into government of the party of a significant proportion of 1992 'no' voters, the Social Democrats. The new government was then apparently able to translate its support into votes for the treaty. At the same time, supporters of the right-wing Progress Party may have been even less sympathetic to the new Socialist government than they had been to the previous Liberal/Conservative coalition, explaining the halving of support for the treaty among this party's voters.

Though we lack panel data to support our contention that voters will have been pulled into line behind their parties, circumstantial evidence is supplied by the way in which opinions changed in all three countries during the run-up to the 1992 referenda, as shown in Table 5. There we see that the rate of EC support (top row for each country) remained remarkably constant over the period surrounding the Maastricht referenda. Opinions about the

PUBLIC SUPPORT AFTER MAASTRICHT 113

referendum itself, however, (when these were first solicited in the Spring of 1992), diverged from these long-term support scores in much the same way in each country, with smaller majorities in favour of Maastricht than were willing to give their support to the concept of European unity. In all three countries, however, the balance of support for the Treaty of Union then worsened considerably, though with a majority in favour still remaining at the time of the referenda themselves. When it came to the actual votes, in Denmark opinion swung against the treaty, in France it remained essentially unchanged, while in Ireland it swung back even farther in favour of the treaty. The implication is that in Denmark and in Ireland government (un)popularity had an effect on the vote even beyond the effect it had already had on opinion about the treaty.

TABLE 5
DEVELOPMENT OF OPINION REGARDING EUROPE AND THE MAASTRICHT TREATY,
AUTUMN 1991 TO SUMMER 1992

Summer '92 Con DK/NA	Autumn '91			Spring '92			Pro
	Pro	Con	DK/NA	Pro	Con	DK/NA	
DENMARK							
EC Support*	52%	15%	32%	50%	18%	33%	56%
12% 32%							
Maastricht**				41	27	32	42
39 19							
Referendum							49
51 --							
FRANCE							
EC Support*	59	4	37	55	8	37	55
9 37							
Maastricht**				48	13	39	43
42 15							
Referendum							51
49 --							
IRELAND							
EC Support*	66	2	32	67	2	31	62
4 34							
Maastricht**				61	6	32	56
28 16							
Referendum							69
31 --							

* Typology derived from 'EC membership a good thing' and 'for/against efforts to unify Western Europe' in EB36, EB37 and EB38 (N=1,000, approx., in each survey for each country).
** For or against ratifying Maastricht treaty EB37 and eve of referendum polls. 31 May Gallup poll in Denmark (n=1,801); 21 Aug., 27 Aug–1 Sept. IFOP/l'Express in France (n=1962); 15 June MRBI/Irish Times poll in Ireland (n=1,000).

CONCLUSIONS

Referenda are primarily devices for legitimating or refusing legitimation for policy or constitutional changes. Seen as such, there is no problem about the Maastricht referenda of 1992. In two countries the Treaty of European Union was legitimated by the process (although not by a very wide margin in France) while in another country legitimation was withheld, only to be granted one year later. If the referenda are seen purely as means of settling political questions, these implications of the Maastricht referenda are inescapable. In this context it does not matter whether people were voting on the ostensible subject at issue or were simply displaying the extent to which they trusted the government which was asking for their support. It is when commentators try to read more into the outcome of a referendum than the simple fact of legitimation or otherwise that problems arise. Trying to infer opinions about Europe from referendum votes implies that the referenda turned on opinions about Europe which it is by no means clear that they did. The fact that people's behaviour may be at odds with their attitudes is a truism that goes back to the dawn of empirical social science.[28]

The implication of referendum votes for the standing of the European project is hard to interpret. We would not want to suggest that votes on the Treaty of European Union in France and Denmark in 1992 were meaningless, but neither were they what they seemed. Table 5 makes it clear that there was never an actual majority against the treaty in either of these countries, much less a swing against the idea of a united Europe, whatever the referendum results. On the other hand, those results certainly do tell us something about the shallowness of opinions that shift so rapidly in response to party cues.

Indeed, it may even be quite dangerous to subject complex matters to a referendum because the very fact that media and politicians are paying attention to the result gives voters an opportunity to 'vote with the boot', indicating by their vote in an area to which politicians seem attached but about which they themselves are much less concerned, what their assessment is of those politicians.[29] This is illustrated by the fact that Mitterrand was unable to prop up his unpopular government on the coat-tails of a popular issue – the thinly disguised agenda when he called for an unnecessary (from a constitutional perspective) referendum. On the contrary, the legitimacy of the Treaty of Union was put into question purely as a result of government unpopularity. In Denmark the consequence was even worse, since the government was led to renegotiate a treaty that would probably have been perfectly acceptable to the Danish people had it been proposed by a different government.

These findings raise the concern that, by giving too much credence to referenda about the future of Europe, politicians and commentators could, in the wrong circumstances, wreck the whole European project – particularly if an unpopular government employs the device to free itself from the consequences of intra-party dissent, as John Major threatens to do in Britain.

More generally, our findings call into question the entire rationale of referenda conducted in parliamentary democracies. If referendum results are so regularly coloured by the standing of the government that proposes them, then their use to ratify government policies will, in many cases, be little more than a gimmick that simply restates the approval of the government whose policies they are. As Gordon Smith has pointed out, a government will normally only initiate a referendum when it expects the outcome to be beneficial to it.[30] However, in cases where a government is unpopular, but has no real choice about holding a referendum, it can tie that government's hands. In preventing the enactment of major policy and constitutional changes by governments that lack electoral support, this brake on government freedom of action may be good for democracy. Moreover, as long as referenda serve to confer a special legitimacy on government actions they may prove useful (provided that governments that call them make sure they are in good standing at the time). However, regarding the result as anything more than a reflection of government support can be dangerous.

Certainly there is little indication in our findings that referendum outcomes should be regarded as necessarily bringing the independent judgement of the electorate to bear on issues of constitutional and political importance. That they do so on some occasions seems undeniable. That they do so at all times seems manifestly impossible. That they did so in regard to the Maastricht referenda seems highly unlikely.

NOTES

An earlier version of this paper was presented at a conference on 'The 1994 Elections and the Crisis of Representation in Europe' held at Nuffield College, Oxford, 7–8 Oct. 1994. The authors are grateful to participants at the conference, and especially to Vernon Bogdanor, for helpful comments and suggestions.

1. David Butler and Austin Ranney (eds.), *Referendums Around the World* (London: Macmillan, 1994); Desmond Dinan, *Ever Closer Union? An Introduction to the European Community* (London: Macmillan, 1994).
2. *Ever Closer Union*, pp.290–1.
3. David Butler and Austen Ranney (eds.), *Referendums: A Comparative Study of Practice and Theory* (Washington, DC: Amer. Enterprise Inst. for Public Policy Res., 1980), p.21.
4 . L. Lindberg and S. Scheingold, *Europe's Would-be Polity* (Englewood Cliffs, NJ: Prentice-

Hall, 1970), p.277.
5. R. J. Shepherd, *Public Opinion and European Integration* (Farnborough: Saxon House, 1975), p.198.
6. The argument in this section is developed at more length in Mark N. Franklin, Michael Marsh and Lauren McLaren, 'Uncorking the Bottle: Popular Opposition to European Unification in the Wake of Maastricht', *Journal of Common Market Studies* 32/4 (1994), pp.455–72.
7. W. Sandholtz and J. Zysman, '1992: Recasting the European Bargain', *World Politics*, 42/1 (1989), pp.95–128; F. Laursen and S. Vanhoonacke (eds.), *The Intergovernmental Conference on Political Union: Institutional Reforms, New Policies, and International Identity of the European Community* (Dordrecht: Nijhoff, 1992).
8. The classic is Philip Converse, 'The Nature of Belief Systems in Mass Publics', in David Apter (ed.), *Ideology and Discontent* (Glencoe: The Free Press, 1964).
9. P. Sniderman, R. Brody, P. Tetlock *et al.*, *Reasoning and Choice: Exploration in Political Psychology* (Cambridge: CUP, 1991). Cf. M. Peffley, and J. Hurwitz, 'International Events and Foreign Policy Beliefs: Public Response to Changing US-Soviet Relations,' *American Journal of Political Science* 36 (1992), pp.431–61.
10. Paul F. Lazarsfeld, Bernard Berelson and Hazel Gaudet, *The People's Choice; How the Voter Makes Up His Mind in a Presidential Campaign* (NY: Duell, Sloan and Pearce, 1944); Bernard R. Berelson, Paul F. Lazarsfeld and William N. McPhee, *Voting; a Study of Opinion Formation in a Presidential Campaign* (Chicago: Univ. of Chicago Press, 1954). Cf. Angus Campbell, Philip Converse, Warren Miller and Donald Stokes (1960) *The American Voter* (NY: Wiley, 1960); David Butler and Donald Stokes, *Political Change in Britain*, 2nd ed. (London: Macmillan 1974).
11. Ronald Inglehart, 'Public Opinion and European Integration' in Lindberg and Scheingold, *European Integration*.
12. Speaking to French voters in 1961, De Gaulle said: 'I need to know how things stand in your hearts and minds. And therefore I appeal to you, over the heads of the intermediaries. . . . The question is one between each man and woman amongst you, and myself'. Vincent Wright,'France' in Butler and Ranney *Referendums* (note 3), pp.139–68.
13. See, e.g., Butler and Ranney, *Referendums*; Austin Ranney (ed.), *The Referendum Device* (Washington DC: Amer. Enterprise Inst., 1981); Butler and Ranney, *Referendums Around the World*; the special issue of the *European Journal of Political Research*, 1976; and papers presented at a workshop on referenda at the Joint Sessions Workshops of the European Consortium for Political Research, 1994.
14. Roy Pierce and Henry Valen, 'Referendum voting behavior' *American Journal of Political Science* 27/1 (1983), p.61.
15. Pierce and Valen, 'Referendum voting behavior', p.61.
16. Harold Clarke and Alan Kornberg 'The Politics and Economics of Constitutional Choice: Voting in Canada's 1992 National Referendum' *Journal of Politics* 56 (1994), pp.940–62.
17. Clarke and Kornberg, 'Voting in Canada's Referendum', pp.957–58.
18. David Butler and Uwe Kitzinger, *The 1975 Referendum* (London: Macmillan, 1976), p.280.
19. British Election Study, Oct.1974; British EEC Referendum Study, 1975.
20. Bo Sarlvik *et al.*, 'Britain's Membership of the EEC', *European Journal of Political Research* 4/1 (1976), p.112.
21. In some ways this is similar to what happened in the Spanish case documented by C. Boix and J. Alt in 'Partisan Voting in the Spanish 1986 NATO Referendum', *Electoral Studies* 10 (1991), pp.18–32. What is interesting in that case is that the Socialist Party, in power, reversed its traditional antipathy to NATO and succeeded in taking its supporters with it just as Labour did in Britain in 1975. It is hard to imagine the same thing occurring with a party in opposition.
22. The swings seen in the government camp among Fine Gael supporters are harder to explain, but our theory says nothing about what is to be expected of supporters of a government party that itself is lukewarm about its own referendum.
23. Karlheinz Reif and Hermann Schmitt, 'Nine Second Order National Elections: A Conceptual Framework For The Analysis Of European Election Results', *European Journal of Political*

Research 8/1 (1980) pp.3–44; Karlheinz Reif , 'National Electoral Cycles and European Elections', *Electoral Studies* 3/3 (1984), pp.244–55; Karlheinz Reif, 'Ten Second-Order Elections', in Karlheinz Reif (ed.), *Ten European Elections* (Aldershot: Gower, 1985), pp.1–36.

24. Karen Siune and Palle Svensson, 'The Danes and the Maastricht Treaty: The Danish EC Referendum of June 1992', *Electoral Studies* 12/2 (1993), pp.99–111.
25. Cf. Mark Franklin, Michael Marsh and Christopher Wlezien, 'Attitudes to Europe and Referendum Votes: A Response to Siune and Svensson', *Electoral Studies* 13 (1994), pp.117–21.
26. In the Swiss referendum on the European Economic Space in 1993, among those having trust in government the yes vote was 70 per cent, while among those mistrusting government it was 27 per cent. The best predictors for the vote were apparently party and trust in government. See Hanspeter Kriesi, Claude Longchamp, Florence Passy, Pascal Sciarini, 'Analyse der Eidgenoössischen Abstimmung vom 6. Dezember 1992', Genève: *VOX-analysen* No.47 (1993).
27. *Irish Times*, 15 May 1993.
28. See, e.g., R. Merton, 'Fact and Factitiousness in Ethic Opinionnaires', *American Sociological Review* Vol.5, (1940), pp.13–27.
29. Cees Van der Eijk, Mark Franklin and Erik Oppenhuis, 'Consulting the Oracle: Consequences of Treating European Elections as 'Markers' of Domestic Political Developments'. Paper presented at the ECPR Joint Sessions of Workshops, Madrid, April 1994; Cees van der Eijk, Mark Franklin *et al.*, *Choosing Europe: The European Electorate and National Politics in the Face of Union* (Ann Arbor, MI: Univ. of Michigan Press, forthcoming 1995).
30. Gordon Smith, 'The functional properties of the referendum' *European Journal of Political Research* 4/1 (1976), pp.1–23.

FURTHER READING

David Butler and Austin Ranney (eds.), *Referendums Around the World* (London: Macmillan, 1994).

Cees van der Eijk, Mark Franklin et al., *Choosing Europe: The European Electorate and National Politics in the Face of Union* (Ann Arbor, MI: University of Michigan Press, forthcoming 1995).

Mark N. Franklin, Michael Marsh and Lauren McLaren, 'Uncorking the Bottle: Popular Opposition to European Unification in the Wake of Maastricht', *Journal of Common Market Studies* 32/4 (1994).

L. Lindberg and S. Scheingold, *Europe's Would-be Polity* (New Jersey: Prentice-Hall, 1970).

Roy Pierce and Henry Valen, 'Referendum voting behavior', *American Journal of Political Science* 27/1 (1983).

Constitutional Reform in the European Community: Are there Alternatives to the Majoritarian Avenue?

RENAUD DEHOUSSE

Traditionally, the weakness of the European Parliament and of European political parties is presented as a central cause of the European Community's legitimacy crisis. This article suggests an alternative reading of the situation. Not only is the legitimacy crisis much more complex than is generally believed, but the strengthening of the Parliament, and the development of party politics that would ensue might ultimately threaten the stability of the Community. The experience of parliamentary federations suggests that the majoritarian features of the parliamentary system may be a source of tension. No matter how necessary the democratisation of the EC's institutional setting may be, reforms must not be detrimental to the quality of centre-periphery relations.

With the conclusion of the Single European Act, it can be said that the European Community (EC)[1] has entered into an era of what Canadian political scientist Peter Russell has called 'mega-constitutional politics': a phase of major constitutional transformations, in which discussions on institutional issues absorb a substantial part of the political system's energy.[2] The EC has gone through two major institutional overhauls – the Single Act and the Maastricht Treaty – in less than ten years, and a third one is already scheduled for 1996. Issues such as the proper use of the subsidiarity principle, or the role of national parliaments in the decison-making process, recurrently re-emerge at the forefront of the political debate. Major political leaders and parties have felt it necessary to make their views on the future of the community known.[3]

So far, whenever the question of the EC's legitimacy has been addressed in academic literature, attention has unavoidably focused on the European Parliament. Its weakness has been seen as the root of the problem, and its strengthening as the main cure for the evils of the Community. In my view, this line of analysis is not satisfactory. On the one hand, the legitimacy crisis of the EC is much more complex – and hence more difficult to solve – than is traditionally thought. On the other, the discussion has often suffered from a lack of critical distance. A comparative analysis would suggest that in fact, if not in law, the European Parliament is often better off than its national counterparts. Moreover, insufficient attention has been paid to the specific nature of the EC, which is not – nor is it called upon to become – a state.[4] Given this *sui generis* character, it could be argued that the strengthening of the European Parliament and of European parties, far from solving the current legitimacy crisis, as is often alleged, might in some respects aggravate it. Indeed, the experience of parliamentary federations suggests that the majoritarian features of parliamentary systems are often detrimental to centre-periphery relations. The negative features of majoritarianism are likely to be accentuated in a divided power system such as the EC. These two arguments are developed in the following pages. The article is structured as follows. Section 1 attempts to show that the EC has moved away from the somewhat formalist model of state legitimacy which dominated its first 30 years of existence. Section 2 discusses the 'classical' analysis of the democratic deficit, which has influenced many proposals of institutional reform. Section 3 reviews the changes in the Parliament's position introduced by the Maastricht Treaty and tries to anticipate what their implications might be on relations between the Community and its Member States. Section 4 sketches an alternative, non-majoritarian avenue for the reform of European institutions.

THE LEGITIMACY CRISIS OF THE COMMUNITY

It has long been held – and is still maintained by some – that the legitimacy of the Community is primarily state-based. The EC has been created by states and its actions are legitimated by their will. Do not the member states, in the shape of the Council of Ministers, occupy a central place in the Community's institutional structure? Do they not designate the members of the European executive? Is their agreement not necessary for most Community decisions? Such a view finds its intellectual roots in De Gaulle's well-known scheme of a Europe of the States.[5]

On this premise, it has been argued that in so far as State organs are legitimated at regular intervals by universal suffrage, it can be concluded that the Community itself indirectly benefits from this ballot-box legitimation. Some, like former French Foreign Minister Roland Dumas, have even argued that the best way to enhance the legitimacy of the European Community would be to strengthen intergovernmental organs like the European Council, since the latter is the 'emanation of the democratic legitimacy of the States', as it is made up of the Heads of State and Government.[6]

However, the relaunch of European integration with the internal market programme has revealed the legalistic character of this line of argument. In fact, for such an indirect legitimation scheme to function, several conditions must be met. First of all, the decisions taken by the Community must be the genuine fruit of the collective will of the member states. Otherwise, it is difficult to see with what authority the Union can claim to base its decisions on some kind of state legitimacy. It is further necessary that the electorate be given the opportunity, when national elections take place, to express an opinion on European issues. Short of this, the legitimacy of Community action would be primarily of a merely formal nature.

Simply listing these conditions is sufficient to perceive how far removed they are from reality. Not only are the member states often tempted to place the responsibility for unpopular decisions on European institutions; they have also witnessed the restriction of their powers of control with the move to majority voting in a certain number of areas laid down by the Single Act. When some of the member states are outvoted, it becomes difficult to claim that the final decision rests on their collective will. The unreality of this inter-state framework becomes greater still when elections are examined. European issues are already singularly blurred in the European elections, which, as explained elsewhere in this issue, are above all an opportunity for wide-scale opinion polls on the popularity of the national governments. Although Europe has become a matter of contention in many national elections, the debate rarely goes beyond the level of shallow statements on the historical meaning or the future of the integration process. Issues relating to the substance of European policies – similar to the kind of issues people vote on in domestic elections – are conspicuous by their absence.

Despite these insufficiencies, the odds are that the question of the legitimation of the European political system would have remained purely academic had the Community concerned itself solely with quotas and tariff restrictions. Indeed, to the dismay of European elites, the question never gained the status of a major political issue in the first three decades of existence of the EC. But the creation of the internal market would not have been possible without 'flanking' policies, such as first the common agricultural policy or competition policy, and subsequently environmental or consumer protection, which affect large numbers of citizens. The Community was also directed to turning its attention to social issues and monetary policy. At the same time, the remarkable marketing success of the 1992 programme and the charisma of Commission President Jacques Delors suddenly enhanced the visibility of institutions that were long ignored by public opinion. An increasing number of European citizens have thus gradually become aware that the decisions of the Community can influence their daily lives, and that it is therefore necessary to take account of its decisions. Some social groupings – farmers and fishermen, for instance – have long been aware of it. As the visibility of European politics increased, the question of the Union's legitimacy became more acute. The Irish have learnt that the EC could impinge upon their anti-abortion laws, the British that it could force them to reconsider their regulations on Sunday trading, the Germans that monetary union could possibly entail doing away with the Deutschmark.

The Maastricht Treaty served as a revelatory mechanism, in furnishing an opportunity for national public opinions to make themselves heard. This exercise clearly indicated that the indirect legitimation of the initial stages no longer appeared to them to be appropriate, given the development of Community activities. In countries where referenda were held, such as Denmark and France, large segments of public opinion voiced their discontent with the current operation of the European political system. In other countries, the ratification debates revealed a similar uneasiness. To the question 'is there a legitimacy deficit in the EC?', European opinion seems to have answered in the affirmative. We shall now try to see how this deficit can be explained – and possibly remedied.

THE DEMOCRACY DEFICIT(S): THEORY AND PRACTICE

Of all the aspects of the legitimacy crisis of the Community, the democratic deficit is undoubtedly the most widely known. The European Parliament made of it one of its chief weapons of battle. As this concept is discussed at length in another contribution to this issue,[7] I shall limit myself here to the few remarks that are necessary for the purpose of this article.

The integration process involves, among other things, a transfer of legislative activity to the European level. Classical democracy deficit analysis starts from the premise that the role of the national parliaments in this process is reduced. Most of them intervene at best in the implementation phase and Community Directives often do not leave them a significant margin of appreciation. At the same time, the European Parliament is far from possessing powers equivalent to those of the national parliaments, even if its situation has been appreciably improved in recent years. At present, the Parliament remains oddly excluded in certain areas (e.g., commercial policy); it possesses only an indirect right of initiative, and even in the framework of the co-decision procedure, its powers are only imperfectly aligned with those of the Council.

Thus, it is argued that, on the one hand, the national assemblies are often presented with a *fait accompli*, while on the other the European Parliament, although it has seen its political standing grow in the last decade, does not yet enjoy the full range of powers accorded to the parliamentary assemblies in the European political systems. In other words, integration is realised by a dispossession of the national legislative powers, which is only partly compensated for by the emergence of the European Parliament. As Community legislation is mainly a product of the cooperation between the national and European administrations, one can say that in overall terms, European integration has led to a weakening of the legislative branch, and to a strengthening of the executive.[8] As a result, Community legislation is often devoid of the legitimacy which attaches to the decisions taken by representatives of the people.

'Classical' democracy deficit theory, which has occupied a central place in debates on the institutional evolution of the EC, suffers, however, from several flaws. It generally overestimates the importance of legislatures in national systems. More importantly in the present context, it is inspired by a somewhat reductive view of democracy, which is implicitly equated with the mere voting of laws by parliamentary assemblies.

In fact, even a vague familiarity with democratic theory suffices to underline the multifaceted nature of the concept of democracy. It entails among other things, the possibility for citizens to choose their rulers and to sanction them if their action is deemed inadequate. It also implies the possibility for voters to control what political leaders do – which, to say the least, is problematic in the European Community. Moreover, the legitimacy crisis is aggravated by structural features: European decision-making processes tend to privilege the technical dimension of problems, rather than their political aspects – a phenomenon which I have labelled political deficit, for lack of a better expression. These three elements are analysed successively.

The Accountability Deficit

In the European tradition, parliamentary assemblies play a central role in the designation of the government. In electing their representatives, citizens participate indirectly in the choice of those who will govern them. As a result, when they are unhappy with the policies pursued by their government, voters can express their discontent at the ballot box.

For a long time, this fundamental aspect of all democratic systems has been absent at European level. Until the Maastricht Treaty, the designation of the Commission was the exclusive privilege of the national governments. True, the Commission could be censured by Parliament, but as the latter was deprived of any real power in the appointment process, this possibility was never used. The Council itself escapes all censure, even if its individual members can be subjected to parliamentary control in their home country. The only institution on which the electorate could have a direct influence was the European Parliament, which is widely reputed to be the most feeble of the political institutions of the European Community. Thus, the electorate have had no possibility of directly expressing their views on the actions of the principal European institutions – the Commission and the Council. The latter could therefore operate without incurring any electoral sanction. This relative impunity has contributed to the creation of a yawning chasm between citizens and the European political system.

However, this situation could well change in the wake of the Maastricht Treaty. As will be analysed in greater detail below, the Commission, henceforth, has to obtain the investiture of the Parliament before it can begin to function. The debate on the appointment of Mr Delors' successor, former Luxembourg Prime Minister Jacques Santer, has clearly shown that the Parliament fully intends to utilise this new power. Furthermore, its powers of control have been strengthened, which should allow it to make its influence felt in a more constant way on day-to-day decisions. One cannot rule out the possibility that the European electorate may eventually become aware of this power shift. This might in turn prompt European parties to nominate their candidates for top Brussels jobs. The question of the executive's composition could thus become one of the issues in European level elections, as it currently is at national level. In voting for one party, citizens will be able to express their preference for Mr X or Ms Y as head of the Commission and, subsequently, their opinion on that person's performance in office. Thus, the strengthening of Parliament's control over the Commission might well sow the seeds of a profound change, which may reduce the gap which currently exists between public opinion and European institutions.

The Transparency Deficit

If Maastricht has undoubtedly contributed to reducing to some extent the democratic deficit, its effects on the transparency of the Community system are clearly less positive. The reflection of laborious compromise, the Treaty has multiplied decisional procedures, carefully measuring out the prerogatives of each institution.

European citizens have already had difficulty in understanding certain peculiarities of the European system, such as the primarily legislative role enjoyed by a body like the Council of Ministers, composed of members of national governments. They are now faced with the growing complexity of this system: no less than 21 different procedures can currently be used by European institutions.[9] In the field of environmental policy, for instance, four different procedures have been laid down in the Maastricht Treaty, not including the possibility of resort to Art.100A, the cornerstone of the internal market. Combined with the secrecy which still shrouds the work of the Council of Ministers,[10] this institutional alchemy makes it somewhat unlikely that European citizens will be able to understand who is responsible for decisions taken at European level.

The system is even more opaque at the level of enforcement. Who can say with exactitude the number of committees of experts in existence at European level? Who can vaunt their knowledge of the rules which govern their composition and mode of functioning? At best, a handful of people. Yet, these committees are called upon to take a range of important decisions in areas which concern the daily life of each and every citizen.

This lack of transparency is at the root of the feeling of distance to which most citizens attest when speaking of the European institutions. In such a context, the idea of political accountability for decisions taken at European level is barely more than illusory. How can the voter be in a position to scrutinise actions at European level, if he is unaware of the roles allotted to the various institutions and how these institutions actually use their powers? Irrespective of the rights citizens may be granted, short of a major effort to simplify and publicise these institutions, they will not be in a position to exercise them in an effective manner.

The Political Deficit

Legitimacy in the European Union also suffers from the way political debates unfold. National politics are characterised by several familiar landmarks. Debate is structured around some large themes: the relationship between freedom and solidarity, the tension between free market and redistributive policies, the left-right cleavage, etc. The citizenship are relatively familiar with the most important rules of the political game (the majority-opposition dialectic) and they often know the principal actors (political parties, trade unions). Finally, a certain number of fora exist within which political debate can build up: the Parliament, naturally, but also, and to an increasing extent, the media.

The contrast with the situation at European level is striking. Technical aspects often dominate the various issues at stake. Rightly or wrongly, public opinion does not often associate Europe with great societal debates. Political actors are weakly organised at European level; European parties cluster together many heterogeneous groups, united only by a relative discipline. As we have seen, the rules of the game are so complex that they are unknown to the general public. Even supposing that genuine political debate could develop, it is difficult to see where it could take place. A real political arena is itself lacking: the Parliament has not yet emerged as a forum; as for the media, they often treat European issues as being of marginal interest.

To what factors can we attribute this striking contrast between European and national levels? Several factors need to be taken into account. First, the European Community only disposes of limited competences. Its primary vocation was an economic one: to integrate the national economies into a single market. It has only gradually extended its activities into neighbouring areas, by reason of the links which unite economic integration with sectoral policies such as social policy, environment policy or consumer protection. This encourages a prismatic approach to problems: many questions are approached in the light of their relationship with the internal market. Without doubt, this fragmentation of competences encourages neither a more global approach nor the starting of work on large societal projects. Consequently, discussion tends to cluster around the technical aspects of Community regulation.

This tendency is reinforced by the diversity of the Community. Dominant values – in terms of social policy or of environmental protection, for example – vary from one country to another, and this is inevitably reflected in their regulatory policies. Economic interests, like political cultures, often differ. All of these elements contribute to the relative complexity of Community decision-making. The same can be said of institutional rules: unanimity is still sometimes required, and more than two thirds of the votes in the Council of Ministers are necessary to obtain a qualified majority. The decision-making process is thus, to a large extent, consensual. The reconciliation of national positions can often only be achieved through laborious compromises, which are difficult for the layman to decipher. The incessant haggling which characterises Community decision-making appears to leave little room for the public interest to be taken into account. In most cases, only the societal groups who are directly affected by the Community measures are sufficiently motivated to follow the long path taken by a draft piece of legislation.

Both the manner in which issues are approached and the bargaining to which these issues are subjected contribute to reinforce the technocratic image of the Community. The European political system is primarily seen as a closed shop, with membership confined to experts espousing the defence of national or sectoral interests, and not as a political arena within which different conceptions of the public interest can be aired and discussed. A real political deficit superimposes itself on the democratic deficit.[11] Can it be otherwise, given the intrinsic diversity of the Community?

The Maastricht Treaty has tried to overcome the difficulties outlined above by consolidating the institutional position of the European Parliament. For the first time in the history of European integration, this is reflected in the establishment of true legislative co-decision making: in some areas, agreement between Parliament and Council is now required for the adoption of Community acts. At the same time, the cooperation and the assent procedures, both introduced by the Single Act, have seen their scope enlarged.[12] Though clearly indicative of an overall trend, this in itself falls short of a proper parliamentary system. However, the Maastricht Treaty also modified the conditions under which the Commission is appointed. This further change, which has so far gone largely unnoticed, possesses the potential to alter considerably the balance of power within the Community. Given its importance it deserves more detailed scrutiny.

Towards a Parliamentary System?

The idea of associating Parliament with the appointment of Commission members had been circulating for several years, well before the present criticisms levelled at the Brussels' bureaucracy had begun to emerge. Over a decade ago, it featured in the Solemn Declaration on European Union adopted in Stuttgart in June 1983, and it has always been high on the list of Parliament's demands. Admittedly, since the introduction of direct elections to the European Parliament, it has been the custom for the newly-appointed President of the Commission to be heard by Parliament's enlarged Bureau, and for the Commission to present its programme to the full house shortly after it took office. Despite the fact that debate on this programme ended in a vote, respect for the forms of parliamentarianism could scarcely conceal the reality: the political will the Commission emerged from was that of the national governments, and not of the Parliament.

The procedure introduced by the new Article 158 involves radical changes. It is only following consultation with the Parliament that national governments can nominate the person they plan to appoint as Commission President. Commission members are then nominated by member states, in consultation with the president designate. However, the whole body must be given a vote of approval before taking office. In other words, the Commission must, as in classical parliamentary systems, have the confidence of a parliamentary majority. This two-stage procedure, singling out the Commission president, while formally recognisng his influence on choosing the body's members, should contribute to establishing his authority over his peers. The model is somewhat reminiscent of the practice followed in many parliamentary systems, where nomination of the head of government precedes formation of the cabinet, for which the prime minister designated by the head of State is often compelled to negotiate with the leaders of the main parties in the majority. The difficulties which have surrounded the appointment of the Santer Commission have shown that Parliament firmly intends to influence the distribution of portfolios among Commissioners. Thus, in the future, the Commission – just like the executive of many parliamentary federations – will derive its legitimacy from a two-fold source: the Member States on the one hand, and Parliament on the other.

Parliament's influence will be increased still further by the link established from 1995 between Parliament's term and that of the Commission. A six-month gap has been arranged between European elections and the setting up of the Commission, to enable the newly elected Parliament to take part in nominating the latter. Any significant changes in Parliament's composition can thus be reflected at Commission level. This development lends new importance to the possibility of a vote of censure, provided for in Article 144. Hitherto, the possibility had remained theoretical, since nothing prevented member state governments from confirming the members of a censured Commission in their posts, as Parliament enjoyed no real influence over the choice of Commission members. Things will be different in the future. In the case of a censure vote, Parliament's new prerogatives will enable it to ensure that its grounds for censuring a Commission will be taken into account in appointing a new one.

The import of these changes is considerable. They augur a deep transformation in the nature of the relationship between Parliament and the Commission. The Commission will henceforth be fully responsible to Parliament, the influence of which will be felt over all its activities, be they administrative or legislative. This will presumably set up a knock-on effect which will reverberate through the whole set of institutional relationships. For instance, one can envisage Parliament playing a much greater role in the cooperation procedure, where to date the Commission has been a necessary intermediary between Parliament and Council. Likewise, given the relationships that are bound to grow up between Parliament and Commission, the right given to Parliament to request the Commission to 'submit any appropriate proposal on matters in which it considers that a Community act is required'[13] may be seen as coming close to a true right of initiative.

These new developments are certainly not without their limits. Both the Parliament's and the Commission's role are fairly limited in monetary policy, where the lion's share goes to the Central Bank. Similarly, censure

is ruled out in relation to the Commission's activities in the context of the
two principal intergovernmental aspects of the Treaty, that is to say, the
newly-established common foreign and security policy, and cooperation in
the field of justice and home affairs. However important these two
reservations may be, it nonetheless appears that the Treaty's signatories, in
their desire to establish the Community's democratic legitimacy, have
radically modified the balance of power between Commission and
Parliament.

Centre-Periphery Relationships

So far, most of my remarks have focused on the horizontal axis of the
institutional system, namely the relations between Community institutions.
It would, however, be unlikely for the reshuffling of the cards among the
Community institutions to take place without affecting relations between
the Community and its member states. Although the model we can see
emerging from the institutional workshop of Maastricht is still a vague
outline, it appears clear that the parliamentary system, in which the
executive is derived from a majority whose confidence it must keep, served
as the reference point throughout the discussion on institutional matters.
Should this evolution be confirmed, centre-periphery relations would be
radically altered.

   The linkage between Parliament and Commission is, in fact, likely to
transform the latter considerably. One of the main features of the
Commission as designed by the original Treaties is its mixed nature as a
multinational and multiparty body. Even under a strong presidency like that
of Jacques Delors, the Commission has remained a collegiate body devoid
of clear political colour. This feature, while largely responsible for the
technocratic profile of integration that some decry, has undoubtedly been a
trump card in its relationships with member states. Its neutrality prevents
the Commission from being perceived as too alien a body in national
capitals despite the institutional autonomy it enjoys. More generally, the
weakness of party politics at European level has helped preserve the
consensual character of Community decision-making.[14]

   It is unlikely that matters will continue in this vein, as the Commission
will henceforth need the support of a parliamentary majority. The resulting
politicisation in both membership and programme will perhaps make things
clearer to the European voter, thereby reducing the 'political deficit'.
However, this may well be at the expense of good relations with national
governments. For instance, imagine the two political groups that currently
dominate Parliament – the Christian Democratic EPP and the Socialist
Group – coming to an agreement on a government programme. What might

the relations be between a Commission born of such an agreement and, say, a Conservative government in London or a Gaullist-dominated one in Paris? Neither would be likely to see the new Commission as in any way 'theirs', even if, as prescribed by Article 157, it contains at least one of their countrymen.

The emergence of a party logic at Commission level is also likely to have effects on its institutional role. Its function as a mediator among national interests, and in particular its mission as a defender of small states, would be made more difficult by such a drift. This is not to say that either function would necessarily disappear. The experience of parliamentary federations shows that party affiliation and representative logic are not, properly speaking, incompatible. However, in the event of a conflict, the former tends to gain the upper hand over the latter.[15]

Underlying these problems is a conflict between two kinds of logic. The logic underlying most parliamentary systems is majoritarian: a majority is to be formed in Parliament and reflected in the composition of the executive. Party lines tend to matter a great deal, as the executive can stay in office only as long as it retains the confidence of its majority. In contrast, federalism is primarily a form of 'anti-majoritarian' government.[16] The component units often owe their separate existence to the necessity of avoiding a domination of minorities by the majority; the same concern has frequently led to the setting up of mechanisms aimed at guaranteeing that even, at national level, decisions require a fairly large degree of consensus. The truth is that these two lines of logic are not easy to reconcile, as suggested by the experience of parliamentary federations like Canada or Australia.

Moreover, the majoritarian logic that characterises parliamentary systems tends to promote the development of a horizontal rationality within the central institutions: coordination among the various departments of the executive and relationships with Parliament move ahead of representing the interests of the federation's components. This clearly does not simplify relationships between the various levels of power. Some studies attribute the relative stability of American federalism to the existence of a tight network of intergovernmental relationships – the 'marble cake' described by Morton Grodzins[17] – in which decisions are taken by specialists in a given area, without too much regard for questions of formal powers or party considerations. By contrast, the 'horizontal' rationality typifying parliamentary regimes, particularly when combined with partisan antagonism, tends to give additional importance to jurisdiction concerns, thereby rendering intergovernmental cooperation more difficult.[18]

Naturally, the kind of parliamentary model that will emerge at Community level will ultimately depend on variables that still remain indeterminate, such as the cohesiveness of political parties or the type of coalition that will be formed. Yet, if the Parliament-Commission axis is as strong as the Treaty seems to want it to be, there is a real risk of seeing tensions develop between the Community and its member states.

As far as we can judge, however, the danger of a major confrontation arising in the near future seems low. The Council, in which national interests are dominant, retains a central role in all legislative procedures. Furthermore, many procedures require the vote of a majority of European Parliament members, in practice amounting to a two-thirds majority of votes cast; these two conditions are even combined in the case of a censure motion. This will probably necessitate the maintenance of a 'grand coalition' in which many diverse interests will be represented. However, the lack of a body charged with reconciling the various interests is liable to be keenly felt. Moreover, the institutional changes which are currently being considered might further accentuate the evolution towards a more clearly majoritarian profile.

THE NON-MAJORITARIAN AVENUE

The 1996 debate is expected to revolve around the question of how the Community's structure must be reformed in order to make possible an enlargement to Eastern European countries without compromising the efficiency of the institutional machinery. In this context, many of the reforms considered in Community circles – a reduction of the Commission, which would no longer include representatives of all member states, the generalisation and simplification of majority voting, a reform of the Presidency which would de facto limit the role of smaller countries[19] – all point in the same direction, that of a strengthening of the majoritarian features of the European political system. Unsurprisingly, smaller countries have a certain concern in this respect.[20]

If these proposals are fleshed out, the Community will find itself in a paradoxical situation. On the one hand, by increasing the European Parliament's powers and by reinforcing the majoritarian element, it will have contributed to establishing the Community's democratic legitimacy, while furnishing a remedy for the political deficit mentioned earlier. On the other hand, one of the pillars of the Community edifice, the representation of member states, will have been seriously weakened. Do the two necessarily go hand in hand, or can we conceive of a system that would allow these two fundamental aspects of the legitimacy of any divided-power system to be reconciled? To my mind, this is one of the major questions that will have to be addressed in the forthcoming institutional debate.

The Community's Twofold Legitimacy

As noted in the first part of this article, for about three decades European integration has primarily derived its legitimacy from the consent of the States which had given birth to it. Post-Maastricht developments have revealed the dissatisfaction of public opinion, and its yearning to be listened to whenever Europe has to address major issues, an increasingly frequent occurrence. The state legitimacy that dominated the early years must therefore be supplemented by another kind of legitimacy, better suited to the current development of the Community's political system.

In today's European politics, public decisions are perceived as legitimate when they are adopted by institutions whose democratic character is recognised. A substantial part of the opposition met by the EC in recent years can be explained by the fact that it was perceived of as insufficiently democratic. Only by bringing it closer to standards of European democracy can one hope to restore its credibility in the eyes of the general public. The days when European integration could be regarded essentially as a 'foreign affair', whose plot was followed by a handful of people, are over.

However, the parallel with the legitimacy of domestic institutions is far from complete. Europe's vocation is not to become a centralised superstate. The EC is the product of a pooling of sovereignties in a limited sphere; it is superimposed on the states, but cannot altogether replace them. The Community is an extremely diverse gathering – it will be even more so after enlargement – in which national traditions remain very strong. In a world where economic and technical transformations have strong centripetal effects, this diversity can be a precious asset, as long as it does not result in boundless competition among states. One of the Community's historical missions is precisely to allow the peaceful coexistence of different national models. Moreover, states still enjoy a primary allegiance in national politics. The Community will only be able to consolidate its own authority if it shows sufficient respect for states, and for national specificities.

It therefore follows that the democratisation of the European political system can only be achieved through the setting up of a pluralist, non-majoritarian model, in which states *as such* will be called upon to play an important role. State legitimacy and democratic legitimacy are the two pillars on which the Community's institutional system must rest. Only a balance between the two will ensure the stability of the whole construction. Changes operated on one front should therefore avoid becoming a source of stress on the other.

Institutional Corollaries

It is not possible here to develop in full the essential features of a non-majoritarian model. Let me, however, point to a few elements which ought to be considered in the construction of such a model.

As already indicated, the strengthening of the European Parliament and the reduction in the number of commissioners, especially if combined, are likely to undermine the representative character of the Community executive, and therefore its relations with national capitals. For the time being, an agreement between the European Council and the Parliament is necessary to give birth to a new Commission. Yet this body will be responsible Parliament only, which may ultimately lead to an unwelcome politicisation. Such an evolution would be a matter of concern, as the Commission enjoys important institutional privileges, such as a monopoly of initiative in many areas, or a guarantee that its proposals will be modified only by unanimous decision of the Council. Such privileges made sense in a situation where the Commission enjoyed the confidence of the member states, but they could become a source of imbalance if the Commission's ties with national societies were to be loosened.

The Community's double legitimacy can only be preserved through some correcting device. The remedy here might be to restore the balance between our two pillars, by also making the Commission responsible to the European Council of Ministers. Naturally, the same conditions could be required for a censure vote as for the appointment of the Commission. Even if censure remains an exceptional event, such a reform would be likely to affect the Commission's behaviour in its day-to-day activities. It might therefore usefully counterbalance the Parliament's growing influence, while softening the effect of a reduction in the number of Commissioners. A country that had no 'representative' in the executive would thus have a way of ensuring that what is decided in Brussels is not detrimental to its interests.

In contrast, the balance still leans in favour of the member states as regards legislative procedures. In most instances, except in the new co-decision procedure established by the Maastricht Treaty, the final say still belongs to the Council of Ministers, while Parliament remains completely excluded from certain areas, ranging from commercial policy to the free movement of capital. Here, the idea of double legitimacy suggests that Parliament's role should be enhanced. The aim would be the establishment of a fully-fledged bicameral system, in which legislative power would be shared between two assemblies – one directly elected, the European Parliament, and the other, the Council of Ministers, composed of members of national governments – much like the German *Bundesrat*, which brings together members of Länder governments.

Turning to decision-making procedures, it is often asserted that a Community of 25 members or more could not survive without a generalisation of majority voting and a lowering of the threshold for majority decisions, which is currently around 70 per cent of the (weighted) votes cast in the Council of Ministers.[21] Undoubtedly, the problem is important. Decision-making, which was already cumbersome and lengthy, in the Community of 12, could be nearly paralysed if Community membership were to double without the necessary adjustments having been made. This fear has led the Institutional Committee of the European Parliament to suggest in its draft European Constitution that all decisions should require a double majority in the Council of Ministers: a majority of states, representing at least a majority of the Community's population.[22] Such a solution would imply great advantages, if only because of its transparency: European citizens would know that no decision could be taken by a minority of States, or against the will of the representatives of the majority of the population. Yet, when considering the kind of coalitions possible, one realises pretty soon that, as most new applicants for membership are small states (and some micro-states), the number of minimum-winning coalitions would be very high. In other words, there would be a serious risk of drifting towards a pattern of strictly majoritarian decisions.

I have suggested elsewhere a form of 'alarm bell' mechanism,[23] enabling a significant minority of states (say, three member states, representing a minimum share of the Community's population) to block a proposal that would in their view threaten their vital interests. Such a veto would only be overcome if the measure at hand was confirmed by an enlarged majority, in order to avoid the possibility that an indiscriminate use of this weapon could result in a complete paralysis of decision-making. Surely other techniques are conceivable which would preserve the consensual character of Community decision-making. The delegation of powers to autonomous institutions, insulated from the electoral cycle, could be envisaged.[24] My concern here is not to advocate any particular mode of constitutional engineering but rather to stress the need to prevent a majoritarian drift that would compromise the stability of the Community.

CONCLUSION

The Maastricht ratification debates have seen an unexpected intrusion of public opinion into Community affairs. The weak legitimacy basis of European institutions, which was at most a matter of academic discussion prior to this development, has suddenly become a dominant issue in European politics. To many, the strengthening of the European Parliament, which has been one of the dominant elements of the last ten years, seems to appear as a natural response to this new situation. If the people want their voice to be heard, then let their representatives play a greater role in the shaping of Community policies. In such a perspective, Parliament's institutional position, still weak in some respects, and the persistent weakness of European parties, unavoidably appears as a matter of concern.

At the same time, certain institutional adjustments are being considered in view of an Eastern enlargement of the Community, which appears unavoidable in the medium to long term. Most of these adjustments, dictated by efficiency concerns – or, to be more precise, by a legitimate desire to limit decision costs – would, in fact, be likely to reinforce the majoritarian character of decision-making.

Although I do not disagree with the analysis that inspires these two sets of proposals, I have tried to show the risks involved in a majoritarian option. The parliamentary system, which is dominant in Western Europe,[25] seems to have been chosen as a model for the institutional development of the European Community. Yet this model, because of its majoritarian aspects, is ill-adapted to the needs of a hybrid creature like the EC, characterised by great diversity and by strong national feelings.

That majoritarian logic may have adverse effects in decentralised systems is by no means a new remark. Discussing the various models that could inspire the American Constitution, James Madison warned two centuries ago that

> [w]hen a majority is included in a faction, the form of popular government... enables it to sacrifice to its ruling passion or interest, both the public good and the rights of other citizens. To ensure the public good, and private rights, against the danger of such faction, and at the same time to preserve the spirit and the form of popular government is then the great object to which our enquiries are directed . . . .'[26]

Replace the word 'faction' by the word 'party', more fashionable today, and you will have a good description of the danger involved in the majoritarian option. The development of party politics at European level might be detrimental to centre-periphery relations, which are crucial for the stability of the Community. Seen in this light, the current weakness of European parties, lamented by some, may appear as a disguised blessing. Yet it is far from clear that the situation will remain unchanged if the institutional system encourages greater cohesion, and there are reasons to believe that Parliament's new prerogatives in relation to the appointment of the Commission may indeed provide that kind of incentive. Certainly, Parliament's involvement in this process must be hailed as a positive development, given the legitimacy deficit of the EC. But the implications of this change ought to be properly assessed and, if need be, corrected. The same is true of the changes considered in view of pending enlargement.

Madison himself wisely suggested that 'factions' could not be avoided, and that the problem was rather to control their impact.[27] Thus, as regards the EC, the 'great object' that will have to be addressed in the institutional debates to come is strikingly similar to the one he described: to carve out an institutional system that will bring a remedy to the current legitimacy crisis of the Community, without at the same time exposing it to the dangers of majoritarian solutions.

NOTES

1. Although the expression European Union seems to be widely preferred in English language literature, I shall stick here to the words 'European Community' as, legally speaking, the questions addressed in this article mainly relate to the structure of the EC rather than to that of the European Union.
2. *Constitutional Odyssey – Can Canadians become a Sovereign People?*, 2nd ed. (Toronto: University of Toronto Press, 1993).
3. Compare for instance British Prime Minister John Major's views in *The Economist*, 25 Sept. 1993, p.19 with French Prime Minister Edouard Balladur's in *Le Monde*, 30 Nov. 1994, pp.1, 9 and 10.
4. For more reflexions on this methodological problem, see my 'Comparing National and EC Law: The Problem of the Level of Analysis', forthcoming in *American Journal of Comparative Law* (1995).
5. Press Conference of 15 May 1962, *Le Monde*, 16 May 1962, p.6.
6. 'Le succès de Maastricht', *Revue politique et parlementaire* (1991), p.43.
7. See the essay by Weiler *et al.* in this volume.
8. The point has been made forcefully by Andrew Moravczik, `Preference and Power in a Liberal Intergovernmental View', *Journal of Common Market Studies*, Vol.31 (1993), pp.473–524.
9. For a detailed analysis, see Jean-Claude Piris, 'After Maastricht, are the Community Institutions more Efficacious, more Democratic and More Transparent', *European Law Review*, Vol.19 (1994) pp.450–87.
10. Limited progress has been achieved in this respect after the Maastricht Treaty. The rules of procedure of the Council of Ministers now provide that votes can be made public when the Council acts as a law-making body, and that public sessions can be held when it engages in programmatic discussions. See OJ N° L304/1 of 10 Dec. 1993.
11. See the debate between Jean-Marc Ferry and Paul Thibaud in their *Discussion sur l'Europe* (Paris: Calmann-Lévy, 1993).
12. For a more detailed analysis, see Renaud Dehousse, 'The Legacy of Maastricht: Emerging Institutional Issues', *Collected Courses of the Academy of European Law*, Vol.3, Book 1, (1992) pp.181–239 at 224–8, on which this section largely draws.
13. Article 138b, second sentence.
14. Unsurprisingly, this element is regarded as essential in neo-functionalist analyses of the integration process. See, e.g., Ernst Haas's preface to the second edition of *The Uniting of Europe*, 2nd ed. (Stanford, CA: Stanford UP, 1968), p.xxv.
15. J. Lemco and P. Regenstreif, 'The Fusion of Powers and the Crisis of Canadian Federalism', *Publius*, Vol.14 (1987), pp.105–13.
16. W.S. Livingston, *Federalism and Constitutional Change* (Oxford: Clarendon Press, 1956).
17. M. Grodzins, *The American Federal System: A New View of Government in the United States*, edited by D.J. Elazar (Chicago: Rand McNally, 1966).
18. The phenomenon has been described by Donald Smiley, 'The Structural Problem of Canadian Federalism', *Canadian Public Administration*, Vol.14 (1971) pp.326–43. See also Watts, 'The Historical Development of Canadian Federalism', in R.L. Mathews (ed.), *Public*

Policies in two Federal Countries (Canberra: Australian National University Press and Centre for Research on Federal Financial Relations, 1982) pp.13–26.

19. See, e.g., Jean-François Guilhaudis, *L'Europe en transition* (Paris: Montchrestien, 1993, pp.131–3; Christian Lequesne, 'Les perspectives institutionnelles d'une Union élargie', *Pouvoirs*, N°69 (1994) pp.129–39.

20. See the memorandum presented by Benelux countries at the Lisbon European Council, *Agence Europe*, Saturday, 20 June 1992, N°5754, 12.

21. See the works by Guilhaudis and Lequesne cited above, supra note 19.

22. Draft article 20, see doc. 179.622, 10 Feb. 1994.

23. R. Dehousse, 'Community competences: are there Limits to Growth?' in R. Dehousse (ed.), *Europe after Maastricht: An Ever Closer Union?* (Munich: Law Books in Europe, 1994) pp.103–25 at pp.121–3.

24. Giandomenico Majone, *Independence v. Accountability? Non-Majoritarian Institutions and Democratic Governments*, EUI Working Papers SPS N° 94/3.

25. Philippe Lauvaux, 'Eléments d'un modèle constitutionnel européen' in Bruno De Witte and Caroline Forder (eds.) *The Common Law of Europe and the Future of Legal Education*, (Deventer: Kluwer, 1992) pp.119–31.

26. *The Federalist Papers*, N°10, ed. by Garry Wills (NY: Bantam, 1982) p.45.

27. 'The *causes* of faction cannot be removed; . . . . relief is only to be sought in the means of controlling its *effects*.' (Ibid)

FURTHER READING

There is no shortage of literature on the institutions of the European Community. Given the rapid pace of change in the last ten years, readers should focus on recent works such as:

Jean-Louis Quermonne, *Le système politique de l'Union européenne*, 2nd ed. (Paris: Montchrestien, Collection 'Clefs', 1994). [A valuable description of European institutions and decision-making processes.]

David O'Keeffe and P.M. Twomey (eds.), *Legal Issues of the Maastricht Treaty* (London: Wiley Chancery Law, 1994).

Renaud Dehousse (ed.), *Europe after Maastricht: An Ever Closer Union?* (Munich: Law Books in Europe, 1994). [Two collections of essays on the innovations introduced by the Maastricht Treaty.]

Joseph Weiler, 'The Transformation of Europe', *Yale Law Journal*, Vol.100 (1991), pp.2403–83. [One of the few systematic analyses of the institutional evolution of the European Community since its inception.]

Andrew Moravcsik, 'Preference and Power in a Liberal Intergovernmental View', *Journal of Common Market Studies*, Vol.31 (1993) pp.473–524.

Renaud Dehousse and Giandomenico Majone, 'The Institutional Dynamics of European Integration: From the Single Act to the Maastricht Treaty' in Stephen Martin (ed.), *The Construction of Europe – Essays in Honour of Emile Noël* (Dordrecht: Kluwer, 1994) pp.91–112. [Two contrasting views on the dynamics of institutional change.]

There is also an abundant literature, mostly of Canadian origin, on the structural tension between federalism and the majoritarian logic of parliamentary systems.

Donald V. Smiley, *Canada in Question: Federalism in the Eighties*, 3rd ed. (Toronto: McGraw-Hill, 1980) provides one of the most complete surveys of the problem.

Democracy or Technocracy?
European Integration and the Problem of
Popular Consent

WILLIAM WALLACE and JULIE SMITH

We trace the historical evolution of the European Communities from the Schuman Plan to the Luxembourg crisis, exploring the underlying assumptions about popular involvement in those formative years. We then consider the theoretical literature developed during that 'classic' period of European integration, and the approach which theorists took to questions of loyalty, identity and democratic accountability. We examine the efforts undertaken in the course of the 1970s and 1980s to reduce the gap between the rhetoric of 'ever closer union among the European peoples' and the reality of popular passivity and growing suspicion. Finally, we raise the question of whether it is possible to reconcile democratic principles or institutions with the approach to international integration represented by the supranational compromise, or whether the historical link between political community, representative democracy and the state does not require Europe's political leaders to make a clear choice between intergovernmental bargaining and federation.

Ideas of popular participation and democratic accountability above the level of the nation state have been themes of idealist approaches to international relations since the time of Kant and the French Revolution. The troops of revolutionary France appealed to the 'peoples' of Europe, against the states, to raise the banner of popular legitimacy against monarchy and aristocracy. Napoleon's armies contained Italians and Germans, Poles and Dutch, fighting for a new order against old regimes. The restoration of monarchic legitimacy across the continent after 1815 could not smother the ideas of popular sovereignty which the French revolution had promoted. But the idea of 'the people' which the romantic movement fostered, in Germany and Italy in particular, reflected the mixed reactions of their liberal intellectuals and middle classes to the French character of this European ideal. For them the 'people' were embodied in 'the nation' and their nations sought to constitute their own states, in imitation of the French and British models of nation states. Industrial modernisation, the growth of the educated commercial and official classes, and of mass movements in large towns, combined to force state after state, from west to central Europe, to shift the criterion for legitimacy to the declared link between state and nation, with the state 'representing' the nation.

Authoritarian states claimed to represent 'their' nation symbolically; democratic states built systems of popular representation. The defeat of authoritarian regimes by a (largely) democratic grand alliance in 1945 might therefore be seen as marking the triumph of the principles of popular legitimacy and representative democracy, within political communities organised as nation states. But the triumph was also a tragedy. One after another, the nation states of continental Europe had collapsed into defeat and occupation, leaving their postwar governments struggling to rebuild the structures of statehood. The revolutionary international ideas of Communism, fostered in anti-Fascist resistance movements and supported by the prestige and military power of the Soviet Union, presented a challenge to liberal democracy within every west European state: the second and third largest Communist parties in Europe in 1945 were in France and Italy.

The liberal superpower which emerged after 1945 as the protector and economic saviour of devastated Western Europe was, furthermore, still partly in the grip of idealist approaches to international relations. The remedy for Europe's repeated wars, based on national rivalries and mistaken balance of power policies, was for Washington's postwar planners to create a European federation. John Foster Dulles himself was the secretary of the US Committee for the United States of Europe; the conventional wisdom of Washington was that Western Europe must unite.[1]

Perhaps the Americans should have pressed their dependent European allies further in the confused and insecure immediate postwar years. Altiero Spinelli, whose passionate campaign for a federal Europe carried him through from wartime resistance to the Draft Treaty on European Union approved by the first elected European Parliament, believed that they missed their opportunity.

> The Marshall Plan represented the one chance for Europe to unite. If the American government had seen through the false European spirit of the British and had granted the aids contingent on the creation of political federal institutions on the Continent, we would now have European union. . . . It is to be regretted that the Americans, on this score, were duped by Great Britain . . . .[2]

Idealists within Western Europe and within the United States could not overcome the countervailing pressures of the emerging Cold War confrontation, and of the efforts of national governments to rebuild their *own* legitimacy against both external and internal challenges. American policy-makers were nevertheless determined to prevent a slide back towards national protection and European power politics, while the European political leaders whom they supported were conscious of the necessity to strike a different balance between sovereignty and international cooperation. 'What we shall have to combine', Paul-Henri Spaak had declared to a wartime meeting of Belgians in exile in London, 'is a certain reawakening of nationalism and an indispensable internationalism.'[3]

What emerged – between 1950 and 1958 – was therefore a delicate bargain between incompatible objectives, which American theorists later labelled 'the supranational compromise'.[4] Substantial authority was transferred, but in strictly limited fields, with the most difficult and divisive issues of national sovereignty and of the future role of national institutions deferred until a later stage. The grand rhetoric of the ECSC treaty preamble was balanced by the modest measures of the text.

> The tactics of M. Monnet and his supporters were clearly designed to reduce to a minimum the likelihood of an inflammatory public debate on the scheme. Thus the bargaining and brokerage that went into the supranational compromise served not only to satisfy but also to quiet major political forces.[5]

American pressure to accept Germany rearmament then forced those promoting the supranational compromise to attempt to strike a similar bargain in a field far more evidently central to sovereignty and statehood, over which it proved impossible to defer issues of authority and legitimacy. But after the collapse of the European Defence Community (EDC) proposals in 1954, bargaining and brokerage returned to the 'low politics' of commerce and energy.

The nature of the supranational compromise, with its inbuilt ambiguities, has bedevilled the evolution of West European integration from the EDC to the Maastricht Treaty. Proponents of an integrated Europe retreated from federation into functional organisation, from political accountability to technocratic administration. Democracy and legitimacy were left in the hands of nation states – at least for the time being. For the idealists who staffed the ECSC High Authority and later the EEC Commission hoped that their successful fostering of faster economic growth and greater welfare throughout the Communities would lead to a progressive shift in perceived interests, and then in loyalties, to this new level of administrative government.

This was a rational vision, propounded in the passionate and irrational circumstances of Cold War confrontation, which saw ideology giving way to enlightened self-interest under the benevolent influence of economic growth. An institutional framework, set up by far-sighted men, could thus set the context for the growth of a wider political community, resting on economic foundations and secured (from the outside) by the United States. Against Spinelli's demand for a leap to federation, in the conviction that popular support would be found, Monnet's strategy was of elite-led gradualism, with the expectation that popular consent would slowly follow that lead.[6] In such an indirect approach to political integration, the locking in of interested organisations – from business, labour, and from national administrative agencies – was a much higher priority than the direct involvement of as yet uninformed publics.

European integration was deliberately negotiated, therefore, as a 'journey to an unknown destination'.[7] Governments and Commissioners, federalists and defenders of national autonomy, could agree on the shared objective of 'European union', each reading their own preferred definitions into that wonderfully imprecise term.[8] Such imprecision, however, made for unavoidable difficulties both in attracting popular support and in building mechanisms to generate popular consent. De Gaulle found it easy to attack the underlying illegitimacy of the EEC Commission's aspirations. From the Luxembourg crisis of 1965–66 onwards, therefore, proponents of closer integration have struggled to build a firmer foundation for popular consent, recognising that the hopes of the federalists that popular opinion would support union against national governments whenever the choice was presented had proved illusory, that the remote and bureaucratic procedures of the Communities had somehow to be made more understandable – 'transparent', in Community jargon – with institutional and policy reforms to construct a real 'political community'. From the Hague Summit of 1969, through the Tindemans Report, the Dooge Committee and many others, to the intergovernmental conferences of 1991 and the Maastricht Treaty, successive groups of ministers, 'wise men' and parliamentarians have grappled with the problem of generating public consent – so far with limited success.

THE HISTORICAL FOUNDATIONS

The contradictions between intergovernmental bargaining, functional administration, and democracy are embedded in the treaties establishing the European Communities. The preambles speak grandly of 'taking the first steps towards a broader and wider community among peoples long divided by bloody conflicts', even of the determination 'to establish the foundations of an ever closer union among the European peoples'.[9] But those who formally make such declarations are the heads of state of the signatory governments, with prime ministers and foreign ministers signing on their behalf. And in the texts which follow, priority is given to administrative bodies, committees and functional consultation with corporate interests, with the 'European Assembly' playing a minor role.

The integration of Western Europe developed in a series of compromises between incompatible pressures and preferences. There were enthusiastic groups of federalists in most West European countries, nurtured on the wartime politics of exile or resistance and on experience of the collapse of most West European nation states.[10] Allied with these were American policy-makers, determined not to allow Europe to sink back into the destructive power politics out of which American troops had rescued them (as it seemed from Washington's perspective) twice in 25 years, and convinced that a United States of Europe would provide both peace and prosperity and build a bulwark against communism.[11]

The Hague Congress of 1948 marked the high tide of enthusiasm for explicit European federalism. Paul van Zeeland, later Dutch foreign minister, declared that

> This Congress has a mission: it is to answer the prayers of the masses of Europe; to give more precise and more concrete expression to their aspirations; to show the governments that even if they are daring in conception, public opinion will follow them, if indeed it is not already ahead of them.[12]

The conviction that the people were really yearning for European unity, and were held back by the short-sightedness of their governments, sustained the dwindling group of federalists through the next 40 years. Altiero Spinelli, above all, clung to

> the view that national administrations are bound to defend the *status quo*, but that there is a large reservoir of popular support for closer unity among the public at large and that the key to successful forward movement is to find ways of bringing this pressure to bear.[13]

Defeated in the Hague and in subsequent Council of Europe Consultative Assembly debates in Strasbourg, Spinelli moved on to organise a 'Campaign for a European Constituent Assembly', which collected 600,000 signatures in Italy. But elsewhere the passive popular consensus in favour of closer European integration remained passive, even in the countries which were to constitute the ECSC six. The Schuman Plan was a response to the contradictory requirements of reviving the West German economy and of containing a reviving German state: an elite enterprise, not a response to any popular pressure.

The Treaty of Paris (1951), which established the ECSC, set the framework within which European institutions have since developed. It struck a balance between an expert and authoritative High Authority and a Council of national ministers, monitored by a Court of Justice to ensure 'that in the interpretation and application of this Treaty, and of rules laid down for the implementation thereof, the law is observed' (Article 31 ECSC Treaty). The High Authority was to act with the advice of a Consultative Committee, which was constituted of 'equal numbers of producers, of workers and of consumers and dealers', to be nominated from lists drawn up by 'representative organizations' (Articles 18–19): functional representation assisting technical experts, on the models of the French Planning system and of practice in the occupation zones of Western Germany. An Assembly of delegates from national parliaments was given 'supervisory powers' (Article 20). The Treaty envisaged an annual meeting to 'discuss in open session the general report submitted to it by the High Authority'. (Articles 22, 24) This marginal body emerged from the Benelux countries' resistance to French and German support for a stronger representative element, for fear that this would lead to Franco-German dominance. Numbers of delegates were therefore heavily weighted in favour of the smaller member states; though a commitment to move towards direct elections (Article 21, which appeared in identical form in the later EEC Treaty) was included on the insistence of the French negotiators.[14]

'Once the Council of Europe included a parliamentary assembly, it was inconceivable that the first European Community should not have one'.[15] But so did the Western European Union, on its reconstitution in 1954, its authority and visibility even lower than that of the Council of Europe Assembly throughout the following 40 years. Those nominated by national parliaments were partly self-selected: the most enthusiastic for European cooperation were happy to volunteer, the most sceptical saw little point in coming forward. In spite of Monnet's vigorous resistance to deliberative institutions without decision-making powers, therefore, 'the High Authority understood right away how attractive an alliance with the Common Assembly could be, in order to ensure that the two institutions, which were genuinely *communautaire*, were on the same side'.[16] This was, however, a secondary matter in the elitist strategy of integration which Jean Monnet was following. Less than half a page in his memoirs is allotted to this auxiliary representative and parliamentary dimension.[17]

Intense American pressure on its European allies to accept a framework for the rearmament of Germany, against the parallel pressures of heightened cold-war tensions within Europe, pushed representatives of these six states towards a more direct approach to European federation. The strength of political resistance to such a great leap forward is indicated by the lack of support from the Benelux governments (and now also from France) for the Italian proposal, during the negotiations on the European Defence Community in 1952–53, that the European Political Authority should be responsible to a directly-elected European Assembly. Proposals for a European Political Community were drafted in an 'Ad Hoc Assembly' constituted on the basis of the ECSC Common Assembly, remote from popular participation and reported only intermittently in national newspapers. The impetus which drove them came from dependence on Washington and fear of Moscow, and the death of Stalin led to their collapse.

> In terms of alternative strategies of integration, the EPC was the first major test of the populist or constituent method favoured by the federalists of giving a major role to a parliamentary assembly. . . . Its failure . . . appeared to vindicate Monnet-type elitist strategies, and it was these which were used in the next stages of the process.[18]

Enlightened administration on behalf of uninformed publics, in cooperation with affected interests and subject to the approval of national governments, was therefore the compromise again struck in the Treaties of Rome. It was the challenge presented by President de Gaulle to this indirect approach to European integration, with the entrenched position it offered to the smaller countries in relation to the large, which transformed the character of the debate and swung the Benelux governments over to become committed supporters of a directly elected Parliament. What became the Fouchet Plan for European Political Union, as first outlined by President de Gaulle in his press conference of 6 January 1960, was a direct attack on the pretensions of the unelected Commission. Characterising the role of the European Parliament as one of 'periodic discussions in an Assembly made up of delegates from the national parliaments', de Gaulle combined an insistence on the reality of nation states as sources of legitimacy and identity with the radical (but characteristic) proposal that plebiscitary democracy might serve instead of representative democracy to legitimise the new structure. He called for 'as soon as possible a formal European referendum in order to lend this new beginning for Europe a sense of belonging and the popular involvement so vital to it'.[19] The 'Five' responded to the revised Fouchet Plan of 1962 with their own Draft Treaty on European Union – defined as a 'Union of States and Peoples'. From then on until the French Government's concession of the principle of direct elections in 1974, the issue of popular involvement was defined in terms of a directly elected European Parliament, and all other governments combined to press this issue against the French.

THEORY AND IDEOLOGY

If the deliberate imprecision of Community objectives presents obstacles to analysis, the contested character and overlapping connotations of the terminology of 'democracy' (and the 'democracy deficit'), 'the people', 'political community', and 'political union' provide greater stumbling blocks. All those engaged in the processes of European integration accepted that the eventual legitimation of European union would have to rest on popular consent. Where they differed was over how that consent should be registered, and over what time-scale it should be sought. European federalists called for an immediate leap to representative government above the nation state, in the belief that this would release latent popular support and so transfer legitimacy and authority. American theorists looked for the emergence of a political community above the state level to provide the foundations for a political union; drawing on the model of the United States itself, and on the integration of nineteenth-century Germany.[20] Jean Monnet and those who supported the technocratic strategy believed that the problem of popular consent could be postponed: that the creation of effective administrative government in discrete policy areas would provide the economic welfare which would in turn generate public support. Ernst Haas described Monnet's technocratic self-confidence in Rousseauan terms.

> In a sense, Monnet considered the High Authority as the repository of the European General Will, with the evil governments merely the spokesmen for the selfish political wills. The Treaty, as administered by the High Authority, *is* the basic European consensus for progress, peace and federation.[21]

All of the above shared the assumption that popular consent *would* be forthcoming, once the new institutions were established and Europe's public had time to understand and appreciate the greater benefits they brought in comparison to those which states acting separately could offer. To this idealist assumption de Gaulle posed the realist answer: that the state and its link with the nation provided the only proven basis for political community and thus for popular legitimation. Even for de Gaulle, however, the legacy of the French revolution and of French dominance of European culture in the eighteenth and nineteenth centuries lingered in assumptions that the interests of France and those of Europe overlapped more closely than those of other states; his proposal for a European plebiscite is explicable only in these terms.

Theories of European integration in the 1950s and 1960s were closely intertwined with perceptions of the Community as seen from the Commission, and with the preferred assumptions and policies of American policy-makers. American in authorship, and idealist in inspiration, they were determinedly rational in their approach to political behaviour, and pluralist in their assumptions about the political process. Nationalism, and nation states, were for their authors part of the baggage of an ideological age which was coming to an end; giving way to the pursuit of prosperity, with loyalty attributed to those institutions which best provided growth and welfare. The neo-functionalists were a small group of academics who exercised a remarkable influence over intellectual approaches to European integration, who were funded by the US government and American foundations, educated in the normative tradition of idealist international relations, attracted by the Commission's sense of mission and welcomed as allies and interpreters by the Commission.[22] The relationship between theory and practice, in Haas's *Uniting of Europe*, is circular: neo-functionalism describes and rationalises what the Commission does, and observation of the Commission in operation validates the theory.

Alan Milward's realist critique ascribes the 'success' of this 'cold war theory of European integration' to

> the fact that neo-functionalism in the 1950s and 1960s became the intellectual foundation for a hegemonic foreign policy architecture. . . Theories which predicted the 'integration' of western Europe, like Rostow's "Non-Communist Manifesto" [*The Stages of Economic Growth*], were essentially models of social engineering for the containment of communism and the promotion of economic growth.[23]

But it was equally important to the intellectual pre-eminence of this theoretical approach in the 1960s that it fitted the Commission's self-image of itself, and justified the Monnet strategy to those who hoped that Western Europe *would* succeed in moving beyond the nation state – which included almost all those who studied the European Community in its early years.

The neo-functionalists were self-confessedly 'economic determinists', seeing in the emergence of an affluent European society a shift away from a politics of 'alienation leading to political mobilization and conflict' to 'a benign social climate in which more and more people will be preoccupied with the satisfaction of material needs'.[24] In this comfortably unmobilised political climate a 'permissive consensus' was all that was needed to signify public consent for elite policies.[25] The incremental strategy of encouraging group interaction among elites, to 'upgrade the common interest' by educating them (as earlier in the French planning process) to understand the advantages of working together, complemented by increasing transborder interactions among the wider public, should in time lead to the emergence of a wider political community: 'a condition in which specific groups and individuals show more loyalty to their central political institutions than to any other political authority'.[26] Thus

> Political integration is the process whereby political actors in several
> distinct national settings are persuaded to shift their loyalties,
> expectations and political activities toward a new centre, whose
> institutions possess or demand jurisdiction over the pre-existing
> national states.[27]

There were several inherent problems in this theoretical approach. First,
the affluence which led to an increase in cross-border transactions also led
to a parallel increase in interactions *within* nation states – as the research of
Karl Deutsch and his followers in the 1960s disappointingly indicated.
Second, the same transactional research uncovered the overwhelming
importance of the United States as sponsor and hegemon, which
neofunctionalist theory with its focus on the Commission and its
enlightened Europeans had underplayed. 'Put quite simply, all the indicators
suggest that Franco-German elites were in 1964 more closely linked to the
United States than to each other or to any other country.'[28] Third, and most
crucially, its reductionist approach to political motivation assumed that
loyalties followed rational perceptions of interest rather than non-rational
assumptions of identity. Against those who argued the end-of-ideology
thesis that 'adherence to a middle class life pattern will enhance the
importance of the business of the Community', Stanley Hoffmann insisted
that politics 'involve the passions that are the stuff of tragedy: prestige and
hubris, domination and independence'.[29]

Monnet and Hallstein, to varying degrees, shared the pluralist/
functionalist assumption that passionate politics was giving way to
administration, as problem-solving replaced ideological clashes.[30] 'In
pluralistic political systems,' the theorists agreed, 'the major problem
becomes one of maximizing wealth – clearly a question for the experts, the
technocrats'.[31] De Gaulle thus posed a problem, an indication that 'domestic
conditions may thrust to the fore a type of nineteenth century nationalism
which disputes the indifference to nationalism displayed by the
instrumentally minded integrationist'.[32] Haas responded to this problem in
his retrospective essay on neo-functionalism, accepting that he and his
colleagues had misrepresented the relationship between ideology and
incrementalism – though he forbore to admit that this misrepresentation also
undermined their crucial assumptions about the instrumental quality of
loyalty, identity and consent.

> ... the triggering of an incremental integration process may require an
> initial dramatic act motivated by passionate ideological commitment.
> Thus the program of the first generation of 'Europeans' was clearly

ideological, and their espousal of incremental methods merely a tactical device.[33]

The collapse of integration theory, and the passing (after the Luxembourg crisis and the departure of Walter Hallstein) of the Golden Age of Commission self-confidence, however, left a void in legitimating the process of integration, which was largely filled by national governments. The Community agenda was redefined, and the integration process 'relaunched' at a summit meeting of heads of government in the Hague in December 1969. The evolution of summits into regular European Councils, and the emergence of the rotating Presidency of the Council of Ministers to compete with the Commission President in steering Community business, seemed to return accountability and representation firmly into the hands of national governments, responsible to national parliaments and electorates.

There was, however, an underlying contradiction in the French government's agenda for relaunching integration, seeking at the same time to entrench the Community budget beyond the detailed control of the Council of Ministers, and to move towards a monetary union which would require 'the transfer of powers to a new decision-taking centre', while at the same time resisting the development of mechanisms of consent and accountability at the Community level.[34] Supporters of a stronger European Parliament soon identified a 'democratic deficit', best defined by a European Parliament committee as

> the combination of two phenomena: (i) the transfer of powers from the Member States to the EC; (ii) the exercise of these powers at Community level by institutions other than the European Parliament, even though, before the transfer, the national parliaments held power to pass laws in the areas concerned.[35]

Commission and Parliament remained allied against the Council throughout the 1970s and 1980s in pressing for direct elections and for greater powers for the European Parliament to fill the gap which they claimed had opened up, with Community legislation emerging out of bureaucratic bargaining in a profusion of intergovernmental committees, to be voted on in overloaded sessions of the Council of Ministers. Moves towards majority voting, under the pressures of rising membership and increased business, made the democracy deficit more apparent: if ministers were outvoted in Brussels on legislation that had direct effect in national law, how could they then be 'held accountable' before their own national parliament?

The Commission after the Luxembourg crisis was also aware of its failure to catch the imagination of the European public with the symbolic importance of the European Community. National governments emphasised the symbolism of bilateral reconciliation, most vividly in the repeated ceremonies and gestures which marked the Franco–German relationship. De Gaulle had taken care to deny the infant EEC the symbolic prestige which Hallstein wanted, provoking a major confrontation over the style and ceremony with which ambassadors of third countries should be received. From the Tindemans Report on, the question of how to encourage the public to identify more positively with the Community exercised working groups, Commissioners, parliamentary committees, even government ministers. The rhetoric of a 'Citizens' Europe' (or a 'People's Europe') has run through each intergovernmental conference. Educational exchanges, rewritten histories of Europe, assistance to 'European' media, have attempted to reshape popular perceptions.[36] The Council of Europe's 12-starred emblem was successfully pilfered, to become first the EC's 'official logo' and then virtually its official flag.[37] Community structural fund-spending has become more and more actively labelled in regions where it is spent, demonstrating how 'Europe helps Bradford (or Barcelona) again'. A more positive image of the processes of formal integration, it was hoped, would emerge from all these, out of which would be generated the passive, permissive consensus which European policy-makers recognised as the basis for public consent. But the sense of European identity which they hoped to encourage has been slow to evolve, despite the explosion of cross-border transactions and the turnover of generations. National identities still constitute the basis for political community, within nation states, in spite of the effective loss of control over central issues of national government and state sovereignty.[38]

CITIZENS AND EUROPE: A CITIZENS' EUROPE?

Attempts to involve citizens in the process of European integration had begun much earlier. If, when they considered it at all, the theorists of European integration took public opinion for granted, parliamentarians and Commissioners did not. Parliamentarians were quick to take the initiative and act on the provision made in all three founding Treaties for direct elections to the Common Assembly. A working group to consider various aspects of European elections was set up in October 1958, only 18 months after the Treaties of Rome were signed. The general report, known as the Dehousse Report, covering various aspects related to the introduction of direct elections to the Assembly, was adopted by the Parliament in February 1960.

The political significance of the proposed elections was not lost on the Working Group, which 'never felt itself called upon to study the problems of elections from a purely academic standpoint. As politicians, its members have always been guided by their concern for political efficacy'.[39] The Working Group argued that the Communities should no longer be treated as the preserve of specialists, saying, 'It is high time, therefore, that the peoples be drawn into this venture, and that they grasp what is at stake and the attendant risks, and make known their will'.[40] This led the Group to the conclusion that elections were necessary since,

> under various forms, we know and practise but a single method of expressing the will of the people and of associating them with the management of public affairs – free elections.

The Council of Ministers did not show such enthusiasm for direct elections, however; the presence of General de Gaulle rendered unthinkable moves which could be construed as leading to a federal Europe. Only with the resignation of the General in 1969, and the enlargement negotiations, was some progress made. While not actually giving any firm guarantees, the Council finally responded to a parliamentary resolution calling on it to introduce direct elections,[41] requesting the Committee of Permanent Representatives (Coreper) to report on direct elections. Following the Hague Summit, the Heads of State and Government announced that 'The problem of direct elections will continue to be studied by the Council of Ministers.'[42]

Such moves were seen as inadequate by the Commission, since, as Jean Rey pointed out, '. . . the Conference, like the communiqué, hardly mentioned political union at all'.[43] Nor had the Council given the commitment to direct elections which the Commission had called for as a way of 'giving the peoples of Europe an interest in the destinies of the Community'.[44]

The introduction of Community 'own resources' meant that the EC now had funds over which there was no parliamentary accountability. Since the EP was composed of elected representatives (albeit with a national, not European mandate), the argument was advanced that Parliament should play a role in the budgetary process. Already the issue of a 'democracy deficit' in European decision-making was troubling the Community. The seemingly obvious solution to a loss of democratic accountability at the national level seemed to be to grant more powers to the Parliament.[45] A problem of priorities arose, however: should more powers be granted to an unelected assembly, or should this weak consultative body first be given the added legitimacy of direct election?[46] The delicate balancing act which the Pompidou Presidency performed, maintaining the Gaullist vision of a European union firmly based on nation states while accepting that some concessions had to be made to the wishes of other governments, blocked any movement on this symbolic issue until the non-Gaullist Valéry Giscard d'Estaing became President of France in 1974.[47]

The commitment to introduce direct elections was thus part of the package agreed at the 1974 Paris Summit, maintaining hopes that the EC was moving towards economic and political union in spite of short-term setbacks in the timetable of monetary union agreed at the two previous summits.[48] Parliament acted swiftly in adopting the *Draft Convention on the election of members to the European Parliament by direct universal suffrage*,[49] emanating from the Patijn Report. Largely based on the Dehousse Report, it laid out guidelines for the elections and expressed the hope that 'the first elections will be held before the creation of the Union, so that the direct cooperation of the European peoples in the Union will be assured to the full'.[50] There was then a clear assumption, reiterated in the Tindemans Report, that European elections would arouse public interest in the EC and endow it with a legitimacy which had previously been lacking.[51] They reality was sadly different (see Appendix).

Only after the signature of the Maastricht Treaty were the democratic credentials of European integration directly challenged. The rejection of the Treaty by the Danes in June 1992 provided irrefutable evidence that the Treaty, the result of compromises between 12 national governments (and associated officials), did not command a permissive consensus throughout the Community. Reactions elsewhere were only slightly more positive. National politicians in several member states were therefore forced to modify their positions in 1992–93. Danish parties in particular were anxious to emphasise how far they had shifted to accommodate the wishes of voters.

Within Germany opposition to the Treaty included an appeal to the Federal Constitutional Court, initiated by a former Chef de Cabinet to a German Commissioner, Manfred Brunner. Its decision, delivered in October 1993, denied that the Maastricht Treaty was unconstitutional, but laid down several conditions for further moves towards European Union to be compatible with Germany's Grundgesetz. In particular, the ruling apparently took a step back from the assumption of the EP as the institution giving citizens their democratic voice. It stated that:

> . . . it was primarily the peoples of the Member States which were called upon democratically to legitimize the exercise of sovereign powers of the community of states by way of the *national parliaments*. With the extension of the tasks and authorities of the Community, there was a growing need for the democratic legitimation and influences channelled through the national parliaments to be 'seconded' by representation of the *nations* by a European Parliament, which afforded 'additional' democratic support for the policies of the Union'.[52] (emphasis added)

Maastricht ratification, therefore, forced European elites to accept that public support for further integration could not be taken for granted. This was reflected in a limited way in the 1994 European elections. There was a burgeoning of new political groups opposed to the accepted model of European integration: Manfred Brunner's Free Citizens' Alliance in Germany, Philippe de Villiers's L'Autre Europe in France, the June Movement in Denmark. Yet these groups achieved only limited success.[53]

Even in the 1994 campaign, the future of the EU thus remained a peripheral issue in the European elections in the majority of member countries. Direct elections had neither interested voters in the future of Europe, nor given them a clear opportunity to express their opinions on the subject had they wanted to. While the question of voting rights in the Council and ideas of a Europe of variable geometry were raised in Britain,[54] the debate was held primarily *within* the Conservative Party. Since there is no way under the first-past-the-post electoral system for voters to express a preference between Tory Eurosceptics and Tory Europhiles, there was little scope for the public to have a say. European elections continued to be fought by traditional national political groupings. Already apparently remote from the citizens at the national level, they served the electorate even less well at the European level. Maastricht may have created 'European citizens', but it has not unambiguously given voters a greater say in the future of Europe.

CONCLUSIONS

European integration started as an elite process, in which popular consent was largely assumed. Even those institutions, notably the European Parliament, which were seen as endowing the European project with democratic credentials, owed little to a desire for a democratic Europe in the full sense of representation and accountability. As we have seen, they have made little progress towards providing even a symbolic sense of public involvement.[55] The initial bargain was elite-led, as all subsequent partial bargains have been.[56]

Some recent observers have seen the signature and ratification of the Maastricht Treaty on European Union, in 1992–93, rather than the introduction of direct elections to the European Parliament in 1979, as marking the transition from a Europe of governments to one based on European citizens. Dominique Wolton goes so far as to suggest that the Maastricht Treaty '. . . symbolised the beginning of democratic Europe, linked with the exercise of universal suffrage'.[57] One of the innovations of that Treaty was the formal establishment of the principle of European citizenship.[58] In practical terms European citizenship, as defined by the Treaty, means little;[59] in symbolic terms it could be claimed to represent a major step forward in the process of uniting Europe.[60]

Democratic legitimacy derives from a subtle blend of legal rules, political institutions, symbols and myths, and the development of a sense of shared political community. Joseph Weiler has drawn the distinction between what he refers to as *formal or legal legitimacy* and *social legitimacy*.[61] In these terms, the European Union can be seen as having legal legitimacy – since national parliaments freely agreed to allow some sovereign powers to pass to the European level – but still lacks social legitimacy. The lack of social legitimacy raises problems for those who claim that granting greater powers to the European Parliament is the natural solution to the weakness of democracy at the European level. One might reduce the democracy deficit in terms of ensuring that there is parliamentary scrutiny at some level; yet this would mean little if the institutions still lack popular support. As he asserts:

> There are several reasons for the crisis of legitimacy in the EC. The first is that the electorate (in most member states) is only reluctantly ready to accept the fact that important areas of public life are decided in a decision-making process in which their national voice can be in a minority; in which it can simply be outvoted by a majority of representatives from other European states.[62]

The problem of one's country being outvoted applies to parliamentary and Council of Ministers' activities, and citizens' anxieties about it demonstrate a lack of social legitimacy. It is not just a question of weak European identity,[63] but also a sense that European decisions are remote, that make it difficult to engender popular support for European integration. For Hallstein, the predicament was that the Parliament's role and democratic credentials prior to direct elections were inadequate:

> The real problem is that the absence of wider powers and the lack of a 'direct' European mandate from the electors undermine the Parliament's ability to dramatize and popularize the great European questions and problems as fully as it could. This may not endanger the development of the Community, but it threatens to make the Community something that will become increasingly remote and incomprehensible.[64]

The need to make the EU more accessible to the people has also been a source of concern for Commission President Delors, who on several occasions warned about the dangers if people did not see the EU as relevant or understandable. Contrary to the aspirations of those who called for direct elections, Quermonne could still conclude after three sets of elections that 'the political system established by the European Communities continues to form a complex whole with a techno-bureaucratic slant'.[65] European policy-making still appears to outsiders to be technocratic and bureaucratic, even though the decisions taken are highly political and are agreed by politicians representing national governments in the Council of Ministers.

National ministers and heads of government thus form a crucial link between national representation and Community legitimation. As political leaders have lost the deferential respect their predecessors commanded from electors at the national level, it has however become harder for them to maintain this representative link. The sense of 'indirect legitimacy', which Helen Wallace has argued characterised the early experience of integration, no longer exists.[66] Thus, despite the introduction of elections, it could be argued that European integration has actually become subjectively more remote from 'the people' – the mass public – over the years.

We are thus driven back to the questions which Karl Deutsch and others posed at the outset of the West European integration process, about the growth – or creation – of political community across state borders.[67] Social legitimacy for the EC depends upon the strength (or weakness) of popular recognition of their shared membership of a broader political community. Deutsch and his 'transactionalist' school looked to a balanced increase in cross-border communications and transactions to foster a sense of shared community and trust. Promoted by affluence and technological advance, eased by the progressive dismantling of border controls, such communications and transactions have increased within Western Europe far beyond what Deutsch can have anticipated 40 years ago. The evidence suggests that this has indeed led to the emergence of a diffuse political community, but not to the 'amalgamated political community' for which he hoped.[68] Neither the pursuit of rational interests nor the growth of new networks of interaction have translated into that 'shift [of] loyalties, expectations and political activities toward a new centre' which integration theorists had predicted.[69]

Further enlargement, moving towards a European Union – and 'Community' – of 20–25 member states, stretching from the Arctic Circle to the Mediterranean and from the Atlantic to the former Soviet border, will make it more difficult to foster a sufficiently strong sense of community to provide popular consent for a more integrated EU. A return to a more clearly intergovernmental, state-based pattern of policy-making and legitimation might therefore seem wise, recognising that idealist hopes of a 'Europe of the peoples' were always illusory. But a larger EU cannot operate effectively on a unanimity/national veto pattern; it requires at least sufficient legitimation to support continuing acceptance of rules imposed by majority vote over national preferences. A Union, furthermore, whose leading members recognise the political desirability – even necessity – of moving towards common policies in security and defence, policing, macroeconomic management, financial transfers, perhaps even a common currency, cannot operate without efficient decision-making rules.

Technocratic policy-making was acceptable among six countries, with a limited agenda and within the wider context of American leadership and the external Soviet threat. For the agenda which an enlarged – and still enlarging – EU now faces, without constructive American guidance or the solidarity engendered by any clear and present external danger, there can be little hope of generating any comparable permissive consensus. Dependence on national sources of legitimation, within a community of 20 or more states, would leave the EU at the mercy of parliamentary crises and repeated national referenda. Some mechanisms for registering shared public consent at the Community level are thus essential.

The European Parliament after four direct elections offers only a weak mechanism for this purpose. It is hobbled by the looseness of its constituent parties, by the diversity of the electoral systems and the national campaigns through which it is constituted and by the resistance of the majority of national governments to any substantial increase in its authority. If there is any reconciliation to be found between popular consent and European integration, however, that reconciliation will have to include both greater visibility and greater authority for this directly elected Parliament of 'the European peoples'.

NOTES

Julie Smith wishes to acknowledge the support of the Economic and Social Research Council for funding her doctoral thesis from which research this study is partly based.

1. Michael Hogan, *The Marshall Plan: America, Britain and the reconstruction of Western Europe 1947–52* (Cambridge: CUP, 1987); Thomas Alan Schwartz, *America's Germany: John J.Mcloy and the Federal Republic of Germany* (Cambridge, MA: Harvard UP, 1991); François Duchêne, *Jean Monnet: The First Statesman of Interdependence* (NY: Norton, 1994).
2. Altiero Spinelli, 'The Growth of the European Movement since World War Two', in C. Grove Haines (ed.), *European Integration* (Baltimore, MD: John Hopkins, 1957), p.54.
3. Quoted in Alan S. Milward, *The European Rescue of the Nation-State* (London: Routledge, 1992), p.320.
4. Leon Lindberg and Stuart Scheingold, *Europe's Would-be Polity* (Englewood Cliffs, NF: Prentice Hall, 1970), p.16.
5. Ibid., p.21.
6. Roy Pryce (ed.), *The Dynamics of European Union* (London: Croom Helm, 1987), Chs.1 and 2.
7. This was the title of Andrew Shonfield's Reith lectures of 1972, published as *Europe: Journey to an Unknown Destination – an expanded version of the BBC Reith Lectures 1972* (Harmondsworth: Penguin Books, 1973).
8. Michel Jobert records in his memoirs a conversation with a young member of the Elysée staff, who had been urging President Pompidou to encapsulate his proposals for the October 1972 European Summit in the phrase, 'European Union'. 'But what does it mean?' the then Secretary-General of the Elysée asked Edouard Balladur. 'Nothing', Balladur replied; 'but

then, that's the beauty of it'. Michel Jobert, *L'autre regard* (Paris: Grasset, 1976), p.164.

9. Preamble to Treaty of Paris (ESCS), 1951; Preamble to Treaty of Rome (EEC), 1957.

10. Walter Lipgens and others, *A History of European Integration, 1945–1947*, Vol.1, *The Formation of the European Unity Movement* (Oxford: OUP, 1982).

11. D. W. Ellwood, *Rebuilding Europe: Western Europe, America and Postwar Reconstruction* (London: Longman, 1992). See also note 1.

12. S. Patijn (ed.), *Landmarks in European Unity: 22 texts on European Integration* (Leyden: Sijthoff, 1970), p.22.

13. Roy Pryce and Wolfgang Wessels, 'Introduction: a framework for analysis', in Pryce, *Dynamics of European Union* (note 6), p.24.

14. Pierre Gerbet, 'The Common Assembly of the European Coal and Steel Community', in *European Parliament: 40th anniversary, proceedings of the Symposium* (Strasbourg: European Parliament, 1992), p.12.

15. Ibid.

16. Albert Coppé, 'The Common Assembly as seen from the High Authority', in *European Parliament 40th Anniversary Symposium*, p.31.

17. Jean Monnet, *Mémoires* (London: Collins, 1978); Kevin Featherstone, 'Jean Monnet and the "Democratic Deficit" in the European Union', *Journal of Common Market Studies* 32/2 (June 1994), pp.149–170. François Duchêne's characterisation of Monnet as a 'creative official . . . an entrepreneur in the public interest' catches the ambivalent career of a man who was firmly rooted in the French republican tradition and who stood firmly against de Gaulle's autocratic tendencies in forming the Free French government-in-exile, but who 'was never voted in by a constituency [and] was never part of an elected government'. Duchêne, *Monnet* (note 1), pp.61, 21.

18. Rita Cardozo, 'The Project for a Political Community', Ch.3 in Pryce, *Dynamics of European Union*, p.72.

19. Cited in Pierre Gerbet, 'In search of political union: the Fouchet Plan negotiations', Ch.5 in Pryce, *Dynamics of European Union* (note 6), p.113.

20. The classic study was Karl Deutsch *et al.*, *Political Community and the North Atlantic Area* (Princeton, NJ: Princeton UP, 1957).

21. Ernst B. Haas, *The Uniting of Europe: Political, Social and Economic Forces, 1950–57* (London: Stevens, 1958), p.456. See also Featherstone, 'Jean Monnet and the "Democratic Deficit"', p.161 and Monnet, *Mémoires*, pp.93, 392–3; cited in M. Burgess, *Federalism and European Union* (London: Routledge, 1989), p.54.

22. Virtually all those who made significant contributions to the field contributed to the special issue of *International Organization* in Autumn 1970, later separately published as Leon Lindberg and Stuart Scheingold, (eds.), *Regional Integration: Theory and Research*, (Cambridge, MA Harvard UP, 1971). It is a measure of the strength of American intellectual hegemony at that time that *all* contributors were American, that the conference out of which the volume grew took place in Wisconsin, and that the editors declare that 'we see this volume as ringing down the curtain on the first act of integration studies'.

23. Alan S. Milward and Vibeke Sorensen, 'Interdependence and integration? A national choice', in Milward and others, *The Frontier of National Sovereignty: History and Theory, 1945–1992* (London: Routledge, 1993), pp.1–3.

24. Lindberg and Scheingold, *Europe's Would-be Polity* (note 4), pp.251–2.

25. Ibid., p.41 and chapter 8. The phrase 'permissive consensus' was taken by Lindberg and Scheingold from V. O. Key, *Public Opinion and American Democracy* (NY: Knopf, 1961).

26. Haas, *Uniting of Europe* (note 21), p.5.

27. Ibid., p.16.

28. Lindberg and Scheingold, *Europe's Would-be Polity* (note 4), pp.52–4.

29. Ibid., p.265; Stanley Hoffmann, 'Europe's Identity Crises: between Past and America', *Daedalus* 93 (Fall 1964), p.1275.

30. Walter Hallstein, *Europe in the Making*, (London: Allen and Unwin, 1972), p.60.

31. Lindberg and Scheingold, *Europe's Would-Be Polity* (note 4), p.269.

32. Ernst B. Haas, *The Obsolescence of Integration Theory* (Univ. of California, Berkeley: Inst. of Int. Studies, 1975), p.8.

33. Ibid., p.13.
34. Quotation from Werner Report, *Bulletin EC*, Supplement 11/70, p.24. See William Wallace, 'The Administrative Implications of Economic and Monetary Union within the European Community', *Journal of Common Market Studies* 12/4 (1974), pp.410–45.
35. Committee on Institutional Affairs, 1 Feb. 1988 PE 111.236/fin. (the 'Toussaint Report'), pp.10–11, cited in Vernon Bogdanor and George Woodcock, 'The European Community and Sovereignty', *Parliamentary Affairs* 44/4 (Oct. 1991).
36. Jean-Baptiste Duroselle, *Europe: a History of its Peoples*, trans. Richard Mayne (London: Viking, 1990).
37. The story is told that a British official argued that his government would be bound to oppose anything so symbolic as a Community flag; but that it would be unlikely to object to the minor adoption of a logo. Both for the British and the French, flags were attributes of states, not of international entities. Despite the despair of American integration theorists, this example of incrementalism in effect gave the Community what has become its flag as well as its familiar logo.
38. Anthony D. Smith, 'European integration and the problem of identity', *International Affairs* 68/1 (1992), pp.55–76; idem., *National Identity* (London: Penguin, 1991), Ch.7; William Wallace, 'Foreign Policy and national identity in the United Kingdom', *International Affairs*, 67/1, (1991); idem., 'Rescue or Retreat? The Nation State in Western Europe, 1945–93', *Political Studies*, Vol.42 (1994), sp. issue on 'Contemporary Crisis of the Nation State?', pp.52–76.
39. Dehousse Report Para. 22, pub. in *Pour l'élection de PEG au suffrage universel direct* (Luxembourg: PEG, Sept. 1969).
40. Ibid., para.24.
41. Resolution adopted by the European Parliament on 12 March 1969 (Doc 214/68–9).
42. Communiqué of the Heads of State or Government para.5 (*Bull-EC* 1/1970).
43. Address by M. Jean Rey to European Parliament, 11 Dec. 1969, *Bull EC* 1/1970.
44. Memo from the Commission to the Conference, 19 Nov. 1969, Para.5. *Bull EC* 1/1970.
45. Report of the Working Party examining the problem of the enlargement of powers of the EP (Vedel Report) – *Bull EC* Supplement 4/72, p.33.
46. The Vedel Report on the powers of the Parliament raises the point that there was a danger that attempts to achieve both desirable aims – increased powers of the EP and direct elections – might result in the achievement of neither.
47. For an outline of the history up to direct elections, see Martin Westlake, *A Modern Guide to the European Parliament* (London: Pinter, 1994), Chapter One.
48. Communiqué of the Heads of Government in Paris *Bull EC* 12-1974.
49. *Bull EC* 1-1975.
50. Patijn Report (Doc 386/74).
51. European Union – Report by Mr Leo Tindemans to the European Council – *Bull EC* Supplement 1/76.
52. Research Services of the German Federal Parliament, Current Court Decisions No.9/93, 22 Oct. 1993, *The Federal Constitutional Court's Maastricht judgment* (2 BvR 2134/92; 2 BvR 2159/92).
53. For further details of the election campaigns and results in the 12 member states, see Julie Smith, 'Twelve into One Won't Go' in this volume and Julie Smith, 'How European are European Elections?', in John Gaffney (ed.), *Political Parties and the European Union* (London: Routledge, forthcoming 1995).
54. At an election rally in Ellesmere Port (Cheshire) Prime Minister John Major voiced the idea that all countries might not proceed with integration at the same speed. Scarcely a new idea in the workings of the EC/U, it serves as a catalyst for the domestic British debate. See *Financial Times*, 1 June 1994.
55. For a strong intergovernmental view of the process of European integration, see Ruggero Ranieri and Vibecke Sørensen, 'The Frontier of National Sovereignty – Nation and Theory' (Paper for Working Group 1, *The Federal Experience: Historical and Comparative Analyses*, at the Second ECSA-World Conference: Federalism, Subsidiarity and Democracy in the European Union, Brussels, May 1994).

56. Helen Wallace, 'Making multilateral negotiations work', Ch.12 in William Wallace (ed.), *The Dynamics of European Integration* (London: Pinter, 1990).
57. Dominique Wolton, *La Dernière Utopie: naissance de l'Europe démocratique*, (Paris: Flammarion, 1993).
58. Article 8 of the Treaty on European Union.
59. For an analysis of this European citizenship and its failings, see Jennifer M. Welsh, 'A Peoples' Europe? European Citizenship and European Identity' in *Politics* 13/2 (1993), pp.25–31.
60. As a symbol however it did not attract universal admiration. The creation of European citizenship, supposed to be a positive aspect of European integration, was one of the reasons for the 'No' vote in the Danish referendum on 2 June 1992.
61. Joseph H. H,. Weiler, 'After Maastricht: Community Legitimacy in Post-1992 Europe' in William James Adams (ed.), *Singular Europe* (Univ. of Michigan Press, 1992).
62. Joseph H. H. Weiler, 'Europäisches Parlament, europäische Integration, Demokratie und Legitimität' in Otto Schmuck and Wolfgang Wessels (eds.), *Das Europäische Parlament im dynamischen Integrationsprozeß: Auf der Suche nach einem zeitgemäßen Leitbild* (Bonn: Europa Union Verlag, 1989), authors' translation.
63. See *Eurobarometer* for attitudes to national and European identity and also Neill Nugent, 'British Public Opinion and the European Community' in Stephen George (ed.), *Britain and the European Community – the Politics of Semi-Detachment* (Oxford: Clarendon Press, 1992).
64. Hallstein, *Europe in the Making* (note 30), p.74.
65. Jean-Louis Quermonne, 'Existe-t-il Un Modèle Politique Européen?', *Revue Français de Science Politique* 40/2 (April 1990), pp.192–211.
66. Helen Wallace, 'Deepening and Widening: Problems of Legitimacy for the EC' in Soledad García, (ed.), *European Identity and the Search for Legitimacy*, pp.95–105.
67. Karl Deutsch, *Nationalism and Social Communication* (NY: Wiley, 1953); Deutsch and others, *Political Community and the North Atlantic Area* (Princeton, NJ: Princeton UP, 1957).
68. Donald J. Puchala, 'International transactions and regional integration', pp.128–59 in Lindberg and Scheingold, *Regional Integration: theory and research* (note 22), provides a useful review of research in this area in the 1960s; several of the chapters in William Wallace (ed.), *The Dynamics of European Integration* (London: Pinter, 1990) provide data on the growth of transactions since then.
69. Haas (note 30).

FURTHER READING

Robert A. Dahl, 'A Democratic Dilemma – System Effectiveness versus Citizen Participation', *Political Science Quarterly* 109/1 (1994), pp.23–34.
Crisis Shore, 'Inventing the "People's Europe": Critical Approaches to European Community "Cultural Policy"', *Man* 28/4 (Dec. 1993).

Economic Recession and Disenchantment with Europe

ANDREW GAMBLE

Recent disenchantment with European integration has been associated with the economic recession, in particular the difficulties in ratifying the Maastricht Treaty and the weakening of the ERM. Cyclical perspectives see integration as driven forward by economic necessities and the present difficulties as temporary; structural perspectives identify recent changes in the political and the economic context as creating political obstacles to the resumption of integration. The structuralist perspective is seen as providing a more plausible account of the present state of the European Union. Evidence on the strength of popular support for European integration and the variations between member states is assessed. It is argued that the limited progress towards the creation of either a European economy or European polity creates serious problems for both the neo-liberal and social democratic programmes for deeper integration.

The process of European integration acquired a new momentum in the 1980s with the signing of first the Single European Act in February 1986 and then the Maastricht Treaty on European Union (EU) in February 1992. The satisfaction which accompanied the successful conclusion of the Maastricht negotiations, however, was short-lived. In the period between the signing of the Treaty and the elections for the European Parliament in June 1994 there emerged widespread questioning, nor merely of the integration project of the 1980s, but also of the meaning and identity of the Union itself and its future. After the optimism and confidence of the late 1980s, fuelled by the progress towards greater integration and the ending of the divisions within Europe after the collapse of Soviet Communism, a mood of pessimism and doubt descended.

The disenchantment with Europe had both economic and political aspects. On the economic side the most obvious cause of the disenchantment was the deep and prolonged economic recession, from which the European economy only began to emerge in 1994. But it also arose from particular events, most notably the crisis in the ERM in September 1992, which forced two members, Italy and the UK, to suspend their membership, and exposed the extreme fragility of the whole system. Since the ERM was a crucial step towards the creation of the economic and monetary union envisaged in the Maastricht Treaty, the inability of the Union to prevent its disintegration was a serious blow to the prospect of creating the kind of supranational institutions required for the next stage of integration. A third economic factor was the long-term economic malaise which afflicted the European economy, making it appear less dynamic and less competitive than either Japan or the United States.

On the political side the disenchantment was associated with the discrediting of old politics, both institutions and policies. Evidence of a growing gap between political elites and popular opinion led to much talk of democratic deficits and legitimacy deficits. Violent swings of electoral popularity, and in some cases corruption scandals, plunged into crisis many of the regimes which had governed since 1945. Several incumbent governments lost office; all were threatened by large swings in electoral support, which went beyond the normal swings of the electoral cycle. The impact on the new EU was considerable. Since the European project had been an elite project from the start, with little popular participation, a crisis of political legitimacy within nation states quickly became a crisis also of the legitimacy of the European Union. The European project has become in some ways the most appealing target for those seeking to highlight the gap between the people and the political elite.

Many new fringe parties outside the political centre have sought to take advantage of the new political climate. They include Fascist and Racist parties, as well as Green, nationalist and regionalist parties. The political turmoil, however, should not be exaggerated. Some incumbent governments most severely affected by the recession, like the British Conservatives, won re-election. In most member states the fringe parties and new parties remained outside government; only in Italy was there a complete breakdown of the old system and the displacement of the old governing parties. Not all the new forces which emerged were hostile to the EU, although many were. A characteristic which they all shared was populism. They made unfamiliar and unsettling demands, and set themselves against the established elites.

The most visible political aspect of disenchantment with the EU was the reception given the Maastricht Treaty itself. Far from being acclaimed as setting the framework for the next phase of European cooperation, the Treaty was widely assailed in many countries as seriously flawed. The ratification process proved tortuous, quite unlike the smooth passage of the SEA six years before. In several countries, particularly Denmark, France, the UK, and Germany, powerful anti-Maastricht alliances emerged. Referenda on the Treaty, far from providing a strong endorsement of what the elites had done, tended to advertise the deep suspicion in which the Maastricht Treaty was held. In Denmark the Treaty was rejected in a referendum in 1992, while the French referendum in the same year produced only a narrow majority in favour. Germany and the UK did not hold referenda, but signs of disaffection were present. In Germany there was a sharp political debate about the potential costs of the Maastricht programme, while in the UK there was a lengthy parliamentary struggle to ratify the Treaty, which exposed deep divisions in the Conservative Party.[1]

The difficulty of winning endorsement for Maastricht reflected popular unease as well as divisions among political elites about the desirability of further European integration, and certainly further integration as envisaged by the Maastricht Treaty. Yet here, too, the political turmoil should not be exaggerated. The various battles to secure ratification of the Maastricht Treaty were eventually won in all member states. The gloom in 1993/94 among supporters of the European project was partly because the process of securing ratification appeared to drain the confidence and energy of the supporters of the EU, resurrecting many issues which had been thought settled, and exposing many disagreements about the future shape of Europe, and the appropriate objectives for the IGC due in 1996.

THE ECONOMIC RECESSION

The favourite scapegoat for these unexpected difficulties in the smooth progress towards ever closer economic and political union in Europe was the economic recession which developed in the early 1990s, and dominated the period between the signing of the Maastricht Treaty in 1991 and the European Parliament Elections in 1994. It was a severe downturn which affected all member states, although not all equally. The particular monetary policies which the UK had pursued outside the ERM before 1990 and the difficulty of adjusting to the ERM regime after entry in 1990 made it the first major European economy to go into recession and the first to emerge from it, while Germany, because of the short-term boost provided by reunification, was the last. Some countries escaped with only a slow-down of economic growth. The biggest contraction of activity was in the UK.

The first signs of the approaching recession appeared in 1990/91, when the rate of growth in most member states began a sharp decline. In 1993 there was an actual contraction of GDP in most states. This followed a period of strong expansion from the bottom of the previous recession in 1981. The slump in activity and growth rates in 1991/92 was more gradual than in either 1974 or 1979/80. In comparison with previous recessions,

1975 was deeper than 1993, but 1981 was shallower. However, the final figures may show the loss of output in the 1993 recession to have been greater than in either 1975 or 1981. There was also doubt in 1994 as to how strong the recovery from the recession would be. The 1975 and 1981 recessions were both triggered by the oil shocks. The initial falls in output were sharp, but so too were the recoveries. The 1993 recession took longer to develop, and some economists feared that the recovery would also be slow, although the European Commission remained optimistic. A slow or patchy recovery would obviously be a difficult background against which to plan the next intergovernmental conference.

The impact of the recession on the EU and the project for ever closer union set out in the Maastricht Treaty has been considerable. Unemployment rose again, reaching 10.9 per cent in 1993, as did budget deficits. Progress towards convergence, particularly of budget deficits, an essential condition for EMU, was thrown off course, although inflation rates did moderate (see Table 1).

TABLE 1
THE COMMUNITY ECONOMY: SELECTED INDICATORS

	1988	1989	1990	1991	1992	1993
GDP	4.2	3.5	3.0	1.4	1.1	-0.3
Inflation	3.8	5.0	4.5	5.4	4.6	3.8
Unemployment	9.8	8.9	8.3	8.7	9.7	10.9
Public Deficits	-3.4	-2.7	-4.0	-4.6	-5.0	-6.0

Source: EC Commission: Annual Report 1994.

Most member states were still growing quite rapidly in 1990. The slow-down really became noticeable in 1991, although in Germany it was postponed until 1992. The major exception to the EU pattern was the UK, which suffered both the deepest and the longest recession. The 2.3 per cent fall in GDP in 1991 was much greater than that experienced by any other economy (although the former West Germany came close in 1993), and was followed by a further fall of 0.5 per cent in 1992. The contractions of most other economies were much milder. Nevertheless, the cumulative impact was considerable, three million jobs being lost, and employment declining by a record 1.7 per cent in 1993. According to the Annual Economic Report of the Commission: 'The total contraction in employment over the period 1992–1994 is likely to reach 2.7 per cent excluding the eastern part of Germany or 3.4 per cent if this area is included. By contrast, employment declined 2.4 per cent over the period 1981–1983 and 1.1 per cent in 1975.'[2]

Unemployment was high in the EU, even during the expansion of the 1980s. The recession led to a new deterioration. All the leading economies had very high unemployment rates in 1993 – Germany 8.1, France 10.8, Italy 11.2, Spain 21.5, and the UK 10.5. The average in the EU as a whole was 10.5 per cent. These figures mask other trends, particularly the concentration of unemployment among certain groups. In France, for example, youth unemployment reached 23 per cent in 1993. The actual number of people registered as unemployed reached three million in France, four million in Germany.

Interpreting the recession has been complicated by the unification of Germany. This both provided the stimulus which kept the German economy, and those economies in the EU most closely linked to it, continuing to expand through 1991 and 1992, when economies elsewhere in the world economy were already turning down. It has also distorted the performance of the German economy, mainly through the very substantial transfers (estimated at five per cent of GDP per annum) which Germany has been obliged to make to the East. This has transformed a government financial surplus into a sizeable deficit (3.3 per cent of the GDP in 1993). The obsolescence of the bulk of the equipment in the East German economy, and the problem of retraining displaced workers (employment has fallen from 9.5 million to 6 million since unification and has not stopped falling); regenerating the East German economy to bring it up to the level of the West, and delivering the promise of wage equalisation, pose difficult policy problems which will take many years to solve.

The political effect has been that the German political elite has become more preoccupied with German internal problems, and has created a political climate in which the 'burdens' of the EU on Germany have become a leading political issue. The difficulty of justifying transfers both towards the East and the poorer states in the EU at a time of stagnation and high unemployment in the German economy, as well as fears about the loss of autonomy implied by the plans for a European Central Bank, has significantly weakened German enthusiasm for the pace of economic integration envisaged by the Maastricht Treaty.[3] The objective of regaining fiscal balance and bringing inflation back below two per cent is being given priority, and this involved the maintenance of high interest rates and a deflationary stance which will mean that the German economy is likely to emerge slowly from the recession.

In Italy the recession began in mid-1992 with a marked deceleration in growth, followed by a contraction in GDP of 0.5 per cent in 1993. The economy has been slow to bounce back, although the depth of the recession has been cushioned by the strength of Italian exports, boosted by the 20 per cent devaluation of the lira after Italy left the ERM in 1992. Unemployment remains high, and continues to be regionally differentiated – in 1993 it was 6.9 per cent in the North compared to 18.9 per cent in the South. Inflation which historically has been high in Italy is being held at just over four per cent, following measures to scrap indexation and impose strict limits on wage increases. At the same time efforts are being made to reduce the fiscal deficit.

In France there was a similar contraction of economic activity in 1993 (0.7 per cent), the first since 1975. The French franc was kept within the ERM, despite severe speculative pressure, (the bands were widened in August 1993), but the French economy became less competitive as a result of the devaluations in Italy and the UK. Inflation, however, because of the exchange rate discipline, remained very low at around two per cent. The cost was felt in high unemployment (3.3 million in 1993, 11.2 per cent) and a rising budget deficit – above four per cent of GDP. (The EU convergence programme requires budget deficits to be kept below three per cent).

THE POLITICAL ECONOMY OF RECESSION

The recession has been the most convenient scapegoat for the political ills which afflicted Europe between 1991 and 1994. It has been blamed as the underlying cause of at least seven different political events and developments: the difficulties in ratifying the Maastricht Treaty; the undermining of the ERM; the distortion of the timetable for economic convergence of inflation rates, interest rates and budget deficits required for economic and monetary union; the electoral difficulties of incumbent governments; the declining legitimacy of established regimes and the rise of populist movements; and the decline in popularity of the European Union and the project of economic and political integration.

Many commentators have linked the political set-backs to the European project to the unfavourable state of the economy, arguing that the fortunes of the European project will revive once the economy does. On this view political support for European integration is cyclical, and is linked directly to economic performance. In times of economic expansion, the gains from cooperation are more apparent and the political task of creation coalitions which will support new initiatives is easier. In times of recession, support is harder to obtain, the costs and burdens of European policies are more apparent, and protectionist, defensive reactions tend to predominate. At such moments the process towards integration is stalled at the political level, but seldom goes into reverse. The gains towards deeper integration made during the period of prosperity are not lost but consolidated. They constitute a higher base from which integration can again proceed once political and economic conditions are more favourable.

This argument assumes that integration is essentially an economic process, driven forward by economic necessities, and that political institutions adjust after a lag. Political will is often weak, affected by transitional factors such as economic recession, but the underlying logic of integration is created through the dynamics of the European economy. Most important here is the argument that expanding intra-Community trade creates a network of interests and interdependence which produces a climate favourable in the long run to political integration, whatever the short-term obstacles. By 1990 only the UK had less than 50 per cent of its trade with other members of the EU, and its proportion had been rising sharply. (See Table 2).

TABLE 2
INTRA EU TRADE AS A PERCENTAGE OF TOTAL TRADE FOR SELECTED EU COUNTRIES

	1960–67	1968–72	1973–9	1980–4	1985–90
Germany	44.8	50.9	50.3	50.5	53.1
France	45.8	57.2	55.0	53.9	61.9
Italy	42.9	49.5	48.7	46.1	55.0
Spain	47.8	44.4	41.3	39.3	56.0
UK	26.7	31.2	37.9	44.1	49.9

Source: Eurostat.

An alternative view is that whatever may have been the case in the past, the cyclical model no longer holds. The EU has reached a watershed in its development, and the political and economic conditions which made possible the project of integration in the past no longer exist. The ending of the Cold War has removed one of the original political reasons for an EC, while the trends towards globalisation in the world economy has made the protectionist bias of the EU in the fields of trade, agriculture, and labour markets anachronistic. Maastricht is regarded not as setting out a new framework for the next stage of integration, but as marking the end of a particular process, a high-water mark on the road to integration that is unlikely to be surpassed.

The assumption behind this structuralist analysis is that the EU was always essentially a political project, and that the economic pressures for convergence and integration do not rigidly determine the response at the political level. They can be accommodated in several different political arrangements. On this view the Franco-German alliance is what has sustained the European project, and it is this alliance which is under severe strain, as a result of the changes that have occurred since 1989. The economic recession is a complicating factor, but it is not the most important. The basic problem will still exist after the recession ends, as to whether the Franco-German alliance can be sustained and a new political purpose for the European Union defined, in the changed circumstances of the unification of Germany, the opening to the East, and the potential dramatic enlargement of the size of the Community.

Two different conclusions can be derived from this analysis. The first is based on the argument that the EU is unlikely to develop further in the direction of transferring powers to European institutions and agencies. If it survives it will do so as a loose trading area, a new EFTA, with very few supranational functions. Power will once again be firmly vested in national governments, and any initiatives for further cooperation will depend on their agreement. The pro-active role of the Commission will disappear.

The second conclusion shares much of this diagnosis, accepts that the process of integration has stalled and will not be resumed automatically, but argues that the momentum can be regained if the project is rethought and resold both to sceptical elites and to sceptical electorates. Such an approach focuses on the need to tackle some of the problems that have accumulated, particularly the lack of legitimacy of EU policies, the weakness of crucial EU institutions like the European Parliament, and the failure to create the institutions and capacities needed for a new economic policy to regenerate the European economy.

For the cyclical view the economic recession is a very important part of the explanation of why the European project is suddenly in trouble after a period of advance, while, for the structural view, it is an irritant but no more. Both seek to analyse elite responses to the problems of the EU, but the cyclical view explores the dynamics of public opinion and policy formation through the economic cycle, whereas the structural view is more concerned to analyse the large structural shifts in political and economic conditions in the world economy and world politics which have changed the contexts in which political elites make their calculations.

The views of elites on the European project are plentiful. Evidence of popular opinion is harder to obtain. The surveys of opinion in all the member states collected by Eurobarometer show that across the Union belief that membership was a 'good thing' climbed from 50 per cent in 1981 to 72 per cent in 1991, and then declined quite sharply to 54 per cent in 1994. The period of decline matches exactly the period of slow-down and then recession, and takes the level of support for membership of the Union almost back to the levels experienced in the last recession. A similar pattern is observable on the question of perception of the benefit of the EU to individual countries. The EU average rises from 52 per cent in 1983 to a peak of 59 per cent in 1991, before falling sharply to 45 per cent in 1993, recovering slightly in 1994. This measure of support for the EU is less positive and more eratic than the membership question, being more prone to particular events and decisions which cause sharp movements in the average. The proportion of those saying that their country had not benefited from EU membership was above 30 per cent between 1984 and 1987, but then fell sharply during the boom years of the late 1980s, before climbing again to 34 per cent in 1994. The proportion saying membership was a bad thing fell steadily from 17 per cent in 1981 to 6 per cent in 1991, before doubling to 13 per cent in 1994.[5]

What the Eurobarometer series indicates is that support for the EU on both these measures has always been positive, even at the trough of the two most recent recessions, but also that the trend of support is broadly in line with the state of the European economy. The cyclical argument predicts that support will rise again once the economy recovers, and that this will create a more favourable climate for renewed moves towards integration. So at this level there is some confirmation of the cyclical thesis.

One of the difficulties, however, in assessing the impact of economic events such as the 1992/93 recession on political attitudes, is the structure of the Community itself. The link that is hypothesised between economic factors and political attitudes in political economy models exists at the level of the national economy and the national political system. There is a substantial literature on how governing parties are judged in terms of economic competence, and how voters' perceptions of the economic prospects of their own households and of the national economy are related to their assessment of political parties. The difficulty with the EU is that it is composed of separate national economies and nation-states. Although there is now a single market, the economic performance of the Union is still presented as an aggregate of the separate national economies. Responsibility for economic performance and economic management is still seen to lie firmly at the national level.

From the beginning the EU and the European project were primarily a project of national elites and the emerging European elite. Many commentators have observed how much the consensus on Europe, which legitimated the participation of member states in the European project, was a permissive and passive consensus as far as national electorates were concerned.[6] The elites were given a relatively free hand in developing the institutional framework of the Community and then the Union. Their legitimacy rested on their conduct of domestic politics and domestic economic management. The trust between electorates and their governments which was established in this way was extended to the institution building at the European level. If the elites judged that participation in the European project contributed to the maintenance of

European peace and domestic prosperity, then the electorates were prepared to endorse it.

The weakness of the political structure of the Community for building something that was more than just an aggregate of the nation-states has long been apparent. But many of the national elites, although well aware of the weakness, were reluctant to propose changes for fear of raising anxieties in their electorates about the long-term implications of the European project. This has always been one of the complaints of the opponents of European Union in the UK. They argue that each proposal for greater European cooperation has been presented to the British people as though it were a small incremental step without wider political implications. In this way it is argued the British have been led step by step towards a goal which has never been presented to them as something they could accept or reject. Instead, as in the 1975 Referendum, the issue has always been presented as a question of trust in the judgement of the dominant section of the political elite. Those sections of the elite which disagreed were successfully characterised as a rag-bag of far left and far right, whose judgement was not as trustworthy as that of the leaders of the three main parties who were urging a Yes vote.

Referenda are a useful device for obtaining national consent and conferring legitimacy on particular decisions taken by national elites. But they also involve risk, since they allow sections of the elite to break away from the elite consensus and present alternatives directly to the people. If the elite has lost legitimacy, or is no longer trusted, a referendum can easily return the wrong answer and discredit the political leadership. But the prize, if it is won, is very tempting, since then it can significantly strengthen the position of the elite and its subsequent freedom of manoeuvre.

Interpreting the meaning of referenda or elections is never clear cut, since voters are being asked to aggregate so many different choices, and establish priority between them. At what point does opposition to a particular policy outweigh the loyalty felt to the party proposing it? Instances of this phenomenon abound. Rational behaviour for voters can mean voting for the party that most directly promises to protect their interests, or is in closest conformity with their opinions, but it can also mean voting for the party that is trusted most over the long term to deliver what voters want.

One of the arguments for direct elections to the European Parliament was to assist the creation of a European public opinion which would be a catalyst for developing the European project, bypassing and isolating national elites, and in time providing a means of making European institutions accountable and therefore legitimate. This hope has only been very partially realised. The turnout in these elections has always been relatively low and the trend has been down not up. Some 63 per cent of EU citizens participated in 1979, compared with 61 per cent in 1984, 58.5 per cent in 1989, and 56.5 per cent in 1989. In some countries the vote was much lower than this average. The elections have been conducted on a national basis – no true European-wide parties have yet emerged – and this has tended to turn the elections into referenda on the performance of the national governments, rather than on attitudes towards the European Union. Surveys before the European election showed that 55 per cent of voters intended to cast their vote on national, rather than on European issues, as against 37 per cent. Only in the Netherlands did a majority of voters (53/38) say that they would vote primarily on European issues.[7]

Despite this evidence, however, there were other Eurobarometer findings in 1994, which indicated broad support for a considerably enhanced role for the European Parliament, and opposition to an intergovernmental conception of Europe. There was majority support for making the European Commission directly accountable to the European Parliament, creating a European Government which would be responsible to the Parliament as well as to the European Heads of Government, and giving the Parliament the same rights in matters of EU legislation, taxation, and expenditure as the Council of Ministers. An important qualification to these findings, however, is that when the figures are disaggregated by country it is clearer that attitudes towards the transfer of powers to the European Parliament are often strongly linked to attitudes towards the national Parliament. The Italians favour more power to be given to the European Parliament by 72 per cent to 7 per cent. Where national parliaments are stronger, support for the European Parliament is less. In 1994 there were majorities against giving more power to the European Parliament in Denmark, the UK, Ireland, Germany, Portugal, and Luxembourg.[8]

The existence of a generalised pro-European sentiment is, however, a consistent feature of the surveys collected by Eurobarometer in 1994. EU citizens are in favour of a common defence policy (75 per cent 'yes'/15 per cent 'no'); a common foreign policy (68 per cent 'yes'/17 per cent 'no'); European Monetary Union and a European Central Bank (65 per cent 'yes'/22 per cent 'no'); and a single currency (53 per cent 'yes'/36 per cent 'no'). Support is very unevenly distributed across the member states. On the single currency, for example, approval in three countries, Germany, the UK, and Denmark, has plummeted and large majorities are now opposed.

Evidence of this kind about support for much closer economic and political union tends to be disregarded, since it is assumed that whatever voters may tell opinion surveys, whenever they are actually asked to vote, domestic issues predominate over European ones. This has been true even of the referenda that have been held on ratification of the Maastricht Treaty. Franklin and Marsh, for example, have argued that even the first Danish

Referendum which rejected the Maastricht Treaty should be interpreted not as a vote on the merits of Maastricht, but as a vote of confidence in the Danish government. The subsequent reversal in the second referendum, they argue, had little to do with changed perceptions of Maastricht or the concessions which the other members of the Union had made to Denmark at the Edinburgh summit in 1992 (few Danish voters could identify what they were), but rather reflected a renewal of trust in the (Danish) government.[9]

The implication of this view of the relation between European and domestic issues is that popular issues to Europe will usually be indirect, mediated through attitudes towards national elites. Europe may be perceived as part of foreign policy. To the extent that this is the case the impact of recession on attitudes to European integration will also tend to be indirect. Recession is unlikely to be blamed on the incompetence of national economic management. At least three possibilities then arise which could weaken popular support: the incumbent party might be closely identified with strong pro-European policies, which then might be blamed as the reason for the economic failure; second, the incumbent government might attempt to deflect criticism of its own performance by making Europe a scapegoat; third, opposition parties might attack the government's competence by linking it with its pro-European stance. In all these ways a fall in a national government's standing might trigger a mood of disenchantment with Europe.

The remoteness of European institutions from the national electorates has two serious disadvantages for the European project. First, it means that there is wide scope for a populist backlash against European institutions like the Commission, which is perceived as powerful and unaccountable and operates in ways that are largely hidden and not easily understood. Second, there is no procedure by which the incumbent Euro elite, apart from the MPs in the European Parliament, can be evicted by popular decision. One of the sources of stability in Western Europe since 1945 has been that electorates have been able to vote against an unpopular incumbent government and elect a new government without needing to install a new political regime. In this way substantial policy continuity has been assured, regardless of the party complexion of the government. No such safety-valve exists at the European level. Since the Euro commissioners cannot be removed by the electorate, hostility towards the current programme of European policies may take the form of rejection of the European institutions themselves. The strain imposed on weaker economies by membership of an exchange rate mechanism whose operating rules reflect the interests of the strong economies is not politically sustainable.

Disenchantment with Europe, therefore, is not directly linked to the economic recession but to the internal politics within each nation-state. One of the most important influences shaping those internal politics is the state of the world and the European economy, particularly when there is either a boom or a recession. But nothing can be read off automatically from economic conditions about political attitudes and responses. These effects will be filtered through the political institutions and culture of each nation-state, and the responses and impact of the same external factors may produce different results.

There is, for example, no consistent relationship between economic performance and attitudes towards the EU in different countries. In Germany support for EU membership has remained very close to the EU average, but on the question of whether (West) Germany has benefited from EU membership, the percentage of those saying it has and those saying it has not (which used to be far apart) rapidly converge in the period 1990–94. By 1994 those claiming the EU had benefited Germany were only three per cent more numerous than those claiming it had not. A similar pattern is observable in France, where again a convergence on the question of benefit produces almost identical percentages on each side, 40 and 39. The vaguer question about whether France should be a member at all produces a reduced but still overwhelming margin in favour – 50 per cent of 13 per cent. The UK has its own distinct pattern. Approval for membership has been consistent since 1983, although it still runs considerably below the EU average, 43 per cent in favour, 22 per cent against. But on the question of whether the UK has benefited from membership, support has fluctuated. During the budget row of the early 1980s a big majority favoured the proposition that the UK had not benefited. After 1988 supporters of the EU outnumbered sceptics, but the position was reversed again in 1992, after Black Wednesday and the exit of sterling from the ERM. The size of the two camps converged again in 1994 to produce a position quite similar to that in Germany and France – a clear majority in favour of continued membership; but an even split over the question of whether the EU as currently organised was providing benefits to national economies like the UK.[10]

THE DEBATE ON THE FUTURE OF EUROPE

The argument of this paper is that there is no simple relationship between economic recession and disenchantment with Europe, and therefore no guarantee that a new momentum towards integration will develop if the economy recovers in the second half of the 1990s. What the recession helped to do was to expose some of the flaws and the faultlines in the European project, and began a series of debates within members of the EU about its future direction.

The structural problems which now confront the European Union have become the focus for a great deal of analysis. Helen Wallace has argued that politics is being renationalised as political parties rediscover the attraction of nationalist and populist themes, in a period of high unpopularity. At the same time the economy is being denationalised because of the increasing impact of global markets and networks in production, finance, and culture. National governments are losing the possibility of maintaining control, but are increasingly reluctant to cede power to European institutions. Wallace interprets the Maastricht Treaty as an attempt to place a ceiling on supranationalism rather than as a new threshold on the way to a European transnational polity. Following Milward, she argues that the creation of the EU belonged to a period when nation-states were strong and extending their control over both economy and society. In the 1980s and 1990s the dominant trend has been for the retreat of state powers, 'the privatisation of public space'.[11]

Wallace sees the problem for the EU after Maastricht as how to create a new system of governance to regenerate and adapt the European economy in the face of global competition, and to reduce the gap between governors and governed. A technocratic and elite driven process can no longer provide an adequate basis for European governance. The growth of lobbying, which gives business groups privileged access to the EU policy-making process, has led to widespread clientelism and regulatory capture. The EU operates too often as a closed system, with no established lines of accountability, and operating in ways that exclude many groups from participating.

The solutions, however, are far from easy. One problem is that there no longer exists a consensus among the political elite within the Union on the definition or desirability of public goods. The integration project of the 1980s was inspired by a neo-liberal agenda, which identified the economic problem facing Europe as removing obstacles and rigidities to the working of markets. This kind of language still dominates the economic reports of the EU. It is based on a defective understanding of the social and political dimensions of markets, and in particular the information and collective action problems which make certain kinds of institutions to promote coordination both possible and necessary. It leads to an emphasis upon privatisation, deregulation, and other supply-side reforms aimed at making labour markets more 'flexible', coupled with orthodox financial policies to maintain price stability. The programme of economic and monetary union aims to create institutions which would establish a common neo-liberal policy regime for the whole of the European economy. Such a regime would be highly deflationary and restrictive.[12]

The implications of deeper European integration have divided national elites along new lines. The Thatcherite wing of the Conservative party in the

1980s divided into those who accepted that the logic of the single market meant the creation of a strong state to police it at the European level, and those who argued that political legitimacy could not be divorced from nation-states, and therefore re-emphasises an intergovernmental conception of Europe to preserve national individuality. An intergovernmentalist programme, however, would be a minimalist one, built on variable geometry; and progress towards tackling some of the long-term problems of the European economy or the European polity would be slow.

The integrationist programme has both neo-liberal and social democratic forms, the latter articulated in particular by Jacques Delors as President of the Commission. Both involve the creation of strong European institutions, but the neo-liberal programme tends to confine these to the institutions required to support the single market, such as a European Central Bank. In the social democratic programme, new institutions would also be required to assist in regenerating the economy and tackling the democratic deficit. The hostility of several member states to any further moves towards deeper integration make it difficult to foresee the circumstances in which the political log-jam can be broken.

There is strong pressure behind the neo-liberal agenda for Europe, but it is increasingly vulnerable to domestic anxieties in several of the larger member states about the erosion of national control over the policies that will influence levels of employment and output, and rates of inflation in the various regions of the European economy. The paradox is that the neo-liberal agenda may only be realisable if substantial parts of the social democratic agenda for Europe are accepted as well. Otherwise Europe may fragment rather than unite.

If integration is to proceed further, European institutions will have to emerge which take responsibility for economic outcomes and are directly accountable to the European electorate. This would signal the emergence of a European economy and a European polity. At the present time the European Union is manifestly neither. Both are needed. One of the difficulties in recent years has been that it has been easier to win support to develop the institutions for a European economy than for a European polity.

The institutions for a neo-liberal Europe cannot be made 'politician-proof' and treated simply as technocratic devices. If they are effective, their impact will be deeply political. If they are not accountable, the problems of maintaining legitimacy in the future will become acute, as many British Conservatives have warned. Harold Clarke and his colleagues explain the political stability of Western Europe in the post-war years by the presence of three sets of beliefs among voters: in the principles of representative democracy; in collectivist social programmes; and the confidence that governments can and should manage the economy successfully.[13]

Transferring this process to the European level has barely begun. Apart from a few areas of subsidy and protection, the EU is not seen as having any responsibility for general economic conditions in the European economy; it does not have responsibility for collectivist social programmes, and the institutions of representative democracy remain very weak.

Wolfgang Wessels has argued that there are five possible strategies open to the European elite.[14] It can press ahead with implementing Maastricht, in the expectation that the difficulties encountered in the last three years will prove temporary. There are few grounds for expecting this will prove viable. Second, it can push for the federalising of Maastricht, seeking to move in one leap to a European state. No one thinks this is a practicable option. Third, there might be a renationalisation of Maastricht. This is the policy of those governments who are most hostile to the supranational elements of the Union. If implemented, it would put the process of integration into reverse. Fourth, Maastricht could simply be abandoned as a treaty too far. This is the fervent wish of the Eurosceptics. A loose trade association would remain, but not an effective single market, because there would be nothing to police it. The fifth alternative, and the one favoured by Wessels, is the rationalisation of Maastricht. This would involve tackling some of the problems, particularly the legitimacy of EU institutions, and seeking to further the process of integration by embracing both a deepening and widening of the Community.

Wessels' analysis is a sophisticated restatement of the cyclical position. He puts his faith in irreversible trends, arguing that:

> this strategy of rationalising Maastricht involves a certain determinist assumption; namely, given the increasing interdependence of European welfare states, it will be rational for governments and administrations to work together via EU institutions, neither the overall legitimacy gap nor the alternative strategies will thus to able to stop this trend towards the fusion of public resources – at least in the absence of unforeseeable shocks.

But the dilemma is this. Moves to implement the neo-liberal agenda for European integration will end by deepening the crisis of legitimacy. Moves to restrict the Union to the intergovernmentalist agenda, perhaps by abolishing QMV, and reasserting the absolute right of veto of national governments, will concentrate legitimacy at the nation-state level and prevent the creation of any institutional capacities at the European level. The language of variable geometry will predominate, and a new and different kind of union will develop around Germany, as it redefines its interests in post-Cold War Europe. The forging of a political will that could create a new dispensation in Europe, based on a vision of a European public good, is formidable, and the task of creating it has hardly begun.

Helen Wallace is right to point to the decline in elite consensus about public goods in Europe, but consensus on public goods such as education, health, and welfare remains strong in the European electorate, as Harold Clarke and his colleagues demonstrate. What is lacking in the European debate is a detailed case as to how the public goods which the European public wants could be secured through action at a European level. One example of how a public good can be defined at the European level and become the basis for policy is environmental protection. The same has not been achieved for industrial policy, social policy, or defence. Progress is likely to be slow unless a fundamental political reform of the Union can be agreed. This structural impasse, and whether it can and ought to be overcome, will dominate the debates on the future of the EU during the preparations for the next intergovernmental conference.

NOTES

I am grateful to Gavin Kelly for research assistance and for comments on an earlier draft of this paper.

1. D. Baker, A. Gamble, and S. Ludlam, 'Whips or Scorpions? The Maastricht Vote and the Conservative Party', *Parliamentary Affairs* 46/2 (1993), pp.151–66; 'The Parliamentary Siege of Maastricht 1993: Conservative Divisions and British Ratification', *Parliamentary Affairs* 47/1 (1994), pp.37–60; '1846 . . . 1906 . . . 1996? Conservative Splits and European Integration', *Political Quarterly* 64/4 (1993), pp.420–34; D. Baker, I. Fountain, A. Gamble, and S. Ludlam, 'Conservative Parliamentarians and European Integration: Initial Survey Results', paper presented to the EPOP Conference, Cardiff (Sept. 1994), 12pp.
2. European Commission *Annual Economic Report 1994*, p.5.
3. E. Kirchner, 'The European Community: Seeds of Ambivalence', in G. Smith *et al.*, *Developments in German Politics* (London: Macmillan 1992), pp.172–84.
4. R. Eichenberg and R. Dalton, 'Europeans and the European Community: the dynamics of public support for European integration', *International Organisation* 47/4 (1993), pp.507–34. They found a significant relationship between the level of intra-EC trade and political support for integration.
5. Eurobarometer 41, July 1994.
6. H. Clarke, N. Dutt, and A. Kornberg, 'The Political Economy of Attitudes Toward Polity and Society in Western European Democracies', *Journal of Politics* 55/4 (1993), pp.998–1021.
7. Eurobarometer 41, July 1994.
8. Ibid.
9. M. Franklin and M. Marsh, 'Attitudes Towards Europe and Referendum Votes: A response to Siune and Svensson', *Electoral Studies* 13/2 (1994), pp.117–21.
10. Eurobarometer 41, July 1994.
11. Helen Wallace, 'European Governance in Troubled Times', *Journal of Common Market Studies* 31/3 (1993), pp.293–303.
12. J. Grahl and P. Teague, 'The Cost of Neo-Liberal Europe', *New Left Review 174* (1989), pp.33–50.
13. Clarke *et al.* (note 6).
14. W. Wessels, 'Rationalising Maastricht: the search for an optimal strategy of the new Europe', *International Affairs* 70/3 (1994), pp.445–57.
15. Ibid., p.457.

Subnational Mobilisation in The European Union

LIESBET HOOGHE

The turbulent ratification of the Treaty of European Union has given a new sharpness to old debates about democratic representativeness in the European arena. The crisis of representation after Maastricht was, however, limited in terms of who and what was criticised: Maastricht was a crisis of intergovernmentalism. There are several alternative ways for establishing links between the citizen and Europe. This paper focuses on the role of subnational intermediaries in day-to-day policy making. The first part of the paper places subnational mobilisation in a broader understanding of the Euro-polity. Three competing conceptualisations: a state-centric model, a supranational model, and multi-level governance make distinct predictions about the features, opportunities and constraints for subnational mobilisation. Next, the contemporary variety of subnational mobilisation is compared with each model. The final section points at some implications for representative democracy in the Euro-polity.

Interests can be represented on the European arena through various channels. One form of representation – through state executives and unelected European institutions – has been heavily criticised during the Maastricht debate. Another way to aggregate interests is through subnational mobilisation in the European arena. Subnational interests encompass all territorial definitions below the national state: regions, local, interlocal and interregional collectivities. In the European reality, regions, in particular those with elected authorities, are the core players. Subnational mobilisation is first placed in a broader understanding of the Euro-polity. Thereafter the varied pattern of subnational-EU links is analysed in the light of three competing conceptions of the Euro-polity.

MODELS OF THE EURO-POLITY AND SUBNATIONAL MOBILISATION

The debate about how the Euro-polity[1] compares with traditional representative democracies is not new. Observers usually agree that it compares poorly. Opinions differ on how interests are aggregated and represented, and how lines of authority and accountability run. These divergent opinions stem from fundamentally different conceptions of how the European Union works.

Some analyses argue that the national state has been strengthened as a result of European integration. They could be grouped under the label of the state-centric model.[2] European integration is perceived as an international regime, designed by sovereign states which each seek to manage economic interdependence by engaging in international collaboration.[3] Control remains vested in the constituent units, the member states.

The traditional competitor of this state-centric model argues that the dynamics of supranationalism are eroding state sovereignty.[4] This is the supranational model: a compound polity has emerged where competencies are distributed among the general European and the constituent governing bodies, and where each is empowered to deal directly with the citizenry in the exercise of those competencies. The European polity has increasingly acquired features of a federation.[5] Control has partly shifted to the supranational level, which has an independent impact on the outcome.

The contrasting descriptions of the state-centric and supranational model have recently been questioned by a third group of scholars, who have put forward a pattern of multi-level governance.[6] They take from the supranational model that European integration has fundamentally transformed the national state in Europe. It has led to a European polity, not an international regime, where the supranational institutions have independent influence on European policy making. However, they also accept from the state-centric model that state executives are unlikely to be superseded by supranational institutions. National arenas are not going to be rendered obsolete by transnational interest mobilisation. State executives have lost their monopoly, though; in fact, decision-making competencies are shared among actors. The emerging picture is that of a polity with multiple, interlocked arenas for political contest. The European level is one of them, where state executives, but also European institutions and a widening array of mobilised interests contend.

The state-centric model leads to a confederal Europe, constructed around essentially voluntary collaboration among powerful national states; the supranational model sketches the contours of a European federation, where an autonomous supranational level has the resources to override national state interests in particular instances; multi-level governance amounts to a multi-layered polity, where there is no centre of accumulated authority, but where changing combinations of supranational, national and subnational governments engage in collaboration. Each model generates distinct expectations about subnational mobilisation.

There is little room for direct subnational mobilisation in the state-centric model. Transnational contacts among local or regional authorities and interactions with the Commission are scarce and peripheral. To the limited extent they have grown, they are likely to buttress state executive power. Subnational actors need member states to further their interests in the European arena, because the latter are and remain the gatekeepers. The relationship between subnational actors and the member state is therefore hierarchical.

National institutions and practices determine the degree and nature of subnational mobilisation, not European or subnational pressure. Hence the differences across the European territory are enormous and are likely to remain so. In other words, the German Länder acquired the right to be involved in European decision making in their areas of competence, because this is in line with how they are entrenched in the German federal system, not because of an alliance between them and European institutions. It is unlikely to be emulated by other subnational actors in a totally different national context.

Subnational interests mobilise predominantly along national lines, not cross-cutting national constituencies. The default standard of aggregation is the member state. So the German Länder participate predominantly through the German channel, essentially through the German Permanent Representation. Finally, subnational input does nothing to mitigate the elitist and bureaucratic nature of European decision making; subnational interests in the European arena are represented by a select group of civil servants and political executives, excluding broader political or social actors. All in all, according to the state-centric model, Europe is and is likely to remain, a *Europe des patries*.

That is in stark contrast to the supranational model, where a European federation compounded of smaller, more natural units (regions) built around a strong supranational core is the most likely outcome: a *Europe of the Regions*. Subnational mobilisation is perceived as an instrument to challenge state power, and to support supranational authority. Subnational units compete with member states for control over territorial interest aggregation. So the relationship is one of contested hierarchy, in which the supranational arena is expected to be on the side of the subnational level.

Subnational interests are mainly mobilised in functional niches around specific policy issues, usually with a European-wide span. They organise around supranational institutions, first of all the European Commission and in the second place the European Parliament, as member state channels tend to be hostile. The European Commission plays an entrepreneurial role in shaping the functional niches, which are expected to spill over into other areas and from there into politics, gradually building an uninterrupted, and uniform, subnational political tier. Hence the uneven pattern of subnational mobilisation will ultimately disappear. In other words, subnational actors are likely to be empowered not only in Germany or Belgium, but also in Portugal, Greece, or France, despite the much stronger national constraints under which the latter operate.

Finally, while member states have an interest in keeping the European decision process elitist to preserve their monopoly of representation over their constituencies, supranational institutions must nurture constituencies and therefore need to exploit any potential counterweight to national power. They are likely to encourage a pluralist setting, which would be open not only to bureaucrats or political executives, but also to regionalist movements, subnational interest groups, local action groups, and other alternative sources of interest aggregation.

Multi-level governance is the only model where regions would be a governmental level of importance next to national, European and local arenas. This Europe cannot be one of the national states, nor of the regions, but only a *Europe with the Regions*. Subnational units do not need member states to have access to the European arena. In fact, regional authorities in particular are important additional channels to tie newly mobilised interests to Europe. Subnational mobilisation does not erode, but complements the aggregating role of member states. Hierarchical relationships are weak but interdependence is high. Actors are linked through networks, which span several levels and in which each actor brings in valuable resources.

Subnational mobilisation has grown considerably, as clear hierarchical lines of authority have been eroded. It is spread unequally across European territory and comes in many guises: narrow functional or political mandate, European-wide associations, or a selection of subnational actors, etc. Like the state-centric model, but for different reasons, the multi-level governance model predicts that this multi-faceted picture is likely to be permanent. That means that German Länder will most likely always participate more strongly and through more channels in European decision-making than Irish, or even French, regions, because they can bring in more resources. Even though subnational actors will undoubtedly converge through transnational learning or competition, it is unlikely to lead to a uniform subnational layer as the supranational model implies.

There is no predominant territorial principle, according to which subnational interests are organised: European-wide, along national lines, various selections of European territory, individually. These various associations are clustered around European institutions, that is to say, the Council, the European Commission and the European Parliament. In addition, they set up independent institutions in the European arena.

The politics of multi-level governance is pluralist but with an elitist bias. There are no gatekeepers to close off the European arena, and resources for effective policy-making need to be collected from multiple arenas and actors. It also has an elitist edge, to the extent that only actors with valuable resources are likely to extract participation. Some subnational actors in Europe are better endowed than others, and, within each, bureaucrats and political executives are usually better bestowed than oppositional forces, collective action groups and movements, or private actors. Multi-level governance does not therefore anticipate a uniformly open playing field for mobilising interests.

SUBNATIONAL PRESENCE IN EUROPE

Mazey and Richardson have argued that 'interest groups ... act as a weather-vane for the locus of political power in society', and Marks and McAdam have refined the logic for subnational interests.[7] So the pattern of subnational interest formation in the European Union should be a reliable pointer to the nature of the Euro-polity: state-centric, supranational, or multi-layered.

First, what is the primary arena for European decision making? To the extent that competencies shift from the national to the European plane, subnational actors can be expected to mobilise into the European arena.

Second, which actors gain from the transfer of competencies? If the Commission or Parliament win, one would expect a circle of mobilised subnational interests around those supranational institutions; if the Council of Ministers gains, subnational interests would cluster around that institution, in addition to existing national channels.

Third, how extensive is the shift of power? Subnational authorities will most likely want to institutionalise their position in the European decision-making process, if it affects a wide range of interests. So, depending on the model, one could expect either the extrapolation of national institutional arrangements into the European arena, or the insertion of special guarantees for subnational interests in the existing supranational institutions, or the creation of another European institution for subnational interests – independent from the existing institution. In other words, in addition to lobbying and pressure politics, subnational actors can be expected to demand some form of shared rule.

Finally, what kind of organisational channels do they use? Do they follow an individual or a collective strategy? Collective channels range from representation in partial (based on geographical, sectoral, or functional principles) or encompassing *national* associations, to representation in partial or encompassing *transnational* associations. National channels are most likely when the Euro-polity resembles the state-centric model; all-European transnational channels would prevail under the supranational model; a mixture would be most likely under multi-level governance. Tables 1 to 3 give a snapshot of the situation as of mid-1994.

Table 1 summarises the forms of institutionalised access to the European arena. The most powerful channel would be representation encompassing the whole EU, independent from other institutions, and with decision-making power. Institutionalisation did not happen until after the Single European Act, the 'sympathetic and lethargic society meeting' of the Parliamentary Intergroup excepted.[8] Two channels were put in place by the Treaty of European Union of 1993, largely as a result of pressure by the German Länder on their federal government; the third one was created a few years before.

Under the new Article 146[9] of the Treaty, a member state can *send regional ministers to the Council of Ministers*, who are allowed to negotiate and bind the member state. So regional authorities can be at the centre of decision making. However, the channel is highly selective. Only Belgian regions (and communities) and German Länder have in practice access to it. The Spanish regions have demanded a similar arrangement, with no success thus far; the Austrian Länder would probably also take advantage of the new procedure. It is unlikely to be of use for subnational authorities in other member states. Furthermore, regional participation is nested in the member state, not independent from it; it does not disturb the delicate balance between member states. Regional ministers from Belgium are first of all Belgian representatives, and only secondly spokespersons for regional territorial interests – and then only of the shared interests of all Belgian regions, not those of their particular region.

The other innovation of the Treaty is the *Committee of the Regions*. Contrary to the Article 146 arrangement, the Committee has a guaranteed representation of all member states. It is independent, be it organisationally associated with the Economic and Social Committee. Several features weaken the Committee's capacity to act cohesively for subnational interests. Subnational representatives are appointed by their member state governments. All operate ultimately as national representatives, but the national mould restricts some more than others. It is fairly constraining in France, where not all regions and only a handful of localities have a representative, and the UK, where the 24 representatives of the UK are picked by the central government to represent a patchwork of local and 'regional' authorities. National constraints are virtually absent for the Belgian, Spanish, and German regions: each region has its own seat (or sometimes more than one) in the Committee of the Regions.

TABLE 1
INSTITUTIONALISED CHANNELS FOR SUBNATIONAL INTERESTS IN THE EUROPEAN ARENA

CHANNELS	ORIGIN	WHO?	ROLE
Article 146 (Council of Ministers)	Treaty of European Union (1993)	Ministers. German Länder and Belgian Regions/ Communities (contested in Spain)	To **decide** (vote) on regional competencies in Council of Ministers. *Collective* strategy (in member state).
Committee of Regions and Local Authorities (**Independent institution**)	Treaty of European Union (1993)	Representatives by and large from elected subnational authorities. **Whole EU.**	**Mandatory consultation** by Council and Commission on five policy areas. **Own initiative opinions** on other matters. *Collective* strategy.
Consultative Council of Regional and Local Authorities (CCRLA) (attached to the **Commission**)	Commission decision (1988) Abolished in 1993	Representatives appointed by AER and CEMR. **Whole EU.** Equal weight for local and regional representatives for each member state.	**Non-mandatory consultation** by Commission on structural funds policy. *Collective* strategy.
Partnership under structural funds (with **member state** and **Commission**)	1990/1991-1993 New round: 1994-1997/99	Civil servants, sometimes social partners. **Part of EU.** 40% population (mainly least developed areas)	**Policy instrument**. *Individual* strategy (in member state).
Intergroup of Local and Regional Representatives in **European Parliament**	1980	MEPs with elected mandate at regional or local level. Variable membership **across EU.**	**Exchange between EP and subnational authorities.** Dormant existence. *Collective* strategy.

Second, the Committee is internally severely divided. The major conflict is between local and regional interests. The representatives are mostly regional in Belgium, Germany, France, Spain and Italy, while local nominees dominate in Denmark, Ireland, Greece, Luxembourg, the Netherlands, Portugal, and the UK. The local-regional divide[10] comes largely down to a conflict between federal or regionalised countries and unitary member states. It is cross-cut by a rift between northern Europe and southern Europe, which is not only about divergent economic interests between contributors and beneficiaries of the EU budget, but also has a cultural-political dimension with a clash between political styles.[11]

Finally and most importantly, the Committee has only advisory powers, not a co-decision right. It must be consulted by the Council or the Commission (not the Parliament) on five matters: education and vocational training, health, culture, trans-European networks, and economic and social cohesion. It may also provide opinions on any other matter. Ultimately, the Committee has to rely on persuasion or on those members who could pressure their national governments (Belgian, German and Spanish regions in particular).[12]

The third significant institutional channel is confined to *structural funds policy*. It consists of several hundred *partnership arrangements* (monitoring committees). The 1988 reform stipulates that the Commission, national authorities, regional or local authorities and social actors work in close, equal and ongoing partnership.[13] The role of the monitoring committees is restricted to policy management, most often of a day-to-day technical-bureaucratic nature, not of a political character. Partnerships compile and organise development programmes (within broadly defined objectives), manage and follow up ongoing projects. Another limitation is the strict national mould in which the committees work. In the most decentralised cases, a committee connects the Commission with an individual region, with or without the presence of national representatives; more often, the Commission's sparring partner is the national bureaucracy, while subnational representatives participate in a junior position. The arrangements provide individual access to Europe, but the operation does not encourage subnational authorities to develop collective strategies.

This uniform set of rules has produced a highly uneven pattern of subnational mobilisation across the Community: partly by design, because regional policy is by definition a discriminatory policy. About 40 per cent of the population is covered by the structural funds, of which the whole of Spain, Portugal, Ireland and Greece (the four cohesion countries), and major parts of the UK, Belgium, Italy, Eastern Germany, and Luxembourg. Within those selected areas, partnership has worked out differently from one member state to another.[14] In Belgium and Germany, national authorities are hardly present. In Spain, the role of Madrid is in general limited for the funds that are divided by region (about half of the budget), although the impact of the centre varies from one region to another. In the three smaller cohesion countries and the UK, subnational authorities are very weak. Yet, even here the impact of EU policy is being felt. Ireland and Greece have set up a regional administrative tier to comply with the EU partnership rules. Although neither of these adjustments have caused an observable shift of power away from the central government, the dynamics of EU cohesion policy-making are rapidly changing. In both cases, the regional monitoring committees have provided subnational actors with fora for closer communication with national and European authorities, and for a greater awareness of their interests in EU cohesion policy and their possible contribution to making policy. Comparison of the negotiation round for the 1994–99 with the 1989–93 period shows that their input has been enhanced.[15] The French case is a difficult one. The complex relations between local and national politics as well as politicians and bureaucrats make an unambiguous assessment difficult.[16]

The Committee of the Regions replaced the *Consultative Council of Regional and Local Authorities* (CCRLA). The latter had been attached by the European Commission to its Directorate General for Regional Policy (DG XVI) in 1988.[17] The members were appointed by two European-wide subnational associations, the Assembly of European Regions (AER) and the Council for European Municipalities and Regions (CEMR). The Council was expected to give greater legitimacy to the Commission's role in the recently reformed cohesion policy.[18] In reality, the Council played an unassuming role until it was abolished in 1993. It lacked independence: the agenda was set by the Commission. There was a major cleavage between regional and local authorities.

TABLE 2

INSTITUTIONALISED CHANNELS FOR SUBNATIONAL INTERESTS IN THE NATIONAL ARENA

CHANNELS	ORIGIN	WHO?	ROLE
Mandatory approval of Treaty revisions by subnational authorities	Germany (from beginning) Belgium (1980, 1989 and 1993)	Elected assemblies.	**Assent.** Germany: *collective* strategy Belgium: *individual* strategy
Regional observer attached to the **member state's** Permanent Representation	Germany (1970s) Belgium (1989-90) Portugal (?) Spain (planned)	Civil servants. **German Länder, some Belgian regions, some Portuguese regions**	Two-way **information.** Right to attend Council meetings. Germany: *collective* Belgium: *individual*
Council working groups.	Germany (1986) Belgium (1993) Portugal (?)	Civil servants. **Germany, Belgium, Portugal**	Germany, Belgium: **decision making** on own competencies (*collective*). Portugal: **advice** (*individual?*).
Commission working groups	idem (not Portugal)	idem (not Portugal)	idem
Regional electoral districts for **European parliamentary** elections	1979	Direct elections. **Belgium and Germany** (partly); Ireland, UK and Italy no national districts, but the districts are not coinciding with regions.	

The institutionalised EU channels have produced a highly uneven pattern of actual subnational mobilisation, even though they are in principle applicable across the EU. Regions with strong entrenchment in their domestic context, that is to say, the Belgian and German regions, have exploited the opportunities; others have not done so. The same bias appears with respect to national channels for subnational EU participation. Table 2 lists the most formalised domestic arrangements. Only Germany and Belgium have systematically taken the route of national institutionalisation. The Spanish autonomous communities are negotiating similar arrangements with Madrid. The surprise is Portugal, where the regions of Madeira and the Azores have obtained some (soft) guarantees. They have a regional observer in the permanent representation, and are allowed to attend certain Council working groups.

Germany and Belgium represent two models. The former has taken a gradual and moderate path, while the latter has changed radically over a short period of time; German regions have also generally worked collectively, while Belgian regions usually link up separately with the European arena. The latter distinction runs through nearly all arrangements. German Länder share a regional observer (Länderbeobachter) in the German Permanent Representation. For Belgium, the Walloon Region and the French Community have each one regional observer, while Flanders has not appointed a representative. The distinction between the two approaches is clearest in the regional role in Treaty ratification processes. While in Germany the Bundesrat (hence the collective chamber) votes on Treaty changes, in Belgium this is not a matter for the Senate only (the Belgian federal chamber), but for each regional and community assembly separately. Within the same logic, the German Bundesrat casts its vote over the whole Treaty – not only matters affecting regional competencies – while the Belgian regions and communities only vote on those Treaty parts affecting their competencies. Finally, the same distinction is reflected in the design of the electoral districts for the European elections. The German system works partly with a national district, partly with regional districts. The Belgian districts are regional.[19]

The distinction between a collective and individual approach rests upon fundamentally different premises. The *German position* accepts that regions are the third level in a multi-layered European polity, and that they are ultimately nested in a national arena. The *Belgian model* discards the national mould; Europe is a polity with multiple actors at multiple levels who act directly with European institutions within their competencies.

Formal channels are by no means the only ways to involve subnational authorities in European decision-making. Most member states have developed practices to take territorially diverse interests into account. In the

UK delegation in Brussels, the Welsh and Scottish administrations are represented indirectly through appointments in functional areas of special concern to them. So European fisheries policy and regional policy tend to be monitored by civil servants from the Scottish Office. However, these civil servants work ultimately within a unitary framework.[20] Similarly, the French system of *cumul de mandats*, in combination with party allegiance, can give regional politicians – not necessarily regional administrations – considerable room to influence the French position.

TABLE 3a

NON-INSTITUTIONALISED CHANNELS FOR SUBNATIONAL INTERESTS

CHANNELS	ORIGIN	WHO?	ROLE
Regional Offices (**Independent actor**)	First two in 1985 Rapid expansion from 1990.	Civil servants, some private input. **Belgian, German, Spanish, French, UK, Danish (cities) authorities, a few transnational alliances** 40-45% population.	**Two-way information and lobbying.** *Individual* strategy (some collaborative efforts).
AER--Assembly of European Regions. (**Independent peak organisation**)	1985	Elected regional representatives. **European-wide membership** (not confined to EU) Weak in Ireland, Denmark, the UK (southeast), Greece. 80-85% population.	Political **spokesman** for regions, **lobbying**, **umbrella** for interregional collaboration. *Collective* strategy.
CEMR--Council for /European Municipalities and Regions (**Independent peak organisation**)	1984 (early roots: 1951)	Confederation of national peak organisations. **European-wide membership.**	Political **spokesman** for local authorities, **umbrella** for collaborative projects, lobbying. *Collective* strategy.

Moving from formal to informal ways of influencing European decisions, the picture changes dramatically. Table 3a and 3b summarise only the most significant instruments, radically simplifying a very complex picture.[21] Three features stand out. Although the informal channels, like the institutionalised forms, produce an uneven pattern of subnational mobilisation, the inequality is less stark. It is more a matter of degree than of kind: regions have more opportunities than local authorities, and the wealthier parts of the EU do generally better than less well-off areas.

Furthermore, subnational authorities mobilise along two distinct paths. Some enter the European arena according to a sort of free market logic. Others are pulled into the European arena by the European Commission and by large encompassing representative associations. The pushing and pulled authorities form relatively distinct groups; together, they cover pretty much the whole EU. Finally, somewhat different from the institutionalised channels, subnational authorities don't choose between collective and individual strategies, but use both.

A spectacular 'push-form' of subnational mobilisation has been the growth of *Regional Offices in Brussels*. There are currently about 70 Offices, up from two in 1985, to 15 in 1988, and 54 in 1993. Their role lies somewhere between an informal 'embassy' for their particular region and a lobbying agency. They provide the Commission and Parliament with regional viewpoints on issues that concern them; they survey the European scene for upcoming issues and bring them to the attention of policy-makers in their home governments; they participate in networks with other regional offices or with other organisations; they provide a rudimentary welcome service to private actors from their region; and they lobby for a greater voice in EU decision-making.

Only a minority of the regions are represented in Brussels, which account for 40–45 per cent of the population. All German, all Spanish, all French regions, one Belgian region, many British local and regional authorities, and three Danish local authorities have set up a regional office. By early 1994 there was not a single office from Portugal, Ireland, and Greece, nor from the Netherlands nor Luxembourg; the Italian office for the Mezzogiorno is run by the national administration. The great majority are individual offices, although there are some collaborative efforts. Two offices represent transnational alliances: the French-Spanish Centre-Atlantique (Centre, Poitou-Charentes, Castile-Leon), and the British-French Essex-Picardie.

The incentives and the capacity to run an 'embassy' in Brussels are unevenly spread among subnational actors. The regions most likely to be present are strongly entrenched in their domestic context (federal or regionalised structure), have a distinct regional identity, or have had a different party-political orientation from the national level over an extended time period. There is no significant relationship between structural funding and regional representation, which suggests that EU funding does not encourage regions to establish *independent* footholds in Brussels. The structural funds have facilitated dependent forms of subnational mobilisation, either institutionalised through the nationally defined partnerships (see above) or informal through Commission efforts (see later).[22]

The regional/ local cleavage among subnational authorities has given rise to two distinct peak organisations at the European level: the Assembly of European Regions (AER) and the Council for European Municipalities and Regions (CEMR). Both emerged independently from EU initiatives, have a membership that reaches well into Scandinavia and Eastern Europe, and staff permanent offices in Brussels.

The *Assembly of European Regions* was founded by nine interregional associations in 1985. The members are the nine founding organisations and regions on an individual basis. The Assembly had some 235 member regions in 1993. The representatives come in principle from elected regional parliaments.[23] The AER members speak for 80–85 per cent of the EU population. The blind spots are in Ireland, Greece, the United Kingdom (mainly the south-east) and Denmark. The organisation has developed a close working relationship with the European Commission, particularly in the area of structural funds but also on institutional issues. It has pushed for an increased involvement of the regions in European decision making, such as a Committee of the Regions, the inclusion of the subsidiarity principle in the Treaty, and the changed wording of Article 146. The AER appointed the regional members in the CCRLA. It was also instrumental in the practical preparation for the Committee of the Regions, although its relations with the new body have become tenuous.[24] The Assembly seems set to become a more traditional interest group organisation as soon as the Committee of the Regions gains greater standing. The *Council of European Municipalities and Regions* (CEMR), the European section of the International Union of Local Authorities (IULA), has early roots in 1951. Although its current name (dating from 1984) suggests differently, it really represents local interests. Its role on the European arena is very similar to that of the AER.

All three channels pursue predominantly a political agenda. While the regional offices allow regional authorities to do that individually, the CEMR and the AER speak for the whole European Union. The next three types of instruments have essentially a functional or policy-oriented purpose. All three focus on transnational collaboration; naturally they use a collective strategy. Yet they are also rather exclusive 'clubs', not encompassing associations, because they bring together subnational authorities that share particular functional characteristics. For all three, access to EU funding is the main goal, although that purpose has variable importance. The main distinction between the three types lies in the role of the European Commission during their creation. The first type is predominantly a spin-off from Commission initiatives; it is the intended result of public policy. The second and third type have emerged bottom-up, often long before the European Commission had a policy for those issues. They became subsequently somehow affiliated with the European Commission, or even incorporated in the Commission networks, hence influencing public policy.

TABLE 3b
NON-INSTITUTIONAL CHANNELS FOR SUBNATIONAL INTERESTS

CHANNELS (continued)	ORIGIN	WHO?	ROLE
Structural Funds networks (**Commission patronship**)	1990s	Politicians and civil servants. **Partial** trans-European associations around **specific** Structural Funds initiatives.	**Exchange of experience, implementors** for Commission, **lobbying.** *Collective* strategy (subset of authorities)
Independent interregional and interlocal associations	1970s onwards	Politicians, civil servants. Partial trans-European associations of **areas with common problems;** mainly in **least developed areas.**	**Aggregation, lobbying and coordination** of collaborative projects; **implementor** for Commission. *Collective* strategy (subset of areas).
Independent collaborative projects and associations	1980s	Business, civil servants, politicians. **Partial** trans-European associations; mainly **in advanced areas of EU.**	**Technical and political** collaboration, lobbying. *Collective* strategy. (subset of areas)

The European Commission manages a budget of 178 billion Ecu for *structural funds* policy over the period 1994–99. The budget falls into three categories. About 90 per cent is allocated to the multi-annual programmes, as agreed by member state, and Commission in the second half of 1993 (Community Support Frameworks). Over the remaining 9–10 per cent the Commission has the last say, as long as the money is spent on broadly defined priority lines (Community initiatives), which have been agreed by the member states, and provided about 70 per cent of the budget goes to the least developed regions. In addition, the Commission has also some pocket money for pilot projects, innovative action and networking. The Commission has been very active in organising subnational interests.

For most networks, it is often difficult to determine whether the initiative came from the Commission or from subnational entrepreneurs. In principle, the goal is to attach a network or organisation to each Community programme or initiative. So there are large associations for objective two regions and for objective one regions, but also smaller ones around Community initiatives like Leader (local networks in rural areas), Rechar (help on coalmining areas), Retex (textile areas), or Renaval (shipbuilding).[25] Some are regional, others composed of local authorities. These networks counteract in a soft way the vertical segmentation of the EU structural funds policy, which keeps the implementation of regional policy-making entirely within the national mould: horizontal coordination across national borders is not required, nor is communication among individual regions within the national framework.

In addition, the Commission runs several specific networking programmes to organise European space beyond the areas of the structural funds. One is the *Exchange of Experience Programme* (EEP), which was initiated by the European Parliament in 1989 and then adopted (and part-financed) by the Commission. The programme aims at promoting the transfer of know-how between developed and disadvantaged regions. The basic requirement is very simple: three regions from three different countries must agree on a project of 12–18 months. In 1993 alone more than 100 of the almost 160 regions of the EU completed over 60 projects. The AER helps the Commission in overseeing the implementation of the programme (AER documentation).

While the networks in the EEP programme may fade when the project is completed, *Recite* (Regions and Cities of Europe, launched in 1991 by the Commission) funds not projects but 37 networks around a broad range of subjects and with a variety of partners. They supplement the more substantial structural funds networks, by giving priority to 'self-help' exchange programmes between unlikely sparring partners in the European Union. So *Roc Nord* is a Danish-Crete network, in which the Danes share know-how in economic and environmental planning with Crete. The *Quartiers en crise* project exchanges experiences between 25 cities on problems of social exclusion. In *Dionysos*, ten French, Italian, Spanish and Portuguese wine-growing regions pool resources to transfer technology to the least-developed regions among them. The CEMR acts as the intermediary between the subnational authorities and the Commission on *Recite* projects.

A second set of networks has *roots outside the European Union framework*. Some go back to the 1970s, such as most networks around the founding members of the AER. Each association brings together regions with common territorial features or policy problems: the Association of European Border Regions (AEBR), the Conference of Peripheral Maritime Regions (CPMR), the three Alpes associations, the Working Community of the Pyrenees, the Working Community of the Jura, and the Association of European Regions of Industrial Technology (RETI – in fact regions in industrial decline). Analyses on whether and how these organisations have made a difference are scarce, and they tend to disagree, depending on whether one emphasises tangible policy outputs or the slower process of changing social and political relations. Some, like the Border Regions, and recently RETI, have become influential pressure groups with the European institutions.[26]

A crucial factor determining their effectiveness as lobbyists is their capacity to recruit widely. And here, most associations face a dilemma. On the one hand, the European Commission has consistently been reluctant to deal with deficiently representative organisations.[27] On the other hand, the Commission is unable to reward organised members and 'punish' non-organised actors; it is committed to a generally applicable and objective policy. That confronts an association often with serious collective action problems, which are worsened by the fact that potential members are usually very unequal (from local to regional authorities, and from weak to very strong authorities) and that there is often no concrete agenda. Regions are therefore not keen to invest energy in a difficult enterprise knowing that they would benefit in any case from the association's eventual success.[28]

The large encompassing associations do not face these collective action problems to the same degree. Even though the diversity of members and interests often causes significant strains within the organisations, they have been accepted by the Commission as the most representative interlocutors for subnational interests. The AER runs now a few policy-specific networks on its own. In 1989 it started the Interregional Cultural Network (ICON) for the exchange of information and the implementation of joint projects. It has intensified collaboration between the European regions' cultural administrations. In 1993 it received some funding from the EU (AER documentation). Similar initiatives emerged around local authorities associations over the past 20 years.

The networks in this second type seem to share a concern to reduce disparities or imbalances. Most focus on, or include, less well-off areas of the EU, which are often in desperate need for EU money for restructuring and development. Hence, they represent the bottom-up cohesion effort by subnational authorities, but have in the process become dependent on the European Commission.

The last category of *networks has emerged from a position of strength in the European Union*. The most famous example is the Four Motors arrangement between Baden-Württemberg, Rhône-Alpes, Catalonia and Lombardy, which combines the most dynamic regions in their respective countries. The purpose of the 1988 agreement is to promote technological collaboration, research and development, and economic and cultural exchanges. The signatories of the agreement explicitly endorse greater European integration. Wales established links with the four in 1990 and 1991. Essentially, the regional governments act as brokers, who set a broad regulatory framework and bring interested parties together, while the decisions about possible collaboration are mainly left to business or other private actors. Other examples are the Euroregio partnerships, such as the Euroregio encompassing the dynamic three-country meeting area of

Maastricht (NL)-Liège (B)-Hasselt (B)-Aachen (G)-Cologne (G). On the local side, many long-standing town-twinning schemes have been extended to economic partnerships and trading and technology transfers. The open-textured nature of networking makes it very difficult to come up with reliable data on the density of the networks. The British Audit Commission estimated that 22 per cent of the British local councils are involved in programmes outside the structural funds.[29]

This third category of networks is more driven by a market logic. Subnational political leaders and civil servants act as 'ministers of external trade' for their subnational territory. That role is in line with the current paradigm in regional development policy, where subnational political leaders are expected to act as brokers rather than development planners.[30] The success of brokers does not depend on their having direct control over services, but on their political connections with those controlling services and money. In other words, leaders from Baden-Württemberg do not have to create new services nor spend large sums on projects, but mobilise resources from the private sector and from the European coffers.

MULTI-LEVEL SUBNATIONAL MOBILISATION AND THE CRISIS OF
REPRESENTATION

Subnational mobilisation has accelerated since the mid-1980s. The pivotal moment is the SEA and the internal market programme. Since then, the European polity has come to resemble multi-level governance much closer than either the state-centric or supranational model. A variety of channels and strategies are available; some are clustered around the Commission, a few weak ones around the European Parliament, others around the Council of Ministers, yet still others are national, and there are several independent channels of subnational mobilisation; the opportunities to use them are unevenly distributed; there are as yet few signs of a 'shake-out' of less efficient forms of representation, suggesting that the uneven and complex pattern of mobilisation has structural rather than conjunctural causes.

Actual access to these channels is determined by three distinct, but interrelated properties. First, institutionalised channels are on average much more effective routes to European decision making than non-institutionalised channels. The latter's role is usually confined to aggregation, consultation, or co-decision on technical and narrow matters. Second, the subnational community is sharply bifurcated between those who have access to the institutionalised channels and those who have not. The 'have's' constitute a very select group: the Belgian and German* regions. The Committee of the Regions is an exception, but it is also one of the weakest institutionalised access opportunities. Third, the overall pattern of mobilisation is one of ordinal hierarchy, in which an actor with access to a stronger channel usually makes use, too, of all weaker routes. So strong and weak actors do not operate in clearly segregated access markets; rather, the more powerful actors have privileged access to a sub-market of a larger, more varied array of participative opportunities.

What does this uneven and complex pattern mean for the democratic representativeness of Europe? It is clear that there are alternative channels to the somewhat tarnished state executives. However, the opportunities for using these channels are unevenly distributed. Some areas are likely to lose out. As a consequence, it may paradoxically be more difficult to arrive at genuinely *representative* policy decisions. The subnational actors most likely to be involved are a privileged subset: regions rather than local authorities, domestically well-entrenched authorities more than weakly institutionalised or contesting regions, resource-rich rather than poor regions, that is to say, the Belgian and German regions, but not the Greek local authorities. Moreover, the *democratic* character, the capacity for the citizens (through their intermediaries) to wield effective power, is low for most channels of subnational mobilisation. There is an inverse relationship between the accessibility of these channels and their decision-making capacity.

How could the lack of open subnational mobilisation against the European Union be interpreted? By and large, subnational authorities and non-secessionist regionalists support a federal-type EU, and by implication a more autonomous supranational core. Secessionist nationalists would like to see a confederal Europe, which brings them closer to the position of state nationalists. Some were originally negatively disposed to European integration, but their scepticism tended to abate when they arrived on the European scene.

Subnational opposition may not be emerging either because institutional hurdles keep opposition out or because the European Commission and the subnational actors have shared interests. Anti-European subnational actors would have to climb many hurdles to stage a persistent, visible, and viable opposition. Thus, the European electoral system tends to favour larger, usually moderate parties.

The possibilities for organised extra-parliamentarian opposition are even more limited. The multi-level political structure does not provide action groups with a clearly identifiable target. It is also very difficult to organise an opposition consisting of territorially dispersed pockets and culturally and ideologically disparate parties. Even the handful of nationalist and regionalist parties in the European Parliament have to date not been able to form a fraction.

Furthermore, the issue of Euro optimism or scepticism is firmly owned by nationally organised groups and political parties. More resourceful national actors have pre-empted the terrain of subnational or European-wide anti-Europeanism. Oddly enough, the national arena seems also the most effective arena for actors without resources, such as fishing or agricultural communities in distress. 'Those without resources have only their numbers, potential disruptiveness, and electoral clout' to make authorities listen to their needs.[31] In Europe, national authorities are responsible for law and order, and the most powerful political leaders are elected nationally. So it makes sense to target national governments even for demands which evolve from European policies (like fisheries).

Another reason for weak anti-Europeanism among subnational actors is the extent to which supranational and subnational actors share certain common interests. Several channels for subnational mobilisation are the outcome of an alliance between the Commission and the larger representative subnational organisations. In addition, the Commission has eagerly subsidised bottom-up subnational initiatives *provided* that these enterprises are transnational and recruit European-wide. The expectation is that these functional ties will pave the way for a greater political role for subnational authorities in European decision making.[32]

At first sight, the creation of the Committee of the Regions and the revised Article 146 on the Council of Ministers seem to make this strategy credible. Yet there are reasons to believe that the coalition between the Commission and subnational authorities may be fragile, especially in a framework of multi-level governance.

The timing and the form of a European institutionalisation of subnational mobilisation was to a significant degree prescribed by the domestic needs of the German federal government, which needed a European solution to break the domestic deadlock with the Länder. Furthermore, the Commission's support for a stronger political presence of subnational authorities was at best lukewarm during the negotiations. Despite earlier statements by Jacques Delors in favour of political representation,[33] it recommended in its Opinion of June 1991 on a Committee of the Regions essentially a polished version of the Consultative Council for Local and Regional Authorities: a composition of regional and local authorities rather than regions only, affiliation with the Commission rather than independent status, no right of initiative, a predominantly technical agenda rather than a political role.

The Commission was faced with a serious dilemma. While a greater *political* role for subnational authorities would in theory undermine state-centric tendencies, an independent political *presence* for subnational authorities would become another form of political *control* on the Commission, weakening the main supranational actor in the arena and ultimately strengthening state-centrism.

This places the Commission for a choice. It could either slow down subnational mobilisation and forsake possible allies against member state executives, or it could promote subnational mobilisation and take the risk of being controlled from either political intermediary. It also forces the dilemma upon subnational authorities, which can either exercise their independent political power and risk weakening the most accessible actor, the Commission, or restraining themselves to functional collaboration with the Commission and improving European access through national channels, hence accepting the unequal opportunities for representation. In the medium-to-long run, the alliance between some, if not all, subnational authorities and the European Commission may simply be untenable.

NOTES

1. As Philippe Schmitter recently reminded us, 'it is the particular mix of territorial and functional constituencies, along with their corresponding relations of authority and accountability that defines the type of polity'. Philippe C.Schmitter, 'Representation and the Future Euro-Polity', *Staatswissenschaften und Staatspraxis* 3/3 (1992), p.383.
2. See, e.g., Stanley Hoffmann, 'Obstinate or obsolete? The Fate of the Nation-State and the Case of Western Europe', *Daedalus,* 85/3, (Summer 1966); idem, 'Reflections on the nation-state in Western Europe today', *Journal of Common Market Studies* 20/1–2 (1982), pp.29–37; Paul Taylor, 'The European Community and the State: Assumptions, Theories and Propositions', *Review of International Studies* 17 (1991), pp.109–25; Andrew Moravcsik, 'Preferences and Power in the European Community: A Liberal Intergovernmentalist Approach', *Journal of Common Market Studies* 31/4 (1993), pp.473–524; Andrew Moravcsik, 'Why the European Community Strengthens the State: Domestic Politics and International Cooperation', Presented at the American Political Science Assoc., New York, 1-4 Sept.1994; Andrew Moravcsik, 'Negotiating the Single European Act', in R.Keohane, S.Hoffmann (eds.) *The New European Community. Decisionmaking and Institutional Change* (Boulder, CO: Westview Press, 1991), pp.41–84.
3. Robert Keohane, and Stanley Hoffmann, 'Institutional Change in Europe in the 1980s', in R.Keohane, S.Hoffmann (eds.). *The New European Community. Decisionmaking and Institutional Change* (Boulder: Westview Press, 1991), pp.1–40; Robert Keohane, *After Hegemony: Cooperation and Discord in the World Political Economy* (Princeton, NJ: Princeton UP, 1984).
4. Ernst B.Haas, *Beyond the Nation-State: Functionalism and International Organization* (Stanford, CA: Stanford UP, 1964); Leon N.Lindberg, S.A. Scheingold, *Europe's would-be polity: Patterns of Change in the European Community* (Englewood Cliffs, NJ: Prentice Hall, 1970).
5. For a definition of federation, see Daniel Elazar, *Exploring Federalism* (Alabama: Univ. of Alabama Press, 1987). On Europe and federalism, see, e.g., Michael Burgess, *Federalism and European Union: political ideas, influences, and strategies in the EC, 1972–1987* (London: Routledge, 1989); Alberta Sbragia, 'The European Community : A Balancing Act,' *Publius* 23 (Summer 1993), pp.23–38; Alberta Sbragia, 'Thinking about the European Future: The Uses of Comparison', in Alberta Sbragia ed., *Euro-Politics: Institutions and Policy-Making in the 'New' European Community* (Washington: Brookings Instn., 1992), pp.257–91; Renaud Dehousse, and Joseph H.H.Weiler, 'The Dynamics of European Integration: The Legal Dimension', in W. Wallace (ed.), *The Dynamics of European Integration* (London: Frances Pinter, 1990), pp.242–60; J.H.H. Weiler, 'The Transformation

of Europe', *Yale Law Journal* 100 (1991), pp.2403–83.
6. For an overview, see James A.Caporaso, and John T.S.Keeler, 'The European Community and Regional Integration Theory', Presented at the Third Biennial International Conference of the European Community Studies Association, Washington DC, 27–-29 May 1993; Liesbet Hooghe, 'EC Politics beyond Maastricht: A Historical Perspective on Political-Administrative Interaction in the European Community', unpub. paper 1993; Gary Marks, 'Structural Policy and Multi-Level Governance in the EC', in Alan Cafruny and Glenda Rosenthal, (eds.), *The State of the European Community II: The Maastricht Debates and Beyond* (Boulder, CO: Lynne Rienner); Gary Marks, Liesbet Hooghe and Kermit Blank, 'European Integration and the State', Presented at 'The Politics and Political Economy of Contemporary Capitalism' Workshop, UNC-Chapel Hill and Duke, 9–11 Sept., 1994; Philippe Schmitter, 'Representation and the Future Euro-Polity', *Staatswissenschaften und Staatspraxis* 3/3, (1992), pp.379–405.
7. Sonia Mazey, Jeremy Richardson, 'EC Policy Making: An Emerging Policy Style?', D.Liefferink and P.Lowe (eds.), *European Integration and Environmental Policy* (Scarborough: Belhaven Press, 1993), pp.14–25 ; Gary Marks, Doug McAdam, 'Social Movements and the Changing Structure of Political Opportunity in the European Union', Paper at the Annual Meeting of the American Political Science Assoc., Washington, 2–5 Sept. 1993; Gary Marks, Francois Nielsen, Jane Salk, 'Regional Mobilization in the European Union', unpub. paper.
8. Hervé Dupuis, 'Committee of the Regions. The Case of France' in J.J.Hesse (eds.), *The Institutionalisation of the EC Committee of the Regions* First Intermediate Report to the German Länder (1993); Francis Jacobs, and Richard Corbett, *The European Parliament* (Harlow: Longman, 1990).
9. Article 146 reads: 'The Council shall consist of a representative of each Member State at ministerial level, authorized to commit the government of that Member State.'
10. The newly elected president M.Jacques Blanc (representing a French regional council) announced immediately that the Committee will advise the 1996 Intergovernmental Conference to divide the Committee into two separate institutions, one for regional and another for local authorities. The regions are currently outnumbered by local representatives (about 45 per cent to 55 per cent).
11. Some observers expect representatives to line up according to party political affiliation, which would constitute a third cleavage.
12. Under the new Article 146, it is conceivable that Belgian and German regional ministers would sit simultaneously in the Council of Ministers and in the Committee of Regions. On culture or regional policy, they would be negotiators in the Council of Ministers, and advisors to the Council in the Committee . . . hence advising themselves. The internal regulations of the Committee have foreseen this situation, and require that members with conflicting interests are replaced by an alternate.
13. The original wording in the regulations spoke of 'competent authorities designated by the member state at national, regional, local or other level' as the third partner, but it was obvious that regional and local authorities were meant. The formulation was strengthened in favour of regional and local authorities in the 1993 regulations.
14. For an overview, see Gary Marks, 'Decision Making in Cohesion Policy: Charting and Explaining Variations', in L.Hooghe (ed.), *European Integration, Cohesion Policy and Subnational Mobilisation* (Oxford: OUP, forthcoming); for systematic case studies, see the country chapters in ibid.
15. On Ireland: Brigid Laffan, 'Ireland, A Region without Regions: The Odd Man Out?' in Hooghe (note 14). On Greece: P.K. Ioakimidis, 'The Implementation of EC Cohesion Policy in Greece: The Tension between Bureaucratic Centralism and Regionalism', in L.Hooghe (ed.); Susannah Verney, Fouli Papageorgiou, 'Prefecture Councils in Greece: Decentralisation in the European Context', in R.Leonardi (ed.), *The Regions and the European Community: The Regional Response to the Single Market in the Underdeveloped Areas* (London: Frank Cass, 1993) pp.109–38.
16. Richard Balme, and Bernard Jouve, 'Building the Regional State. French Territorial Organisation and the Implementation of Structural Funds', in Hooghe (note 14); Hervé Dupuis,

'Committee of the Regions...'; Robert Ladrech, 'Europeanisation of Domestic Politics and Institutions: The Case of France', *Journal of Common Market Studies* 32/1 (1994).

17. In a way, it replaced an earlier consultative committee of local and regional institutions (created in 1977), in which the representatives had been appointed by the member states. That committee had not met since 1986.

18. The president of the Commission, Jacques Delors, considered the CCRLA more ambitiously as the first step towards a wider and more political involvement of subnational authorities in European decision-making. Delors spoke on the inauguration of the Council: 'Ce geste n'est donc pas simplement de procédure. C'est un geste politique qui en annoncera d'autres.' (Discours du président Delors à l'occasion de la réunion constitutive du conseil consultatif des collectivités régionales et locales, Bruxelles, 20 Dec. 1988.)

19. Strictly speaking, the electoral constituencies in Belgium are based partly on territory and partly on language: 15 seats are distributed among votes in the Flemish region and on Flemish candidates in Brussels; 11 seats among votes in the Walloon region and on Francophone parties in Brussels; one seat for the German-speaking region. On Belgium, see L.Hooghe, 'Belgian Federalism and European Integration' in B.Jones and M.Keating. (eds.), *The European Union and the Regions* (Oxford: Clarendon, forthcoming). On Germany see Richard E.Deeg, 'Germany's Länder and the Federalization of the European Union', presented at the Annual Meeting of the American Political Science Association, NY, 1–4 Sept. 1994; Rudolf Hrbek, 'The German Länder and EC Integration', *Journal of European Integration* 15 (Winter/ Spring 199?); pp.173–193.

20. Mette Jensen, 'Regional Mobilisation in Response to European Integration. The Potentiality of a Europe of the Regions' (unpub. MPhil. Th., Oxford, 1994); James Mitchell, 'Lobbying Brussels: The Case of Scotland Europa,' presented at the European Consortium for Political Research Workshops, Madrid, April 1994; Sonia Mazey, James Mitchell, 'Europe of the Regions? Territorial Interests and European Integration: The Scottish Experience' in S.Mazey, J.Richardson (eds.) *Lobbying in the European Community* (Oxford: OUP, 1993); Barry Jones, 'Wales and the European Union: The Development of a Regional Political Economy', presented at the Eur. Consort. for Political Res. Workshops, Madrid, 17–22 April 1994; Michael Keating, 'Le Monde pour Horizon. Québec, Catalonia and Scotland in the European Union', presented at the Int. Political Science Assoc., Berlin, Aug. 1994.

21. This is just one of many possible classifications. Bennington and Harvey made a useful one for local authorities, see John Bennington and Janet Harvey, 'Spheres or Tiers? The Significance of Transnational Local Authority Networks', in P. Dunleavy, J. Stanyer (eds.), *Contemporary Political Studies, 1994,* (Political Studies Assoc. of Britain, 1994), pp.943–61.

22. Relying on a statistical analysis of survey data encompassing all regional offices, an American research team has explored which factors correlate significantly with the presence or absence of particular regions. See Gary Marks, Francois Nielsen and Jane Salk, 'Regional mobilisation in the European Union', (Chapel Hill, unpub. paper, 1993); Jane Salk, Francois Nielsen and Gary Marks, 'Patterns and Determinants of Cooperation Among Subnational Offices in Brussels: An Empirical Investigation' (Duke Univ., unpub., 1994).

23. Failing this (which is the case in six member states), they are appointed by an association or body constituted at the regional level by the local authorities at the level immediately below. *AER documentation: Visiting Cards. European Regions* (Brussels: AER, Dec. 1992, Dec. 1993).

24. Interview with a spokesperson of the AER in Brussels, June 1994. The AER considers it as its role to promote the interests of the weaker regional authorities in particular. It had therefore asked for a privileged link with the Committee as institutionalised 'patron' for the weaker regions, but was rebuffed. Confirmation from an interview with a Commission official, June 1994.

25. Liesbet Hooghe and Michael Keating, 'The Politics of EU Regional Policy', *Journal of European Public Policy* 1/2 (1994); John Bennington and Janet Harvey, 'Spheres or Tiers?...'; Paul McAleavy, 'The Political Logic of the European Community Structural Funds Budget: Lobbying Efforts by Declining Industrial Regions', Eur. Univ. Paper RSC No.94/2 (1994).

According to McAleavy, the objective 2 network had its origins in a meeting held in Brussels in July 1991, which brought together the 60 regions eligible for objective 2 assistance (regions in industrial decline). It was organised by the European Commission. Ostensibly a gathering of experts in regional economic development, it had also a clear political goal: to put pressure on the European institutions as well as the national governments to support further funding for objective 2. The Commission let it be known that further initiatives would have to come from the regions. Within two weeks, eleven objective 2 regions got together to organise a follow-up meeting. That second gathering appointed a core group of eight regions to represent the interests of the objective 2 regions in meetings with Commissioners and representatives of other EU institutions.

26. See Susanna Borras, 'The Four Motors for Europe and its Promotion of R&D Linkages Beyond Geographic Contiguity in Interregional Agreements', *Regional Politics and Policy*, 3/3, (1993), pp.163–76.

27. W. Averyt, 'Eurogroups, Clientela and the European Community', *International Organization* 29/4 (1975), pp.949–72; Justin Greenwood, Jürgen Grote, and Karsten Ronit (eds.) *Organised Interests and the European Community* (London: Sage, 1992); Robert Hull, 'Lobbying Brussels: A View from Within' in S. Mazey and J. Richardson (eds.), *Lobbying in the European Community* (Oxford: OUP, 1992), pp.82–92.

28. The difficult and uncertain ascendancy of RETI illustrates the dilemma. RETI was formed in 1984 as the Assoc. of Traditional Industrial Regions of Europe. The European Commission was present at its first meeting. From the beginning, its membership was flawed. The core consisted of such diverse partners like the French region of Nord Pas-de-Calais, the Belgian province of Hainaut, the German Land North Rhine-Westphalia, and the British local authority West Yorkshire Metropolitan County Council. Moreover, the association was not representative, in the sense that it was numerically dominated by UK local authorities, and had no representation of a number of member states. The Commission took a very cautious stand throughout the 1980s, even to the point that it decided in 1991 to persuade the objective 2 regions (de facto the RETI constituency) to form a new representative lobby (see footnote 12). The challenge transformed RETI in 1992. RETI changed its name to the more optimistic European Regions of Industrial Technology and declared it sought to encompass all objective 2 regions. The new objective 2 lobby and RETI are now working closely together to lobby the European Commission. However, the basic collective action problem deriving from unequal members, diverse interests and absence of clear membership advantages remain alive. One outcome is that the most powerful member, Nord Rhine-Westphalia, allowed its membership to lapse, implying that it has much more effective channels for defending its interests in the European arena than the troubled association. RETI is dispensable. The RETI tale illustrates also how the survival of these networks seems to depend on the receptiveness of the Commission. The European Commission is centrally placed to encourage or discourage, direct and shape interest formation. (P. McAleavey, 'The Political Logic of The European Community Structural Funds Budget: Lobbying efforts by declining industrial regions', European Univ. Paper RSC 94/2, 1994).

29. Quoted in Stephen George, Ian Bache, and Rod Rhodes, 'The UK and the Committee of the Regions' in J.J.Hesse (eds.) *The Institutionalisation of the EC Committee of the Regions.* First Intermediate Report to the German Länder, 1993. Further sources: Peter John, 'The Presence and Influence of United Kingdom Local Authorities in Brussels' P. Dunleavy, J.Stanyer (eds.), *Contemporary Political Studies, 1994.* (Political Studies Assoc. of Britain, 1994), pp.906–22; Barry Jones, 'Wales and the European Union: The Development of a Regional Political Economy', Presented at the Eur. Consort. for Political Res. Workshops, Madrid, 17–22 April 1994.

30. See Udo Bullmann, Michael Goldsmith and Edward C.Page, 'Subnational Government Autonomy and Political Authority: Regions, Localities and the Shifting Balance of Authority in Europe', Presented at the American Political Science Assoc., New York, 1–4 Sept. 1994; Michael Goldsmith, 'The Europeanization of Local Government', *Urban Studies* Vol.4/5 (19??), pp.683–99; Raffaella Nanetti, 'Cohesion Policy and Territorial Restructuring in the Member States', Presented at the Conference for 'Policy Networks and European Cohesion Policy', Nuffield, Oxford Univ., 2–5 Dec. 1993; Robert Leonardi, and Raffaella Nanetti

(eds.), *The Regions and European Integration. The Case of Emilia-Romagna* (London: Pinter Publishers, 1990).

31. Sidney Tarrow, 'The Europeanisation of Conflict: Reflections from a Social Movement Perspective', *West European Politics* 18/2 (April 1995), pp.223–51.

32. This reliance on a neo-functionalist logic is not new. It has been observed throughout the Commission's history. See Frank Wilson, 'Interest Groups as Domestic Political Actors in the European Union', Presented at the American Political Science Assoc., New York, 1–4 Sept. 1994; David Coombes, *Politics and Bureaucracy in the EC. A Portrait of the Commission of the EEC* (London: Allen and Unwin, 1970). It has become particularly pronounced under the presidency of Jacques Delors. See on networking as Commission strategy: Les Metcalfe, 'Après 1992: la Commission pourra-t-elle gérer l'Europe?', *Revue française d'administration publique*, 63, (1992), pp.401–12. See on the concept of 'espace organisée': George Ross, 'Sidling into Industrial Policy: Inside the European Commission', *French Politics and Society* 11 (1993), pp.20–44. For the Commission's application in cohesion policy see: L.Hooghe, 'Building a Europe with the Regions. The Politics of the European Commission Under the Structural Funds', presented at the Council of Eur. Studies, Chicago, 31 March–2 April 1994.

33. As late as Oct. 1990, he seemed to lean towards a body representing regions only, not local authorities. He admitted that the diverse regional structures in Europe would make its creation difficult, but believed that a harmonisation in ten years time would be possible. See J.J. Hesse, A. Benz, C. Onestini, 'The Institutionalisation of the EC Committee of the Regions', First Intermediate Report to the German Länder, 1993.

Appendix
The 1994 European Elections:
Twelve into One Won't Go

JULIE SMITH

The first three sets of European elections were easily dismissed as second-order: the campaigns were predominantly nationally organised and focused on domestic issues, turnout was low and small and protest parties performed well in elections to an institution widely perceived to be weak and ineffectual. By 1994 the European Parliament had acquired significant powers and the European Union was facing important questions concerning both its own institutional development, enlargement and issues of public policy such as unemployment. This situation might have led to greater public interest in the elections and more closely co-ordinated transnational campaigns. Considering the electoral system in force, the nature of the campaigns, issues on which the elections were fought in the 12 member states and the final outcome, there was no major shift to more integrated European elections in 1994.

European elections, which were first held in 1979, can be seen as an attempt to extend representative democracy 'beyond the nation state'. However, as Deutsch points out, theorists have typically confined their considerations to the nation state.[1] When European elections were introduced, the assumption therefore seemed to be that they would look rather like national elections. Former Commission President, Walter Hallstein, for example, argued prior to the introduction of direct elections, that:

> What is lacking under the present system is an election campaign about European issues. Such a campaign would force those entitled to vote to look at and examine the questions and the various options on which the European Parliament would have to decide in the months and years ahead. It would give the candidates who emerged victorious from such a campaign a truly European mandate from their electors; and it would encourage the emergence of truly European political parties.[2]

Hallstein believed that the introduction of elections to the European Parliament (EP), prefigured in the 1951 Treaty of Paris, would enable such developments to occur. Have such expectations been met?

How far can European elections be seen as a single election, rather than as 12 national elections? We consider the electoral systems in the European elections, transnational party activity, manifestos, issues raised and results. The elections vary significantly between countries: in the relative attention paid to them by politicians and voters, the issues raised, and even the electoral rules used. In general, however, turnout has been lower than in national general elections, small, new and protest parties have done well at the expense of larger parties of government and opposition, and the main thrust of the campaigns has focused on national issues: a far cry from Hallstein's expectations.

Thus, by 1994, European elections could still best be characterised as simultaneous national second-order elections.[3] This was despite changes arising from the Single European Act (SEA) and the Maastricht Treaty, which means not only that the EU plays a huge role in the lives of its citizens, but also that the role of the European Parliament in the decision-making process has increased greatly. The prevalence of protest voting, success for new, small and extreme parties and low turnout can be seen as part of the 'crisis of representation' affecting western democracy. Yet, I shall argue that, since the elections are qualitatively different from national elections, such an analysis is inappropriate.

ELECTORAL ARENA

The intention implicit in the Treaties was that the Common Assembly should represent the peoples of Europe.[4] States did not receive an equal number of seats in the Assembly, but neither were seats allocated solely on the size of the member states; rather a system of 'degressive proportionality', similar to that introduced for the Council of Europe Assembly, was used. As Table 1 shows, the small member states have therefore been significantly over-represented in the European Parliament in terms of size of population.[5]

With the question of numbers of seats at least partially resolved, the appointed Parliament turned its attention in 1958 to the EC treaties' requirement that it 'draw up proposals for elections by direct universal suffrage, in accordance with a uniform procedure in all Member States.'[6] Efforts were made before the introduction of direct elections to find a common system, but the near impossibility of finding one led to the compromise suggested in the 1960 Dehousse Report that 'uniformity was not synonymous with identity'.[7]

TABLE 1
ALLOCATION OF SEATS PER COUNTRY

	No. of seats	Population (January 1994)
Belgium	25	10 083 600
Denmark	16	5 195 200
Germany	99	81 096 400
Greece	25	10 390 000
Spain*	64	39 114 200
France	87	57 803 600
Ireland	15	3 571 000
Italy	87	56 960 300
Luxembourg**	6	389 000
Netherlands	31	15 354 000
Portugal	25	9 868 000
United Kingdom	87	58 276 000
EC	567	348 102 100

* = January 1993   ** = January 1992

Source: *Info Memo 'Special Elections' No.2* (Brussels: EP – Directorate of the Press, 10 Feb. 1994).

Two problems in particular emerged:
– There was a general issue of the relative merits of proportional and majoritarian electoral systems. The former seemed more appropriate to reflect public opinion; the latter to elect a Parliament capable of producing a strong, homogeneous government. (Since the working group was to consider what the Parliament might become, not simply what it was in the late 1950s, the question was not entirely vacuous, even though no government was to emerge from the Parliament.)
– More specifically, electoral practices varied considerably between the

member states, leading to a situation where, 'Although most of the politicians consulted favoured the same electoral system for all six States, they were not slow to add that they could only accept a uniform system if it were broadly in line with their own.'[8]

In order that elections should be held at all, it was decided that member states should be allowed to adopt their own electoral rules, based on certain 'fundamental principles of democratic elections, ie. elections must be equal, free, universal, direct and secret'[9] and leave the first directly elected parliament to propose a common system. Of course, the difficulties surrounding the negotiations prior to the elections did not diminish after the elections. Three serious attempts to devise a common system had come to nought by 1994. The most recently adopted, the De Gucht Report, awaited the consideration of the Council of Ministers at the time of the elections.[10] Thus, as Table Two shows, the elections were fought under thirteen different sets of electoral regulations.[11]

TABLE 2
ELECTORAL RULES IN EUROPEAN ELECTIONS

Country	Number of seats (1994)	Electoral system	No. of const.	Choice of candidate?	Compulsory voting?	work rest day
Belgium	25	Proportional: regional lists	4	Yes from party list	Yes	Rest
Denmark	16	Proportional: national list	1	Yes from party list	No	Work
Germany	99	Proportional: regional lists	1	No - strict party list	No	Rest
Greece	25	Proportional: national list	1	No - strict party list	Yes	Rest
Spain	64	Proportional: national list	1	No - strict party list	No	Rest
France	87	Proportional: national list	1	No - strict party list	No	Rest
Ireland	15	Proportional: single transferable vote (STV)	4	Yes - no list	No	Work
Italy	87	Proportional: regional lists	5	Yes - flexible list	No	Rest
Luxembourg	6	Proportional: national list	1	Yes, open lists	Yes	Rest
Netherlands	31	Proportional: national list	1	Yes from party list	No	Work
Portugal	25	Proportional: national list	1	No- strict party list	No	Rest
UK	87	Plurality in GB	85	Yes - no list	No	Work

Source: Compiled by the author from various sources including her own unpub. MPhil thesis, *The European Parliament and Direct Elections* (1993) and T.T. Mackie, *Europe Votes 3 - European Parliamentary Election Results 1989* (Aldershot, UK: Dartmouth, 1990).

It is impossible to say precisely what the full consequences of the lack of a common electoral system are. Certainly, the use of the 'first-past-the-post' system in Britain has led to a situation where a small shift in votes can have a disproportionately large effect on the balance of the party groups in the Parliament. It has also been argued that the problem makes it harder to conduct transnational election campaigns or to view the elections in anything other than national terms.[12] This may also help explain the inability of the transnational parties to field slates of candidates for the Commission, as some had hoped to do in 1994.[13] How transnational were the election campaigns?

TRANSNATIONAL PARTIES

Political parties at European level are important as a factor for integration within the Union. They contribute to forming a European awareness and to expressing the political will of the citizens of Europe.[14]

This extract from the Maastricht Treaty might well appear to be the triumph of hope over experience. European party federations, based on existing party internationals, were created in the run-up to the first direct elections.[15] By the 1994 elections, the centre-right European People's Party (EPP), Party of European Socialists (PES) and European Liberal, Democrat and Reform Party (ELDR Party) had all formally become parties. In addition, the Federation of European Green Parties was established in 1993. The role of these parties in the electoral sphere remained limited, however.

As on previous occasions, so in 1994, the three European parties, plus the Greens for the first time, produced transnational manifestos. The need to reconcile the wishes of 12 or more political parties,[16] often themselves broad churches comprising a range of views, plus the necessity of translating proposals, meant the manifestos were generally superficial. Thus, although the European Union faced huge problems – unemployment, enlargement, institutional reform and security questions, especially immigration – there was little emphasis on these issues in the manifestos. Indeed, the EPP's four page manifesto scarcely did more than highlight a few of its key principles, notably the Party's commitment to a federal Europe.

The manifestos did not give voters any clear or distinctive policies for the future direction of the EU, either in terms of institutional change or policy options. The parties all asserted their support for further integration, with commitments to more powers for the European Parliament and a written constitution for the EU, but there was little in the campaigns to arouse public awareness of 'Europe'. Perhaps not surprisingly, given the attitudes of most European parliamentarians, it was easier to point to similarities than differences, at least between the three largest parties' manifestos in this area.

In terms of policies concerning unemployment and the environment, there was a fair degree of overlap in the manifestos. Yet, when one remembers that the legislative agenda is still set by the European Commission, this is probably also to be expected.[17] Indeed, the preface to the PES's manifesto went as far as to state that the document was 'not a detailed programme, but rather a framework in which our future policies will be fleshed out.' This approach, while appropriate to the powers of the EP, meant there was little scope for the parties to mobilise public will across the Union.

Apart from the manifestos, the transnational parties played little part in the elections. Although the transnational parties could arrange speakers from one member state to speak in another, logistical constraints, ranging from the need to campaign in one's own country to linguistic difficulties, meant that such activity was limited. The PES did arrange pre-election rallies; the ELDR Party found itself unable to agree on a venue or a time and did not.

NATIONAL PARTIES

Since transnational party activity in European elections[18] was still weak by 1994, it is important to consider the role of national parties in the elections. The most obvious aspect to note here is just how little the elections had in common across the Union. Although there was a proliferation of parties in most member states, the nature and extent of the proliferation differed widely. For example, Denmark had only eight lists compared with 37 in Spain (see Table 4 below). In several countries, including France and Germany, the proliferation arose primarily from changing attitudes towards further European integration; in others, especially Italy, domestic factors were more significant in this respect.

Whereas in earlier European elections, only voters in Denmark had a chance specifically to vote for or against further European integration, 1994 saw the emergence of more 'Euro-sceptical' parties in other states as well.[19] The ratification process of the Maastricht Treaty had an effect not just on those countries, Denmark, France and Ireland, which held referenda, but on other EU states as well. Thus, Germany saw the emergence of Manfred Brunner's *Free Citizens' Alliance*, France had an anti-Maastricht list, *L'Autre Europe*, headed by Philippe de Villiers and Sir James Goldsmith, while in Britain the UK Independence Party provided an anti-EU choice in some constituencies.

In addition, several countries witnessed a change of focus from the traditionally strongly pro-European parties. Ireland, Portugal and Spain all saw a weakening of public support for European integration in the period prior to the elections in June. This shift may have been due partly to the influence of the British media in the two former countries,[20] and to the high levels of unemployment in the last. Yet, although the pro-European rhetoric of the parties was often tempered, this did not lead to a shift to a clear choice for voters on issues concerning the development of the EU; parties were at most responding to perceived public opinion, without offering definite strategies for European affairs.

France saw the emergence of a left-wing challenger to the Socialists, Bernard Tapie's *Energie Radicale*, as well as the list proposed by a group of intellectuals calling for the arming of Bosnian Muslims, 'Europe starts at Sarajevo', which was withdrawn before the election.[21] The Italian party system had collapsed between the 1989 and 1994 elections. Silvio Berlusconi's *Forza Italia*, fresh from success in the general election, which took place in March, put forward a list for the first time in a European election.[22]

In most cases the parties standing in the European elections were broadly similar to those standing in national elections. Some fought on the transnational manifestos of the European parties of which they were members. Several chose not to refer, or to refer only in passing, to the transnational documents. The Socialist parties were broadly supportive of their manifesto. The British and Spanish parties fought primarily on that manifesto. British Liberal Democrats preferred to ignore the ELDR manifesto, concentrating on their own national manifesto, which played down its federalist sympathies.

The EPP member parties were in a slightly odd position. The British and Danish Conservative Parties are not members of the EPP, although MEPs from these parties sit with the EPP Group in the EP as 'allied members'. This association meant that the British Conservatives could campaign on their own manifesto, with no commitments to the EPP document. An alliance between the French Centre-Right parties, the UDF and the RPR, constructed for domestic political reasons, led the Gaullist RPR to give at least rhetorical support to the federalist EPP manifesto.

ISSUE DIMENSION

The Dehousse Report argued that European elections should be held on the same day in the then six member states, but that they should not coincide with national elections, general or local, in any of the member states, since,

...there would be a real risk that the distinctive character of European elections would be overshadowed by local or national issues brought forward by parties or candidates during the electoral campaign. This would undoubtedly imperil one of the principal aims of European elections – to increase the peoples' interest in European unification.[23]

However, when direct elections were finally introduced, it was decided that the benefits in terms of higher turnout which might accrue were such that simultaneous national and European elections should be permitted.[24]

Experience shows both arguments have some validity. Turnout has typically been higher when national and European elections have coincided.[25] The Irish case is particularly noteworthy in this respect: turnout fell 24 per cent between 1989 when the European election coincided with a general election and 1994 when it did not. National issues *have* dominated in such cases, but then they have also dominated European elections which did not coincide with national elections.

Thus, despite the fact that in 1994, for the first time since the introduction of direct elections to the European Parliament, only Luxembourg had a general election on the same day as the European election,[26] this did not lead to greater emphasis on European issues, either in terms of institutional change or policy issues best tackled at the European level. To varying degrees across the EU, domestic issues were to the fore, admittedly often intermingled with European issues.[27]

In France, Germany and Belgium the elections have to be seen against the backcloth of impending national elections. The joint UDF/RPR list in France was part of a deal on the Right prior to the presidential election scheduled for May 1995. Since the parties have traditionally differed over attitudes towards European integration, the result was a list headed by the Europhile Dominique Baudis, with alternating pro and anti-EU candidates, all notionally supporting the EPP manifesto. The reward for the RPR from the pact was intended to be that they should nominate the presidential candidate of the Right. Even the 'Europe starts at Sarajevo' list, which was primarily concerned with foreign affairs, had a domestic impact, Socialist leader, Michel Rocard, being anxious to placate the demands of its candidates. As already noted, the presence of *L'Autre Europe* provided the opportunity for voters to vote against the Europe of Maastricht, without voting for Le Pen.

While Chancellor Helmut Kohl's Christian Democrats (CDU) put forward a positive European programme, their chief strategy was to emphasise Kohl's leadership, pending the general election due the following October. Since unification it has become much harder for the CDU's sister party, the Christian Social Union (CSU), which only presents a list in

Bavaria, to reach the 5 per cent *national* threshold. Bavarian Minister President, Edmund Stoiber, therefore made some rather Euro-sceptic remarks in the hope of maximising support in Bavaria, home of Brunner's list and the far-right *Republikaner*, but at the same time putting himself somewhat at odds with Kohl. Yet, the elections were not totally devoid of European issues: bananas emerged as a major question following the GATT agreements, which would increase the cost of the fruit. A European issue with a direct impact on the people was thus on the agenda.

Disillusionment, with local politicians reputedly being less noticeable than at the national level, meant that the European elections, which have never attracted much public interest in Belgium, were used as a test for the governing parties before the October municipal elections. The opposition Liberal Party certainly campaigned this way. With increasing hostility to the large numbers of foreign nationals resident in Belgium, the far-right *Vlaams Blok* presented a list in Brussels for the first time and the *Front National* in the francophone constituency.[28]

Italian voters, just emerging from a general election which had highlighted the collapse of the postwar party system, paid little attention to the European elections. While there appeared to be a subtle shift away from Italy's traditional support for the EU among the politicians, the extent of this change was unclear, and certainly had little impact on the election campaign. Similarly in the Netherlands, only a month after the general election, government formation was the prime concern. One interesting point about the Dutch campaign was that voters appeared to be interested primarily in issues such as foreign affairs, immigration policy and drugs, that is to say, second and third pillar issues over which the EP has only a consultative role. This situation has potential implications for future European elections.

Spanish support for the EU, almost unchallenged in 1989, had declined in the face of high levels of unemployment. Coupled with corruption in the Socialist Party, this enabled the right of centre Popular Party, which is internally divided on European affairs, to fight on domestic issues, primarily the standing of the Gonzalez government. The change in public opinion had apparently by-passed Prime Minister Felipe Gonzalez, however, as he continued to preach the Euro-idealism of the 1980s. Domestic issues and foreign policy dominated a lacklustre campaign in Greece. Since the Macedonia question is crucial to Greek foreign policy, there was a European dimension to the elections in this respect at least.

Britain for once did have a debate on European affairs. While the Liberal. Democrats tried to play down their European credentials, the Labour Party was keen to show its new-found Europeanness and campaigned on the PES's manifesto (albeit in an election overshadowed by the death of their leader, John Smith, in May 1994, and the quest for his successor). It was from the Tory ranks, however, that the European dimension emerged. Anxious to reconcile the different factions of his party, John Major discussed ideas of a *Europe à la carte*, and accused the two opposition parties of being prepared to surrender Britain's veto in European decision-making.

This situation highlights one of the key problems associated with European elections: divisions on European integration frequently arise within parties rather than between them. Where this is the case – for the parties of the centre-right in France, the Spanish Popular Party (PP) and traditionally both major parties in Britain – national considerations typically mean that differences on European issues are largely papered over. In France the desire to demonstrate agreement prior to the Presidential elections meant divisions were little discussed, while in Britain the electoral system ensured that voters had no opportunity to choose between, say, pro- and anti-Maastricht Conservatives. Debate is therefore often limited to national issues, even in countries such as Germany where support for the European Union, at least at the elite level, is high.[29]

Issues which can arise in European elections can be characterised as falling broadly into three categories: domestic (national or local); European in terms of public policy formation; or European in terms of the construction of Europe. Whereas in domestic elections, national or local, the nature of the institution to be elected is unlikely to feature in the elections, at the European level it may well do so. Generally, national and local issues feature in varying proportions in both national and local elections. Yet the fact that national issues tend to characterise European elections has led to the implied criticism that the elections do not appear to be 'European'.

One underlying feature of such criticisms is, perhaps, the belief that the issues raised should reflect the electoral arena in which the elections take place. Such an assumption is dubious if one considers that national issues are frequently raised in local elections in Britain, while local issues form the basis of US Congressional campaigns. Thus, within traditional states, different sorts of issues can emerge, regardless of the electoral arena. Why should the European arena be any different in this respect?

What the appropriate focus of attention should be at any election partly depends on what functions one thinks an election plays. In most modern democracies, elections can be seen as electing a government, contributing to the public policy agenda and/or providing 'a recognisable human face for government in the form of a political leader'.[30] European elections fulfil these criteria only to a very limited extent. No government or political leader emerges from EP elections and their impact on the direction of EU decision-making is indirect. Changes arising from the Maastricht Treaty have had only a small effect in this regard: M. Santer was not chosen as nominee for the Commission presidency as the result of popular elections, nor was the choice of the whole Commission the result of public will. And, while national political parties might have argued the need for a left or right wing majority in the Parliament, the requirement for an absolute majority in votes in several policy areas means that the party group balance in the EP is not of major importance in securing a particular set of European policies, since on major decisions the PES and EPP groups vote together.

European elections may, however, serve a different purpose, which Niedermayer refers to as the 'legitimation function'.[31] Indeed, it was assumed that both the EP and the EU would gain in legitimacy as a result of direct elections. If the simple fact of holding an election is sufficient to confer legitimacy, this would have been a valid argument. But if, as appears to be the case, low turnout and protest voting have been the result of dissatisfaction with the EU, debate over the future direction of the Union would seem to be desirable. It was not just the campaigns, but also the results of the elections which largely reflected national political affairs, a situation which does little to confer legitimacy on the EU.

RESULTS

Unlike previous European elections, when there were some transnational trends, such as the rise of the Greens in 1989, 1994 saw few similarities between countries. Average turnout continued to fall, as it had done on each occasion, yet this disguised increased turnout in some member states. Turnout in Germany held up reasonably well, following a campaign urging people to go and vote; in the Netherlands and Portugal turnout actually fell below levels in Britain for the first time. (See Table 3).

The anti-government pattern which characterised earlier European elections was less clear-cut in 1994. In Italy and the Netherlands, support continued for those parties which had been successful in recent national elections: *Forza Italia*, the National Alliance and the Lega Nord performed well in Italy, while the two liberal parties, the VVD and D'66, gained six seats in the Netherlands. While this could have been predicted,[32] the strength of support for Helmut Kohl in Germany was more surprising. Following a period when the opinion polls had indicated a loss of support for the CDU, the outcome was 38.8 per cent for the CDU/CSU, not enough to give Kohl a clear victory in the general election, but generally seen as a good indicator for the October poll.

Governing parties did perform badly in Greece, Spain and the UK, however. For the first time since the death of Franco (1975), the Popular Party were able to defeat the Socialists in a national election in Spain.

TABLE 3

TURNOUT IN EUROPEAN PARLIAMENT ELECTIONS 1979–1994

	1979 %	1981 %	1984 %	1987 %	1989 %	1994 %	Average[1] %
Belgium*	91.4		92.1	90.7	90.7	91.2	
Denmark	47.8	-	52.3	-	46.2	52.5	49.7
Germany	65.7	-	56.8	-	62.3	60.1	61.2
Greece*	-	78.6	77.2	-	79.9	71.2	76.7
Spain	-	-	-	68.9	54.6	59.6	61.0
France	60.7	-	56.7	-	48.7	52.7	54.7
Ireland	63.6	-	47.6	-	68.3	44.0	55.9
Italy	84.9	-	83.4	-	81.0	74.8	81.0
Lux*	88.9	-	88.8	-	87.4	86.6	87.9
NL	57.8	-	50.6	-	47.2	35.6	47.8
Portugal	-	-	-	72.6	51.2	35.6	53.1
UK	32.3	-	32.6	-	36.2	36.4	34.4
EC	65.9[2]	-	63.8[3]	-	62.8[4]	58.3	62.7[5]

Sources: European Parliament: *Results and Elected Members* (Provisional ed. 15 June 1994) and *Info Memo 'Election Special' No.1* (Brussels: EP Directorate General for Information and Public Relations, 1994).

NB. Unweighted figures used. Weighting gives slightly lower turnout figures.
* = voting is compulsory.

Notes
1. The average figures refer to the average turnout for the elections of 1979, 1984, 1989 and 1994, except for Greece, where they refer to 1981, 1984, 1989 and 1994, and Spain and Portugal, where they refer to 1987, 1989 and 1994.
2. The average for the EC9.
3. The average for the EC10.
4. The average for the EC12.
5. The figure is an average based on all the elections which have occurred between 1979 and 1994, i.e. four elections except for Spain and Portugal.

Although their success was not enough for the party to push for an early dissolution of Parliament, it was significant for the confidence of the PP. In Greece it was the new Popular Spring Party which achieved most success, with both the ruling *PASOK* and main opposition, New Democracy, faring badly. In the UK, Prime Minister Major's attempts to woo Euro-sceptics failed and the Tory Party won only 18 seats and 26.8 per cent of the vote.

TABLE 4
LISTS PRESENTED AND ELECTED IN THE MEMBER STATES

	Number of lists presented	Number of parties/lists elected
Belgium		
Flanders (14 seats)	11	6
Wallonia (10 seats)	11	5
German-speaking (1 seat)	7	1
Denmark	8	7
Germany	26	4
Greece	50	5
Spain	37	5
France	19	6
Ireland	11	5
Italy		14
North-west (23 seats)	17	
North-east (16 seats)	17	
Centre (17 seats)	16	
South (21 seats)	16	
Islands (10 seats)	18	
Luxembourg	10	4
Netherlands	11	6
Portugal	14	4
United Kingdom	na	7

Sources: *Election Special June 1994 The Outgoing Parliament/1989–1994/The Candidates* (European Parliament, 1994, Doc EN\DV\252\252337); *Info Memo 'Special Elections' XVIII Session Constitutive Le Nouveau PE au 19 Juillet 1994* (Brussels: EP, Directorate of the Press, 1994).

The proliferation of party lists did not necessarily lead to an increase in the number of parties represented in the Parliament. In Germany, only 4 parties succeeded in winning seats, despite 26 lists being presented. This contrasts with 14 Italian parties securing seats, a sign of the splits in domestic Italian politics. The success of two new groups in France, *L'Autre Europe* and *Energie Radicale*, had a significant impact on the group formations in the incoming European Parliament, if anything out of proportion to their popular support. However, formation of the *Europe des Nations* Group (of which the *Europe des Nations* MEPs are the main force) does seem to fill a gap in the EP: if there is a trend away from popular support for further European integration, the formation of an anti-Maastricht group may be a desirable innovation.[33]

TABLE 5
SEATS BY PARTY GROUP AND COUNTRY – 19 JULY 1994

	PES	EPP	LDR	EUL	FE	EDA	Greens	ERA	NE	IND	TOTAL
B	6	7	6	-	-	-	2	1	-	3	25
DK	3	3	5	-	-	-	1	-	4	-	16
G	40	47	-	-	-	-	12	-	-	-	99
Gr	10	9	-	4	-	2	-	-	-	-	25
S	22	30	2	9	-	-	-	1	-	-	64
F	15	13	1	7	-	14	-	13	13	11	87
Ire	1	4	1	-	-	7	2	-	-	-	15
I	18	12	7	5	27	-	4	2	-	12	87
Lux	2	2	1	-	-	-	1	-	-	-	6
NL	8	10	10	-	-	-	1	-	2	-	31
P	10	1	8	3	-	3	-	-	-	-	25
UK	63	19	2	-	-	-	-	2	-	1	87
Total	198	157	43	28	27	26	23	19	19	27	567

Source: *Strasbourg Notebook* (Strasbourg: EP, 19 July 1994, PE 177.794)

PES	Party of European Socialists	**EDA**	European Democratic
EPP	European People's Party		Alliance
LDR	Liberal, Democratic and	**Greens**	Green Group in the
	Reformist		European Parliament
EUL	Confederal Group of the	**ERA**	European Radical Alliance
	European United Left	**NE**	Nations of Europe
FE	Forza Europa	**IND**	Non-attached

NB. The minimum number of MEPs required to form a political group is 13 from four or more member states, 16 from three member states, 21 from two member states or 26 from just one member state.

As Table 5 indicates there were few trends in support for the transnational parties and groupings. Following the election, the PES group remained the largest group, retaining the same absolute number of seats (a drop in real terms since the Parliament was enlarged at the time of the election) by virtue of the strength of the British Labour group, itself the beneficiary of Britain's electoral system. The EPP Group is more fragmented following the elections and may become more so after Germany's general election, since it is believed that the *Forza Europa* group established in the new Parliament, and composed solely of *Forza Italia* MEPs, will seek EPP membership. The ELDR group, always rather fragmented, enjoyed very mixed fortunes. For the first time the British Liberal Democrats secured seats in the directly elected Parliament, and there were gains for the Danish and Dutch Liberals. As in 1984, however, the German Free Democrats failed to clear the five per cent threshold, and so are absent from the 1994–99 Parliament. While the Greens did not attract the levels of support across the Union that they did in 1989, they succeeded in gaining representation in Ireland and Luxembourg for the first time. By and large, far right parties had little success, although in Belgium *Vlaams Blok* and the National Front each gained a seat.

WHAT ARE THE IMPLICATIONS OF THE EUROPEAN ELECTIONS?

What was the impact of the lack of common patterns in the elections? What does it suggest for representation? A crisis? Or is the EU too different from nation states for representative democracy to make sense? The parties which fight the elections are based on traditional national alignments. If such parties contribute to a crisis of representation at the national level this situation is likely to be exacerbated at the European level, since they are even further away from the people. Should we then favour lists like that of de Villiers as offering a real choice?

Vernon Bogdanor has suggested that, 'The party system in the European Parliament is one that is mainly carried over from domestic party politics.'[34] In many ways, the European parties can best be seen as fora for national political parties to meet with other like-minded parties. Thus, while European political parties exist, in many ways they are less than the sum of their parts. Despite some convergence between states, for example over class alignments, which enable transnational parties (and, more importantly, party groups in the European Parliament) to exist at all, such groupings are arguably not the most relevant at the European level.

To a certain extent, the different electoral outcomes across the Union can be seen to arise from the electoral rules; it is, for example, far easier to secure representation in Italy than in Britain. However, the determination of national politicians to maintain their positions means that it is also difficult to get a sense of the importance of European elections. The outcome of EP elections is of increasing importance in terms of the impact on Community decision-making and the composition of the Commission, but this significance does not yet seem to have become apparent to the voters.[35] Or perhaps the elections do not seem to be of great importance to an electorate more interested in foreign affairs or crime. Certainly this thought appeared to have occurred to John Major, who suggested to colleagues at the June 1994 Corfu Summit that placing the emphasis on controlling drugs might have increased interest in the elections.[36] The fact the EP has little to do with this policy area had apparently escaped his notice.

If in the first direct elections there was little to discuss in terms of the Parliament's work, by 1994 the results could have had a decisive effect on the composition of the Union's (at least nominal) executive and the political balance could have had an impact on the direction of Europe as a market-led or socially conscious Europe. Moreover, the lessons of Maastricht suggest that there is little support for a political Europe.[37] Until this begins to change, it will be difficult to alter the electoral processes in such a way as to generate transnational campaigns fought on European issues.

Considering the apparent 'crisis of representation' which seems to be affecting most Western democracies, one might view European elections as part of the same phenomenon. Certainly low turnout and the propensity to vote for small and protest parties would suggest such an analysis might be fruitful. But there are further problems which emerge in the European context.

In the first place, if we accept the idea that 'Representative government is a system of national government in which representative institutions play a crucial role in the decision-making process, so that few political changes of any importance can be made without the authority of the central legislative assembly,'[38] it becomes immediately apparent that elections to the European Parliament do not yield such representative government. At most, the EP contributes to an overall system of European government, whose nature is not well defined.[39]

Furthermore, the nature of the EU is itself disputed in a way that the nation state, at least in EU member states, is not. Bhikhu Parekh has suggested that, 'Every polity has a more or less coherent conception of the kind of collectivity it is, what it means to belong to it, who belongs to it or is an outsider, and how it differs from others.'[40] While the membership of the EU is clearly defined, precisely what that membership entails remains the subject of heated debate. Moreover, there is no single vision of how the Union should evolve over the coming years. These differences are not simply differences of emphasis, but in many cases reflect fundamental disputes over what the EU should be. Such issues potentially could offer scope for debate in European elections which has so far been lacking.

Indeed, the failure of politicians and the media to raise institutional questions in European elections has been perceived by many as a problem for European democracy. Decisions on the future of the EU are taken by members of national governments, themselves with national mandates, in the Council of Ministers. European integration, while playing an increasing part in the national agenda, still does not form a major issue in national elections in the nation states; neither does it play much of a part in European elections. Thus, there seems little scope for voters to express their views about the future of Europe.

Whether any of this matters, partly depends on one's conception of representation and the functions of elections.[41] If MEPs are to be the agents of the electors, then it is necessary for them to know the wishes of the voters in the policy areas with which they are dealing. Naturally, the more diverse the issues tackled become, the harder it is to reconcile views on different policy areas, making this form of representation difficult.

If, however, we assume a Burkean view of representation, where the representative should not act on a specific mandate, but rather as a trustee of the electors, free to act as he or she felt best for the nation, then the fact that the question of the sort of EU desired is not debated is less of a problem. Indeed, the European approach to representation, as Birch points out, holds that it is '. . . undesirable that the representative should be too closely tied to the interests and opinions of his constituents.'[42] Surely, MEPs would use their judgement to make decisions which would be in the best interests of Europe. Here again we hit the problem noted earlier. If there is only a limited sense of what it means to be European and the nature of the EU remains contested, obviously it is almost impossible to formulate a concept of what is in the best interest of 'Europe'. Thus, the fact that certain issues are not broached at European elections should be of fundamental concern to politicians, political scientists and, perhaps most importantly, the media which are best placed to inform European citizens of the functions and activities of the EP and the EU.

NOTES

This article is partly based on research for a doctoral thesis funded by the Economic and Social Research Council.

1. Karl W. Deutsch, *Political Community at the International Level* (NY: Doubleday, 1954) p.26.
2. Walter Hallstein, *Europe in the Making* (London: Allen and Unwin, 1972) p.74
3. To use the term coined by Reif in his analysis of the 1979 and 1984 elections. See, e.g., Karlheinz Reif, 'National Electoral Cycles and European Elections 1979 and 1984', *Electoral Studies* 3/3, (1984), p.244–55.
4. The European Parliament was officially known as the Common Assembly under the Treaty of Paris, which created the Coal and Steel Community, and the European Parliamentary Assembly under the Treaties of Rome. From 1962, MEPs referred to it as 'European Parliament'.
5. This pattern has been followed for each enlargement of the Union, including the 1995 enlargement. With the accession of Austria, Finland and Sweden on 1 Jan. 1995 there are now 624 MEPs.
6. Article 138(3) of the EEC Treaty.
7. Dehousse Report (1960) para.18.
8. Report on questions relating to the electoral system of the Parliament to be elected, para.8, 1960.
9. Patijn Report (Doc 368/74) Article 7.
10. The Seitlinger Report was passed by the EP in 1982, but did not get through Council. The Bocklet draft was shelved by the Parliament. The De Gucht Report was finally passed by the EP on 10 March 1993. Despite its flexible provisions, the proposal did offer a greater degree

of uniformity than the existing system.

11. The UK has two systems: single member plurality in Britain and single transferable vote proportional representation in a single three-member constituency in N. Ireland.

12. See Juliet Lodge and Valentine Herman, 'Direct Elections to the European Parliament: A Supranational Perspective', *European Journal of Political Research* 8 (1980), pp.45–62; Andrew Duff, 'Building a Parliamentary Europe', *Government and Opposition* 29/2 (Spring 1994), pp.147–65.

13. Article 158 of the Maastricht Treaty gives the Parliament a vote of approval on the Commission and some MEPs expressed the hope that the elections might be fought in such a way that the outcome might directly affect the composition of the Commission, for example by each of the transnational parties putting forward a slate of Commissioner candidates. This scenario did not occur in 1994, but should not be ruled out as a possibility in future European elections.

14. Article 138a of the TEU.

15. For the history of early transnational party links, see Geoffrey and Pippa Pridham, *Transnational Party Co-operation and European Integration* (London: Allen and Unwin, 1981).

16. In some cases there are two parties from the same country in a transnational party and some non-EU states were able to vote on manifestos, hence the large number of parties.

17. The Parliament does have an opportunity to vote on the Commission's proposed agenda.

18. The parties play a growing role in European politics outside the electoral arena, particularly in the run-up to European summits, as Simon Hix points out, 'The Emerging EC Party System? The European Party Federations in the Intergovernmental Conferences', *Politics* 13/2 (Oct. 1993), pp.38–46.

19. In earlier elections, the anti-EC French electors could vote for Le Pen's *Front National* and Communist parties in several member states gave an anti-EC choice, but there were no pro-system anti-EC parties. In 1981 Greek voters had some choice between *Pasok*, which was originally anti-EC, and the strongly pro-EC New Democracy Party.

20. Information from officials in interviews with the author in July 1994.

21. There was some confusion as the list was proposed and then apparently withdrawn, only for some on the list to claim it had not been.

22. The traditional system of regional proportional representation with preference votes was used for the European elections, whereas the national election was fought on a plurality system. This difference in electoral regulations freed the governing parties – *Forza Italia*, the National Alliance and the Northern League – from the constraints of electoral pacts and they therefore fought the European elections on separate lists.

23. Report on questions relating to the electoral system of the Parliament to be elected (explanatory statement to Chapters II and III of the draft Convention), para.23.

24. Patijn Report, Article 9, p.26 (Doc 368/74).

25. Greece and Luxembourg have compulsory voting. Hence, on the occasions when national and European elections have coincided in these states, the high levels of turnout are the result of two interacting factors. The same caveat would apply to Belgium if the elections were ever held on the same day there.

26. Luxembourg deliberately schedules its five-yearly general elections to coincide for reasons of financial and administrative efficiency.

27. The distinction between domestic and European issues is frequently contested, however.

28. Belgium's 25 seat allocation is divided between 4 constituencies: Flanders which has 14 seats, Wallonia with 10 seats, a seat elected by German-speakers and Brussels where voters may choose whether to vote for the francophone or Flemish list.

29. It is interesting to note that the Schauble/Lamers paper on the future of the EU was published after the European elections. Had it been produced earlier, it could have led to fruitful debate during the campaign.

30. Vernon Bogdanor, *Democratising the Community* (London: Federal Trust, 1990), pp.4–5.

31. Oskar Niedermayer, 'Turnout in the European Elections', *Electoral Studies* 9/1, (1990), pp.45–50.

32. Support for government parties in the so-called 'honeymoon period', i.e., shortly after

national elections, tends to be high. See, e.g., Karlheinz Reif, 'National Electoral Cycles and European Elections 1979 and 1984.'

33. This implies nothing about other policies that any of the member parties may have.
34. Vernon Bogdanor, *Democratizing the Community* (note 30), p.7.
35. For an assessment of the powers of the Parliament after Maastricht see Martin Westlake, *A Modern Guide to the European Parliament* (London: Pinter, 1994) and Francis Jacobs, Richard Corbett and Michael Shackleton, *The European Parliament* [London: Longman, 2nd edition, 1992; 3rd ed. forthcoming 1995].
36. *The Times*, 25 June 1994.
37. One might argue with Hallstein *(Europe in the Making* (note 2), p.301, that *Eurobarometer* or other opinion polls are a better indicator of public opinion than are the results of European elections. However, one can scarcely credit such results when compared with use of instruments of direct democracy.
38. A.H. Birch, *Representation* (London: Pall Mall, 1971), p.30.
39. Helen Wallace, 'The European Parliament: The Challenge of Political Responsibility', *Government and Opposition* 14/4 (1979), pp.433–43.
40. Bhikhu Parekh, 'Discourses on National Identity' in *Political Studies* 42/3 (Sept. 1994) pp.492–504.
41. For the different types of representation, see A.H. Birch, *Representation*; for representation and the functions of elections, see the *International Encyclopedia of Social Science* (London: Macmillan, 1968).
42. Birch, *Representation*, p.81.

Notes on Contributors

Jack Hayward is Professor of Politics and Director of the Centre for European Politics, Economics and Society, Oxford University.

J.H.H. Weiler is Manley Hudson Professor of Law, Harvard Law School, Co-Director of the Harvard European Law Research Center, and Co-Director of the Academy of European Law, European University Institute, Florence.

Ulrich R. Haltern LLM, Yale Law School, is Visiting Researcher at the European Law Research Center, Harvard University.

Franz C. Mayer LLM, Yale Law School, is Rechtsreferendar in Berlin.

Peter Mair is Professor of Political Science, University of Leiden.

Rudy Andeweg is Professor of Political Science, University of Leiden.

David Judge is Professor of Government, Strathclyde University.

Mark Franklin is Professor of Political Science at the Universities of Houston and Strathclyde.

Cees van der Eijk teaches at the University of Amsterdam.

Michael Marsh teaches at Trinity College, Dublin.

Renaud Dehousse is Professor of Law at the European University Institute, Florence.

William Wallace is Professor of International Studies at the Central European University in Prague and Walter F. Hallstein Fellow at St. Antony's College, Oxford.

Julie Smith is a Lecturer in Politics at Brasenose College, Oxford.

Andrew Gamble is Professor of Politics, University of Sheffield.

Liesbet Hooghe is Assistant Professor of Political Science, University of Toronto.

Index

EDITOR'S NOTE: TABLE 5 on p.113, Summer '92 heading should be on the right side of the table with the final pair of percentages (Con and DK/NA headings) to the right of the last Pro column.